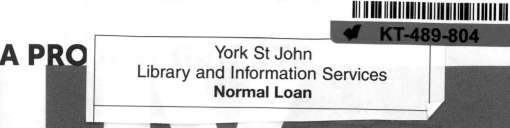

A PRO

UX DESIGN

FOR USER EXPERIENCE DESIGNERS IN THE FIELD OR IN THE MAKING

RUSS UNGER AND **CAROLYN CHANDLER**

 PEACHPIT PRESS

A Project Guide to UX Design:
For user experience designers in the field or in the making
Russ Unger and Carolyn Chandler

New Riders
1249 Eighth Street
Berkeley, CA 94710
(510) 524-2178
(510) 524-2221 (fax)

Find us on the Web at: www.newriders.com
To report errors, please send a note to errata@peachpit.com

New Riders is an imprint of Peachpit, a division of Pearson Education.

Copyright © 2009 by Russ Unger and Carolyn Chandler

Acquisition Editor: Michael J. Nolan
Project Editor: Becca Freed
Production Editor: Tracey Croom
Development Editor: Linda Laflamme
Copyeditor: Leslie Tilley
Proofreader: Suzie Nasol
Compositor: Danielle Foster
Indexer: Valerie Perry
Cover design: Mimi Heft
Cover production: Andreas deDanaan
Interior design: Mimi Heft

ISBN-13 978-0-321-60737-9
ISBN-10 0-321-60737-6

9 8 7 6 5 4 3

Printed and bound in the United States of America

Praise for A Project Guide to UX Design

If Russ Unger and Carolyn Chandler were magicians, the Alliance would be after them for revealing their best secrets. Fortunately for you, they're not. Russ and Carolyn have collected up sage wisdom previously only known to the most experienced UX project leaders and codified it for all to see. Now you can learn the secrets necessary to running great user experience projects.

Jared M. Spool, CEO and founding principal of User Interface Engineering

Is there one book that can tell you everything you need to know about designing user experiences? No. Is there a book that get you most of the way there? There is now. Carolyn and Russ have laid a solid foundation for planning and managing design projects. This is an essential handbook for anyone mired in the competing methodologies, the endless meetings, and all the moving parts of user experience design.

Dan Brown, author of *Communicating Design*

This book is a fantastic introduction to how to design great products for real people. But it covers much more than just design—it also includes all the things around design: managing projects, working with people, and communicating ideas. A great all-rounder.

Donna Spencer, author of "Card Sorting: Designing Usable Categories"

This is a practical, accessible, and very human guide to a very human activity: working together with people to make great things for other people.

Steve Portigal, Portigal Consulting

If you've heard of Wil Wheaton the author, you understand why I hold Russ Unger in such high regard. Russ's experience and guidance was fundamental to the construction and design of Monolith Press, and he's been one of the most valuable collaborators I've ever worked with.

Wil Wheaton, author of *Dancing Barefoot*, *Just a Geek*, and *The Happiest Days of Our Lives*

Acknowledgments

Russ Unger

This book would never have come close to being completed without the support of my family, friends, colleagues, and a host of people who were completely unknown to me prior to typing the first few keystrokes.

My beautiful wife, Nicolle, who willingly and knowingly married a geek with an overachiever bug, managed to double up on parenting duties through-out most of the writing of this book. Our daughters, Sydney and Avery, often poked and prodded their near-comatose father to life to get him to dance, sing, and play Spore. I unwittingly thought that writing a book with a newborn in the house would not be that big a challenge. I quickly learned otherwise. And Nicolle stepped up to bat, time and time again, to rescue me and allow me to have the focus that I needed to complete this project. She's the hero I rely upon the most; she keeps our house in order amid the chaos. She's the center of our world here, and she lets us all off the hook entirely too easily. Nicolle, along with Sydney and Avery, manage to make me look like a pretty good father, and I'm grateful for that. I live in a house with three girls, and I couldn't imagine loving any of them with anything less than all I have to give.

Carolyn kept me on track. There were times when it seemed that this project would never begin or end. She always kept things moving, explored ideas, and moved us in the right direction. The collaboration has been great, and I've learned a lot through this! She's definitely a great UX yin to my UX yang.

Michael Nolan was our acquisition editor, and he has been the perfect guide. Michael is honest and kind, and he has really helped to keep things moving smoothly. Rebecca Freed has been the juggler, managing every aspect of the book, keeping us on task, and often sending e-mails to us late, late at night. Sadly, she often got near-immediate responses from me! Linda Laflamme was our development editor and once I got used to her Red Pen of Doom, it was pretty clear that was she steering me in the right direction, no matter how hard I tried to drown her in incomplete thoughts and run-on sentences. Leslie Tilley gave the words a final polish; Tracey Croom brought production, layout, and graphic elements together; and a real book appeared.

Steve "Doc" Baty read every chapter before it ever saw light of day in the Peachpit offices. I would often send Steve chapters around 2 a.m., and he would send his feedback by 5 a.m., which is no small feat. Mind you, Steve's in Australia, but it's impressive nonetheless. Without Steve's constant willingness to help and his quick turnarounds, it's hard to believe that this book would have found its way to a shelf.

Brad Simpson (www.i-rradiate.com) took all the graphics I threw at him and turned them into beautiful, print-ready images, often while juggling his own life with two teenage sons and a busy work schedule. It would have been easy for Brad to walk away at any time, but he's a true friend who had interest in the project and wanted to support me. I'm not sure there will be enough steak dinners to pay back this effort, but I'm going to work hard to get there. Thank you, Brad, for giving up many of your days off and late nights to supporting this.

Mark Brooks found me in panic mode a few times as I was trying to convey messages that required a visual component beyond my time and/or capabilities. Mark jumped in and saved the day on more than one occasion and I'm indebted for this. Talented and giving of himself to a fault, Mark is the type of person I aspire to be.

Jonathan Ashton wrote the entire chapter on search engine optimization for us. After 5 minutes of talking to Jonathan, I knew he was the right person for the job. His chapter alone is a great reason to buy this book, and it's been great to have him on board.

Jono Kane jumped in at the last minute and on a moment's notice. Jono is a Web developer, interaction designer, and prototyper at Yahoo and was invaluable in his support and assistance in authoring Chapter 12.

Lou Rosenfeld really helped get this ball rolling. Besides coauthoring the famous "Polar Bear Book," (O'Reilly's *Information Architecture for the World Wide Web*), Lou is brilliant, kind, approachable, and always willing to help others in our field. You'll be hard pressed to find many folks as generous of self as Lou is.

Christina Wodtke helped make introductions and connections for me. Without Christina, I'm not sure where we'd be today, but it probably would not be "in print." Besides being an "author that you should read," she's someone who has always been available to give advice and provide insight. Many in the UX design field owe a lot of what they know to Christina's tireless efforts to expand our horizons by constantly innovating.

Will Evans and Todd Zaki Warfel generously supplied high-quality deliverables that you can use as templates for your own deliverables. They were true bro's, and gave of their time and talents without question or concern, often at a moment's notice. They are great members of our UX community—ones you want to know and work with—and I'm blessed to be friends with them. I certainly cannot do justice to the debt of gratitude I owe these two.

David Armano, Chris Miller, Kurt Karlenzig, Livia Labate, Matthew Milan, Michael Leis, Mario Bourque, Troy Lucht, Ross Kimbarovsky (and the gang at crowdSPRING), and Wil Wheaton served me well as good friends and true supporters and believers. I'm fortunate just to be able to type those names together as a list of people I know, and I'm a big fan of everything that they do. Their support has been an immeasurable benefit to me in all that I do.

These fine folks went out of their way to help me, generously contributing input, anecdotes, and access to their resources, and I wholeheartedly thank them: Tonia M. Bartz (www.toniambartz.com), chapter 7; Steve "Doc" Baty, (www.meld.com.au), chapters 3, 11, 14, and "A Brief Guide to Meetings"; Mark Brooks (www.markpbrooks.com), chapters 3 and 11; Leah Buley (www.adaptivepath.com), chapter 11; Dave Carlson (www.deech.com), chapter 11; Will Evans (www.semanticfoundry.com), chapters 7, 10, and 11; Christopher Fahey (www.behaviordesign.com), chapter 14; Nick Finck (www.nickfinck.com), chapter 10; Jesse James Garrett (www.adaptivepath.com), chapter 10; Austin Govella (www.grafofini.com), chapter 11; Jon Hadden (www.jonhadden.com), chapter 12; Whitney Hess (www.whitneyhess.com), chapter 11; Andrew Hinton (www.inkblurt.com), chapter 10; Gabby Hon (www.staywiththegroup.com), chapters 3 and 11; Kaleem Khan (www.uxjournal.com), "A Brief Guide to Meetings"; Ross Kimbarovsky (www.crowdspring.com), chapter 14; Livia Labate (www.livlab.com), chapter 7; Michael Leis (www.michaelleis.com), chapter 11; Troy Lucht (www.ascendrealtysolutions.com), chapter 14; James Melzer (www.jamesmelzer.com), chapter 10; Matthew Milan (www.normativethinking.com), chapter 7; Chris Miller (www.hundredfathom.com/blog), "A Brief Guide to Meetings,"; Maciej Piwowarczyk (www.linkedin.com/pub/3/a74/a66), chapter 11; Stephanie Sansoucie (www.linkedin.com/in/smsansoucie), chapter 11; Kit Seeborg (www.seeborg.com), chapters 3, 11, and "A Brief Guide to Meetings"; Josh Seiden (www.joshuaseiden.com), chapter 7; Jonathan Snook (www.snook.ca), chapter 12; Joe Sokohl (www.sokohl.com), chapter 12 and "A Brief Guide to Meetings"; Samantha Soma (www.sisoma.com), "A Brief Guide to

Meetings"; Donna Spencer (www.maadmob.net), chapter 7; Jared M. Spool (www.uie.com), chapter 7; Keith Tatum (www.slingthought.com), chapter 12; Todd Zaki Warfel (www.messagefirst.com), chapters 7, 12, and 14.

I also would like to thank Andrew Boyd, Dan Brown, Tim Bruns, Christian Crumlish, Bill DeRouchey, Brian Duttlinger, Jean Marc Favreau, Hugh Forrest of SXSW, Peter Ina, Alec Kalner, Jonathan Knoll, Christine Mortensen, Steve Portigal, Dirk M. Shaw, and Paula Thornton—as well as the Manifest Digital folks.

It is inevitable that I've missed someone, and I hope it is not taken personally. There are an abundance of folks in the "crowd" that were sourced, and I have tried to keep track of everyone. If I've missed you, let me know and I'll find a way to make it right!

Finally, it is important to note that without organizations like the Information Architecture Institute, Interaction Design Association, and others, it would have been impossible for me to make the connections with many of the people mentioned. If you're at all curious about the field of UX design, go explore these organizations, join them, and get involved!

Carolyn Chandler

A lot of us dream of writing a book at some point in our lives. Without Russ, I don't know if I ever would have gotten the motivation to jump in and do it. His energy and enthusiasm helped us find the right people at the right time, from the Peachpit team to leaders in the UX industry, all of whom have had a huge impact on what you see in these pages. He's truly one of the great connectors in our field, and he thrives on bringing people together day and night. Plus, I think he posts more tweets in a single day than I have since I joined Twitter!

Russ has thanked many of the people who helped us both immensely. I won't repeat all those names other than that of Steve Baty, who read all of our chapters in whatever raw form we could throw at him and still managed to sound enthusiastic at 2 a.m. (his time). John Geletka also provided thoughtful feedback and intriguing discussions with a spark and a perspective that crosses several disciplines. And of course, the Peachpit team; I'll never forget getting my first chapter back from Linda Laflamme. It wasn't pretty (though she delivered the suggestions with great tact). She patiently took me through the edits and helped me improve my flow, which was originally more suited to writing one-off white papers than a full-length book. Now, I even find myself adding transitions into my casual conversations with colleagues! Speaking of which …

Christine Mortensen, a.k.a. Morty, was my partner in crime when it came to the visual elements. The icons and diagrams you see in my chapters are a result of her hard work—and I know how hard, because she and I were working on many of the same client projects at the same time that we were trying to meet chapter deadlines. Morty is one of those visual designers who can plant her feet solidly in both visual and interaction design, cheerfully collaborating with everyone on the project and bringing concepts to vivid life. She has an integrity and a focus on quality that make her a pleasure to work with, and it's been an honor to have her as a partner on this.

Many thanks also go to all of the folks at Manifest Digital, who have been so supportive during the past few months. Jim Jacoby brought a special blend of business savvy and UX perspective, with his trademark zenlike calm, which got me through some stressful moments. Jason Ulaszek is one of the most enthusiastic people I know in the UX field, and he has an endless knowledge of tools and techniques; I have no idea where he makes room for it all! Also, Brett Gilbert and Jen O'Brien provided valuable input into some of the many roles that collaborate with UX designers.

I'd also like to thank the members of the Manifest UX team, who have provided inspiration and who have been so patient with my constant references to progress on "the book": Brian Henkel, Chris Ina, Haley Ebeling, Jenn Berzansky, Meredith Payne, and Santiago Ruiz. You are a constant joy to work with. Every day I appreciate your humor and insight.

To my fellow members of the Interaction Design Association, thank you for sharing your experiences and for being active members of the UX community that I love. In particular, I'd like to acknowledge Janna Hicks DeVylder and Nick Iozzo, who were key in the development of the Chicago chapter and who continue to find new ways to grow a vibrant network of smart people.

Last but not least, I want to thank my family, my friends, and Anthony, who have all borne with my disappearing act patiently and kept checking in to make sure I was still alive. You have a lot of rain checks to cash in, and I look forward to spending them with you!

Contents

Introduction

Why We Wrote This Book

Welcome to *A Project Guide to UX Design*.

Somewhere there's a student in user experience design losing sleep because he doesn't know what it will be like to work on a real project at his new company. Across town, there's a visual designer with plenty of project experience who yearns to take on new responsibilities in defining her site's user experience. These are two people at different points in their lives but with a similar need: to understand how to integrate user experience practices within the context of a living, breathing project.

Our goal with this book is to give you the basic tools and context that will help you use UX tools and techniques with working teams. As you'll see in many of these chapters, we're not trying to be everything to all people, but we're trying to provide you with the core information and knowledge that you should have to perform many of the duties you'll be assigned as a UX designer. Beyond our own examples, we provide you with examples that help you identify ways to jumpstart the basic materials and allow you to mash up the information and create something newer, better, or even more suited to your own purposes.

We hope we've done a decent job of articulating that this is a pretty good approach to UX design projects.

We're nothing if not constantly trying to learn and improve *(whatever we do)* with each iteration. That's why, to a degree, we're in this field.

A Word from Russ

As a mentor for the Information Architecture Institute (www.iainstitute.org) I've noticed a pattern among the people I have worked with: Most were either having difficulty landing jobs or were not aligned with the expectations of prospective employers. Some had outstanding education but not always enough practical application of their UX design skills in a project-based setting.

The same themes resonated in many of the conversations I had at Information Architecture Summit (www.iasummit.org) in 2008. It was then that the idea for this book—which addresses many of these common issues—began to take shape. I don't remember whether Carolyn or I sent the first e-mail, but I do know that in her I found a willing and capable co-author who helped me sand the corners off the idea that eventually became this book.

A Word from Carolyn

For many years now, I've been in the lucky position of building and managing UX teams. I say "lucky" because I find that UX designers in general have a great balance of characteristics that make them plain fun to work with, mixing right-brain intuition and left-brain logic.

As I've conducted interviews to build these teams, one thing has really stuck out: A related educational background, like human factors or communication design, is a great indicator that someone is committed to the field of UX design, but it's not the number one indicator of whether someone would be a good fit within the team or on a project. Just as important—if not more so—is the person's ability to have a consultant's mind-set. This means a positive attitude, a drive to understand and include others throughout a project, and—above all—a focus on making a real impact for users and clients.

This mind-set means taking the time to understand the perspectives of other roles on the project, making cases, and making compromises where necessary. It takes experience and effort to get this mind-set down really well, but having an open mind, a strong foundation, and a good set of questions (with the courage to ask them) can take you a long way. This book may not supply all "the answers," but it will give you the questions to ask to help you find them.

Who Should Read This Book

A Project Guide to UX Design provides a broad, introductory overview to UX design within the context of a project. Anyone with an interest in UX design should find something useful here. We focused on the following groups in particular:

Students taking UX design courses (such as human-computer interaction or interaction design) who want to supplement their coursework with information on how to apply their learning to real-life situations, where communication and collaboration are vital.

Practitioners who would like to deepen their knowledge of the basic tools and techniques of UX design and improve team communication about the roles involved. Chapter 3 is also particularly geared toward freelancers who need to create their own proposals.

Leaders of UX design groups who are looking for a book that will help their teams integrate project best practices with UX design activities.

Leaders of any project teams who are interested in learning more about how UX design integrates into their projects, what the value is, and what to expect from UX designers.

IF YOU NEED TO...	THEN YOU SHOULD READ...
Define user experience design and understand what draws people to the field	Chapter 1: The Tao of UXD
Ask the questions that are important to have answered before the project begins (or at least before you start to work on it)	Chapter 2: The Project Ecosystem Chapter 3: Proposals for Consultants and Freelancers
Start things off right with efficient meetings, clear objectives, and well-understood approval points	Online chapter: A Brief Guide to Meetings Chapter 4: Project Objectives and Approach
Define project requirements that are unambiguous and easy to prioritize, drawn from business stakeholders and users	Chapter 5: Business Requirements Chapter 6: User Research Chapter 9: Transition: From Defining to Designing
Learn about your users and represent their needs throughout the project	Chapter 6: User Research Chapter 7: Personas Chapter 13: Design Testing with Users
Choose and utilize the tools and techniques that enable you to bring visual ideas to your project team quickly	Chapter 10: Site Maps and Task Flows Chapter 11: Wireframes and Annotations Chapter 12: Prototyping
Ensure your site is easily found and searched by users and by search engines	Chapter 8: User Experience Design and Search Engine Optimization
Communicate and evolve your design with the project team once development begins	Chapter 14: Transition: From Design to Development and Beyond

Be sure to visit www.projectuxd.com to read the bonus chapter "A Brief Guide to Meetings" and to download other bonus materials such as templates.

A Note on Methodology

There are a variety of approaches and methodologies out there. We aren't proponents of one approach over another. Our goal for this book is to focus on the steps that are common to most projects: defining the project needs, designing the experience, and developing and deploying the solution. The amount of overlap between these steps will vary greatly depending on the project approach you use (see Chapter 4 for more detail). For the most part, our framework is a loose, linear approach, where the definition step comes first—but in each step we take advantage of facilitation and design techniques where they're most helpful.

What This Book Is *Not*

An encyclopedia of all techniques. The UX field has an enormous number of creative people, and they're always trying new approaches to design problems. Including all of those approaches here would make a much larger book—and one that would quickly be outdated. What we've included here are the most commonly used techniques, the nuts and bolts of UX design. We've tried to provide enough information to both intrigue you and allow you to communicate the activities to other project members—including the basic process for each technique and additional references to books or sites that will help you implement it once you choose your path.

A guide to being a project manager. Good project management (including setting and tracking project objectives, timelines, and budgets) is key to any project's success. We don't cover specifics on how to be a project manager or how to choose a particular project methodology. We do discuss the skills that a UX designer brings to a project that allow it to run effectively, such as facilitation and communication, as well as the ability to clarify and maintain focus on project objectives. These skills will help you become a partner in project management.

The only or the perfect process or methodology for *you* to follow. We don't have all the answers—no one does, today. The UX design field is relatively young, and we're all working to improve upon where we are. You will probably find that trial and error, enhancements and improvements, and feedback from others will help you tailor a process to fit your needs. When you find something that works for you—share it! Let us know!

How to Use This Book

There are many excellent resources out there for UX designers. We cover topics broadly here but point you to references that will allow you to explore topics at a deeper level depending on how much time you want to dedicate to them. To help you understand the amount of time generally needed for each reference, we've split them out into three major categories:

Surfing
References called out with the surfboard are shorter features (usually online) that will take 5 to 30 minutes to read.

Snorkeling
Those called out with the snorkel are longer online articles, white papers, or short books that take anywhere from an hour to a weekend to read.

Deep Diving
Those called out with the diver's helmet are longer books that will probably take more than one weekend to read; they give you in-depth coverage of the topic.

1 The Tao of UXD

Curiosity Meets Passion Meets Empathy

The important thing is not to stop questioning. Curiosity has its own reason for existing. One cannot help but be in awe when he contemplates the mysteries of eternity, of life, of the marvelous structure of reality. It is enough if one tries merely to comprehend a little of this mystery every day.

Albert Einstein

A sense of curiosity is nature's original school of education.

Smiley Blanton

Passion and purpose go hand-in-hand. When you discover your purpose, you will normally find it's something you're tremendously passionate about.

Steve Pavlina

The great gift of human beings is that we have the power of empathy.

Meryl Streep

Quite simply, this chapter is about you—and about others who are drawn to the field of user experience design (or UX design, for short).

If you're reading this sentence, you're a curious person.

You want to know how things work—anything from doorknobs to airplanes to that thing in the back of your throat. Most of all, you want to know what makes people tick.

You don't see things as black and white; there are a whole lot of shades of gray to explore! Sure, sometimes you may drive your peers a little crazy by always volunteering to play the devil's advocate, but it's not like you can stop yourself from trying to look at the other side of the coin.

Lucky you!

The user experience design field attracts curious folk who are comfortable working with many shades of gray.

We seek out patterns and thrive for organization and structure. We connect the dots. We relentlessly pursue the next piece of the puzzle, and when the puzzle is solved, we look for ways to improve it!

We can be analog or digital. We are at home with pencil and paper, whiteboards and dry erase markers, Post-it notes, and Sharpie pens. We talk in terms of Visio and 'Graffle, and we live in a world of boxes and arrows connected on the multiple screens of our computers.

We are not only curious. We are passionate!

We have passion for brainstorming ideas and facilitating discussions. We have a passion for creating things that make a difference for those who use them—and those who create them. Oddly enough, we're most proud when something we create is so good that people don't realize how good it is!

And, of course, we have empathy.

We can feel it deep within the core of the fabric of our being when we encounter a bad experience. Even worse, we instantly try to find solutions to solve the problems.

We know what it's like to have an unexpected response to what seems like a simple request—and we don't like it! We don't want users—people just like us—to have to endure the confusion and feelings of inadequacy that often go hand-in-hand with a poor experience.

When you combine that almost constant, childlike curiosity with an unrivaled passion for "doing what we do" and a sense for how others feel, you end up with a lively community of professionals who are comfortable speaking their minds, asking questions, sharing solutions, and being wrong—all in the name of getting to what is right.

Welcome to the UX design community.

What Is User Experience Design?

There are many definitions for user experience design. After all, it's a field that thrives on defining things. Admittedly, sometimes we don't do such a good job of "defining the damn thing" when it comes to the various parts of the whole, but we at least know what the whole is.

In this book we'll be focusing on two definitions in particular: the broadest sense of the term *UX design* and the definition we will use in the context of this book.

The Broad Definition

User experience design is

> The creation and synchronization of the elements that affect users' experience with a particular company, with the intent of influencing their perceptions and behavior.

These elements include the things a user can touch (such as tangible products and packaging), hear (commercials and audio signatures), and even smell (the aroma of freshly baked bread in a sandwich shop).

It includes the things that users can interact with in ways beyond the physical, such as digital interfaces (Web sites and mobile phone applications), and, of course, people (customer service representatives, salespeople, and friends and family).

One of the most exciting developments of the past few years has been the ability to merge the elements affecting these different senses into a richer, integrated experience. Smell-o-vision is still far in the future, but otherwise products continue to blur the traditional lines.

Don't Forget the Tangible

Although we're focusing on the digital aspects of the user experience, these types of interactions don't occur in a vacuum. Be sure to consider the effects of the tangible experience when designing your digital products. The environment your users are working within matters, as do the physical products (screens, keyboards, and other input devices) that affect the way your users will interact with your design. Chapter 6 offers techniques to help you understand the impact of context.

Also, don't forget the other touchpoints a product or company has with those who interact with it. After all, the brand of the company is affected by many things, and the brand experience doesn't end at the screen of a computer or a mobile phone. The best Web site design possible can't make up for a reputation for poor customer service or provide the satisfaction of well-designed packaging when a product gets delivered.

Figure 1.1 *A modern classroom experience blends the analog and the digital.*

Tangible experiences, such as learning in a classroom, are increasingly being influenced by digital applications. Likewise, experiences that used to be individual, such as choosing which at-home karaoke machine to buy, are increasingly becoming enhanced through social interaction.

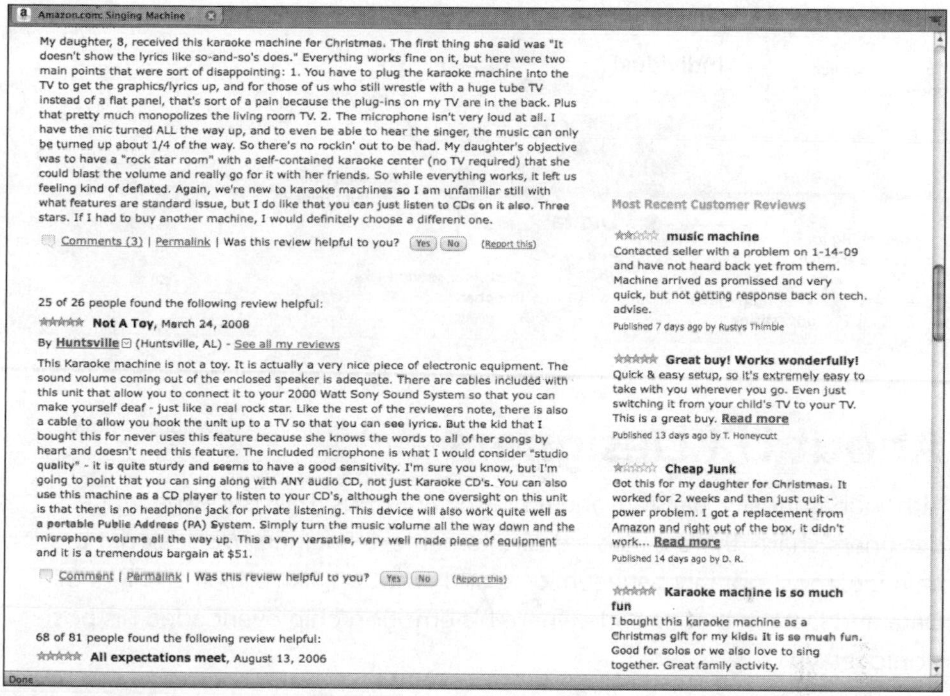

Figure 1.2 *Online reviews are a major influencer of consumers.*

Our Focus

As you can see, the scope of UX design is large, and growing. For the purposes of this book, we'll be focusing on projects centered on the *design of digital experiences*—in particular, such interactive media as Web sites and software applications. To be successful, the user experience design of these products must take into account the business objectives of the project, the needs of the product's users, and any limitations that will affect the viability of product features (such as technical limitations or constraints around project budget or time frame).

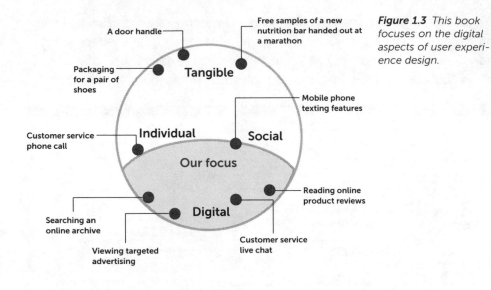

Figure 1.3 This book focuses on the digital aspects of user experience design.

The labels on the figure:
- A door handle
- Free samples of a new nutrition bar handed out at a marathon
- Packaging for a pair of shoes
- Tangible
- Mobile phone texting features
- Individual
- Social
- Customer service phone call
- Our focus
- Reading online product reviews
- Searching an online archive
- Digital
- Viewing targeted advertising
- Customer service live chat

About UX Designers

Although curiosity, passion, and empathy are traits that user experience designers share, there is also a desire to achieve balance. We seek out a balance, most notably between logic and emotion, like Spock and Kirk or Data and Data in that episode where his emotion chip overloaded his positronic relays.

You get the idea.

To create truly memorable and satisfying experiences, a UX designer needs to understand how to create a logical and viable structure for the experience *and* needs to understand the elements that are important to creating an emotional connection with the product's users.

The exact balance may shift according to the product. An ad campaign for a child's toy will have a different balance than an application for tracking patient information at a hospital. A product designed without understanding the need for both is likely to miss opportunities for a truly memorable experience— and the resulting benefits to the company behind the product.

Note For additional information about emotional design, check out Donald Norman's *Emotional Design: Why We Love (or Hate) Everyday Things (Basic Books, 2005).*

Achieving that balance requires a heightened sense of empathy: the ability to immerse yourself in the worlds of potential product users to understand their needs and motivations. User experience designers perform research to reach this understanding (see Chapter 6) and create such tools as personas (see Chapter 7) to help the rest of the project team focus their efforts.

Remember, emotion is just a part of the overall picture. Use the logical side to bring you back from the edge and keep your mind on the tasks at hand. In most cases, you will be working against a budget that is based on the time and materials required to complete the project. You'll need to understand that sometimes you need to fish or cut bait.

Where UX Designers Live

You're not alone in this. Look around and you'll find a number of organizations and communities that can foster your development as a user experience designer. In addition to offering mailing lists, online resources, and a whole slew of really smart people, many of these organizations sponsor events or conferences that can help you broaden your horizons and narrow your career focus all at the same time. A number of companies host events geared to providing continuing education, including User Interface Engineering's Web App Summit and User Interface Conference, Adaptive Path's UX Intensive, and the Nielsen Norman Group's Usability Week. There's also a growing number of "unconferences" in different cities; these are created by a collection of motivated individuals independent from any particular company or association.

Several professional organizations sponsor yearly conferences, as well. Table 1.1 provides a short list of some of the more well-known organizations, their Web sites, and events that they host.

TABLE 1.1 A Sampling of UX Organizations		
ORGANIZATION	WEB SITE	MAJOR CONFERENCE (TYPICALLY HELD)
Interaction Design Association (IxDA)	www.ixda.org	Interaction (early February)
The Information Architecture Institute (IAI)	www.iainstitute.org	IDEA Conference (September/October)
American Society for Information Science and Technology (ASIS&T)	www.asis.org	IA Summit (March)
ACM Special Interest Group on Computer-Human Interaction (SIGCHI)	www.sigchi.org	CHI (early April)
The Usability Professionals' Association	www.usabilityprofessionals.org	UPA (June)

Let's Get Started!

You've made it this far. It's time to get into the reason you picked up this book in the first place. Turn the page and take a dive into how user experience design exists within the realm of projects.

But don't stop there—this book is a guide to get you started. It has a lot of examples that can help you deliver on many of the activities you will be tasked with. We've also tried to provide additional examples to help you expand and find your own best approach for creating deliverables that are useful to your team and your clients.

Keep your curiosity, passion, and empathy alive! Challenge yourself to find new ways to inspire others to build that ideal user experience.

That is, of course, before you set out to improve upon it.

2 The Project Ecosystem
Planning for Project Needs, Roles, and Culture

Are you about to start a brand new project? Or are you in the middle of one? Either way, take a moment to consider the dynamics and context of the project— the issues that will affect you and the rest of the project team. What type of sites or applications are involved? Which roles and skills are needed? What is the company culture? Answering these questions will help you define the project and ultimately determine the tools and skills you need to bring to the table to be successful.

Carolyn Chandler

E ach project has its own unique challenges. If you're designing Web sites or applications, many of those challenges will involve specific features and functionality, such as building a method for a user to share photos with friends and family online or restructuring the information in an intranet so that content can be more easily found and shared.

Around those specific design goals, however, all projects have a larger context that you need to understand and integrate into your planning. This context is the project's "ecosystem," and it includes the environment you're working within (the company culture), the general type of work you will all be engaged in (such as the type of site you're designing), and the people you'll be interacting with (including their roles and responsibilities).

If you take the time to understand the project ecosystem you'll have knowledge that will help you throughout the project. You can communicate your responsibilities and ideas more effectively, and you can help others on the team anticipate project needs they may not have considered.

To help you, this chapter identifies different types of projects you may work on, as well as the roles you may play, the people you may depend on and how their involvement tends to vary by the type of site or application being designed. Finally, the chapter discusses some elements of company culture that may affect how you work during the project.

Note *Depending on how your client company structures its projects, a particular project may involve the design of more than one site or application. For the sake of simplicity, this book assumes that a project involves the design of a single type of site. If you have more than one site, consider each separately to make sure you have the right roles represented on the project team.*

Identify the Type of Site

Although no black-and-white distinctions exist between one type of site and another, some relative differences in site focus and characteristics are identifiable. Understanding these similarities and differences can help you

▶ Set design goals for yourself. These are the general problems that need to be solved (such as "explain the company's business model") or the attributes that need to represented (such as "demonstrate the company's responsiveness to its customers") within the site's visual design and interaction design.

- ▶ Solidify the primary objectives of the project (see Chapter 4).

- ▶ Understand which departments or business units may (or should) be involved as you gather business requirements (see Chapter 5).

- ▶ Determine the best methods for incorporating user research (see Chapter 6).

- ▶ Ask questions about which systems and technologies may be involved.

Your site will probably associate strongly with one of four types:

 Brand presence—a constantly present online platform that facilitates the relationship between the company and a general audience (anyone interested in its products or services)

 Marketing campaign—a targeted site or application meant to illicit a specific and measurable response from a particular audience or from a general audience over a limited period of time

 Content source—a store of information, potentially composed of several types of media (articles, documents, video, photos, tutorials) meant to inform, engage, or entertain users

 Task-based application—a tool or collection of tools meant to allow users to accomplish a set of key tasks or workflows

The next sections take a closer look at each of these types, discussing their characteristics and the impact they'll have on your challenges during the design of the site or application. We'll also discuss the most common *cross-over projects*—e-commerce, e-learning, and social networking—which have characteristics of more than one type.

Brand Presence

What do you think of when someone says the word *brand*? Often the first thing that comes to mind is a company's logo, such as the Nike Swoosh or the Coca-Cola script emblem. A company's brand is much more than their logo, however; it's the entire series of impressions that a particular person has about the company.

Dirk Knemeyer presents some excellent definitions of brand in his article "Brand Experience and the Web":

> Brand represents the intellectual and emotional associations that people make with a company, product, or person...That is to say, brand is something that actually lies inside each of us.

> The science of branding is about designing for and influencing the minds of people—in other words, building the brand.

Surfing

For more information on the distinctions between a customer's *experience* of a company's brand and a company's efforts to *build* their brand, read Dirk Knemeyer's explanation in "Brand Experience and the Web": www.digital-web.com/articles/brand_experience_and_the_web.

For an excellent discussion of how a site's UX design can influence an individual's brand experience, read Steve Baty's article "Brand Experience in User Experience Design": www.uxmatters.com/MT/archives/000111.php.

A company can do a lot to influence the associations made with its brand, from running memorable advertising campaigns to expressing brand traits (such as "responsiveness" or "value") through the features and design of its Web sites.

All sites within a company are likely to have some impact on a company's brand, either directly (by presenting a site that customers can visit) or indirectly (by enabling a key service that customers rely on, such as customer support). Brand presence sites, however, are the most focused on presenting the company's brand messages and values. They provide channels that interface directly with customers and serve as a broad online funnel for those interested in finding out more about the company or its offerings.

A brand presence site is often the company's primary .com or .org site, such as GE.com, or for larger and more distributed companies, are the primary sites for business units of varying sizes, such as GEhealthcare.com. Distinct product lines also often have their own unique brand presence online. For instance Pepsico.com has one brand presence, while Pepsi.com has its own distinct presence.

If you're working on a brand presence site, you'll probably be designing for a variety of user groups, including current and potential customers, investors, partners, the media (such as news organizations and authors of prominent blogs), and job seekers.

Common Brand Presence Sites

▶ A company's main home site (company.com, company.org, company.net, etc.)

▶ A site for a primary business unit of the company (often a unique site for a particular industry, region, or large suite of products)

▶ Sites for prominent sub-brands within a company

Brand Presence Design Goals

The design goals that are often of most importance in a brand presence project are these:

▶ Communicate the brand values and brand messages of the company, either explicitly (perhaps a statement about the importance placed on being responsive to customer needs) or through the overall experience upon entering the site (such as ensuring it performs well and prominently offers features that encourage customers to communicate with the company).

▶ Provide quick and easy access to company information. You want to answer the questions "What does the company do?" and "How do I contact someone for more information?"

▶ Present or explain the business model and value proposition of the company: "What can the company do for me?" and "How does the company do it?"

▶ Engage a set of primary user groups and guide them to relevant interactions, functionality, or content.

▶ Help the company attain goals being set against key metrics, such as the number of unique visitors. Often this is one part of an overall marketing strategy.

Later, in the section "Choose Your Hats," you'll learn the various roles that may be involved in designing a brand presence site. For now, let's take a look at the other types of sites you may work on, including one that has a close relationship with brand presence sites: the marketing campaign site.

Marketing Campaign

Marketing campaign sites are similar to brand presence sites, as both are focused on engaging users with an experience that influences their perception of the company's brand. Marketing campaign sites, however, tend to be evaluated on their ability to achieve very specific actions within a set focus (such as within particular time frame or with a targeted audience). Rather than serving as a funnel for channeling interest, they are meant to be the engines that *generate* interest. From an online standpoint this generally means they are aligned with an overall marketing strategy and may be run in conjunction with other marketing efforts using different channels, such as TV or radio commercials, print ads, and other promotions.

Common Marketing Campaign Sites

▶ A landing page that promotes a specific offer. The page is reached via a banner ad from another page.

▶ A small site (or microsite) promoting a particular event.

▶ A game or tool that has been created for the purpose of generating buzz or traffic.

The primary purpose of a marketing campaign site is to create a narrowly *focused campaign* usually targeting a specific set of *metrics*. The focus is often narrowed by one or more of the following:

▶ **Time**—for example, a campaign centered around an event (such as a conference) or a season (such as the Christmas shopping season)

▶ **User group**—such as a campaign targeted to teenagers or teachers

▶ **Product, product suite, and/or a specific use for that product**—for example, a site that highlights kitchen appliances by showing virtual kitchens with matching ovens, dishwashers, and stoves

A campaign using a mix of these strategies would be a spring campaign targeted to selling patio equipment, combining time and product suite. See Figure 2.1 for an example showing a mix of product suite and user group.

A marketing campaign site may be as simple as a banner ad leading to a landing page in the company's .com site, or it could be a *microsite*, a small site that often veers away from the branding apparent on the .com site to provide a tailored experience according to one or more of the areas of focus. "Small" is relative here—some microsites are only one page and others have many, but either way the microsite is smaller and more focused than the company's main brand presence site.

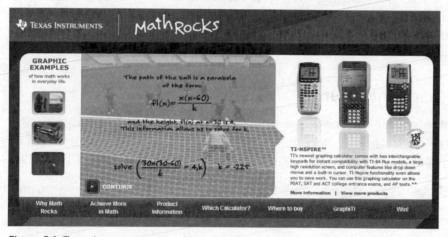

Figure 2.1 *Texas Instruments uses this education-focused microsite, http://timathrocks.com/ index.php, to present information on the company's graphing calculators. The product suite is used primarily by high school and college students in algebra classes. The microsite maintains general ties to the Texas Instruments brand but is intentionally distinct in order to attract a younger audience and organize content and features according to their needs.*

Marketing Campaign Design Goals

For the person or team responsible for designing and implementing a marketing campaign site, the design goals that are often of most importance are these:

▶ Generate interest and excitement, often by presenting a clear and immediate *value proposition* (the value that a product or service brings to the user, such as the possibility of quick loan qualification) or some kind of incentive (a special offer, entry in a contest, or entertainment such as an online game).

▶ Engage a set of primary user groups in order to illicit a particular action, such as clicking through to a specific location on a brand presence site, signing up for a newsletter, or applying for a loan. When this action is performed by a user it's called a *conversion.*

▶ Help the company attain goals being set against key metrics, such as number of unique visitors. Often this is one part of an overall marketing strategy.

Deep Diving

For more on designing pages to support marketing campaigns, see *Landing Page Optimization: The Definitive Guide for Testing and Tuning for Conversion,* by Tim Ash (Sybex, 2008).

Content Source

A content source site contains a store of information, potentially in several types of media (articles, documents, video, photos, tutorials), and is meant to inform, engage, and/or entertain users.

Common Content Source Sites

▶ A company's intranet

▶ An online library or resource center for members of an organization

▶ Sites or areas of sites that are focused on providing news or frequently updated posts (large commercial blogs may fall into this category)

▶ Customer support centers

All sites and applications have some content, of course, but some sites place a particular emphasis on the presentation and structure of their content. The emphasis may come about because the site has such a large amount of content that it poses its own challenge or because specific types of content carry a high degree of importance; they might, for instance, support critical decisions or draw users back to the site frequently.

The primary purpose of a content source site is to increase user knowledge and self-sufficiency by providing relevant content (an intranet, for example). They often also encourage some kind of action, such as sharing information or purchasing a product after reviewing its description.

Content Source Design Goals

A content source site often has to do one or more of the following:

▶ Present content that is the primary draw for first and repeat visits to the site.

▶ Demonstrate a company's thought leadership capabilities, for example, by providing access to ideas and perspectives held by the CEO or other subject matter experts within the company.

▶ Support critical decisions among the user base.

▶ Increase a company's enterprise knowledge, by bringing out ideas that may be buried within individual departments. This may be part of a larger goal to identify more opportunities for innovation.

▶ Support users who are seeking information in different ways. For example, some don't know what specific product they need yet (and are more likely to browse), while others may know exactly what they're looking for (and are more likely to use a search field).

Surfing

For more information on the different ways users tend to seek information, read "Four Modes of Seeking Information and How to Design for Them," by Donna Spencer: http://boxesandarrows.com/view/four_modes_of_seeking_information_and_how_to_design_for_them

With regard to UX design, some of the tasks that are most common in a content source project are:

▶ Creating a categorization structure that fits the mental models of your users

▶ Determining how to incorporate a system for organic growth of content (for example, functions such as tagging and filtering)

▶ Designing an effective search tool

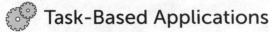 # Task-Based Applications

Task-based applications can vary from a simple calculator embedded in a mortgage site to a full system handling multiple critical workflows. If your project involves the latter, there will be more roles involved and, most likely, a substantial requirements-gathering process (for more on this process, see Chapter 5).

Common Task-Based Applications

▶ A software application that supports the creation of a particular type of item (such as a spreadsheet or print piece)

▶ A Web tool or application that supports a critical workflow within a company (such as a ticket-management application for an IT support group or a customer tracking application for a call center)

▶ A Web site that allows for access to, and management of, personal data (such as Flickr)

The primary objective of a task-based application is to allow users to perform a set of tasks that are aligned with their needs and, ultimately, with the client's business goals.

Task-Based Application Design Goals

Most task-based applications need to

▶ Enable users to do something they couldn't do elsewhere—or if they can, to do it better ("better" can mean more efficiently, more effectively, with a higher degree of satisfaction, or more conveniently)

▶ Support novice users with easy-to-access instructions and visual prioritization of key tasks

▶ Support intermediate and advanced users with access to shortcut features and deeper functionality

▶ Reduce the load on the user and make the best use of system resources (for example, reusing data versus requiring duplicate entries)

- Be designed and deployed with attention to the degree of change required of the application's users—ideally, with a design that facilitates learning and a communication plan that demonstrates the value to the user

One of the biggest challenges of designing a task-based application is to keep "feature creep" under control. As a project is being developed it's very common for great ideas to come up at later stages of the design, or even during development. User experience design is well suited to guarding against feature creep because user models such as personas can be used to identify high-value features and to keep focus throughout the project.

If a truly great idea does come up later in the process, *and* it meets the needs of a high-priority user group, *and* it aligns with the business goals of the site, your team may be able to build a case for changing direction. If an idea can't make it through that wringer, it may not be worth the delay and cost.

E-Commerce Sites

E-commerce sites can include elements of all four project types, because a site that is primarily intended for e-commerce needs to have its own brand presence, provide content (usually product specs or descriptions of product usage), and facilitate tasks (searching, comparing, writing reviews, checkout). Marketing campaigns are often closely tied into these sites as well and may involve multiple marketing groups within the organization.

Common additional design goals for e-commerce sites are

- Explain the model for the site, if it's nonstandard. As online marketplaces are constantly being reconceived, this explanation will help set expectations (for example, eBay, Amazon, and Craigslist have very different models).

- Support decision making as the user moves from learning to consideration to comparison to purchase, with helpful content and features.

- Make use of points in the experience where cross-selling and upselling is possible, and place those suggestions in a way that is eye-catching without being disruptive.

- Create a communication flow from the point of purchase through the point of delivery. Communication needs to happen not just within the site but also with other channels, such as integration with delivery tracking systems and e-mailed communications about order status.

E-Learning Applications

E-learning applications are crossovers between a content source and a task-based application. Content for lessons must be generated, which often requires that the team add the roles of learning specialist and subject matter expert (SME) for the topic being covered. The product is task-based in that the user usually follows a flow through the lesson and may also need to track progress or explore related topics. Some hands-on lessons may also require tasks to be completed.

Common design goals are

▶ Set an understanding of the baseline knowledge needed to start a course and who it is targeted to.

▶ Provide content in manageable chunks that are paced for comprehension.

▶ Engage the learner in activities that simulate hands-on learning.

▶ Communicate performance and progress and, if applicable, suggest next steps for continuing the educational process, such as more advanced courses.

Social Networking Applications

A social networking application is primarily a task-based application, because users need to be able to find and add friends, manage their profile, connect, post, and search. They also contain challenges associated with content sources, however, especially the need for an organic framework that can handle a potentially very large amount of user-generated content. If the site is essentially given its own identity, it will also have the characteristics of a brand presence site.

Snorkeling
If you're working on a social networking application or trying to integrate social features into another type of site, this book will help you on your way: *Designing for the Social Web*, by Joshua Porter (New Riders, 2008).

Common design goals for social networking applications are

▶ Focus potential users on the purpose and the values of the network.

▶ Facilitate meaningful interactions between users that support, and are supported by, the features presented (such as image sharing, video sharing, and discussions).

▶ Protect the integrity of the site by ensuring those within the network understand how to control their information and respond to inappropriate behavior.

▶ Harness and display the power of the community to bring forward features that are only possible with active members, such as popular features and reviews.

Identifying the type of site or application you may be working on during a project is only the first step. Next, you should consider the different roles that are often needed and how their involvement may vary based on the type of project.

Choose Your Hats

When you become the UX designer on a project, you often end up having to play several roles. Whether they're formally defined within your client organization or not, the roles you will play depend on the type of project and the makeup of the rest of the team, as well as a client's experience with each. It's good to know which roles you're already comfortable taking on and which you think you can learn on the job. It's also helpful to find out what expectations others may have about the responsibilities covered by these roles. With this understanding, you can represent yourself more clearly from the beginning of the project.

What are the most common roles expected of a UX designer? Each client company you work for may have different titles for those roles (or no name at all, if it's not a formal job in the organization). In general, you can expect to encounter the big three: information architect, interaction designer, and user researcher.

Note *Few companies have the size or budget to split these common roles among different individuals. Keep the role names in your mind when defining a project, but speak in terms of needs and responsibilities when talking to the client—otherwise they may think you're building a very large team! This focus on responsibilities rather than titles will also help keep you sane: If you're performing several of these roles, it doesn't necessarily mean you're doing the job of many people, because responsibilities ebb and flow through different parts of the project.*

Information Architect

An information architect is responsible for creating models for information *structure* and using them to design user-friendly navigation and content categorization. During the design of sites and applications, common responsibilities include creating detailed site maps (discussed in Chapter 10) and ensuring that categories and subcategories of information are distinct and user-friendly.

Understanding Expectations

Within the UX field, distinctions are made between the roles of the information architect and the interaction designer (discussed next). At a particular company, however, there is seldom a common distinction between the two roles, at least when it comes to what is stated as a need for a particular project. For example, you may end up on a team with the title of information architect because that's the historical term for the role, whether or not that truly fits your responsibilities.

Should you correct the project team if the title you're given doesn't match the main role you're taking on? If this is a shorter term project (say, four months or less) and the title you have is widely accepted within the organization, with clear responsibilities outlined, it may not be worth the potential confusion you'd be introducing to try to change it. If there is no widely accepted title, however, and you think there's a chance you'll need both roles to be represented—potentially by different people—then it's worth making a distinction early in the project when you're planning your involvement and communicating your responsibilities.

Essentially, for more task-based applications it makes sense to emphasize the role of interaction designer, and for more content-based projects it makes sense to emphasize the role of information architect. But what may make the most sense of all is to use the term familiar to the client organization and ensure the team understands how you're defining the role with regard to the responsibilities you're taking on. This definition is something you'll want to make clear in the statement of work (see Chapter 3).

The responsibilities of an information architect can also blur with those of a content strategist (see below, under "Other Roles"). If these roles are represented by different people on the project team, be sure to discuss how you'll be collaborating at the beginning of the project.

Interaction Designer

An interaction designer is responsible for defining the *behavior* of a site or application in accordance with user actions. This includes flows in the site across multiple views and interactivity within a particular view. During the design of sites or applications, common activities are to create task flows showing interaction across pages or components within the site (see Chapter 10) and to create wireframes showing in-page interactions such as dynamic menus and expandable areas of content (see Chapter 11).

Understanding Expectations

If you're working on a small team or on a project that isn't highly focused on creating new task-based functionality (for example, if you're working on a brand presence site that mainly includes some content categories, a contact form, and a sign-up form for a newsletter) interaction designer may be the main role responsible for capturing the project requirements (see Chapter 5).

If you're working as the interaction designer on a project with a high level of new functionality, most likely you'll have a separate person on the team in charge of outlining detailed requirements (for example, a business analyst or product manager). The process of gathering and detailing functional requirements can be helped greatly by the skills of a UX designer, and documents such as functional specifications and use cases are affected by experience design. Be sure to sit down with the person in charge of gathering requirements to discuss how you can best work together.

User Researcher

A user researcher is responsible for providing *insights* regarding the needs of end users, based on information that is generated from, or validated with, the research that person conducts with users. There are many types of activities that can fall into the category of user research, and they can occur at several points in the project timeline. (See Chapter 6 for a description of common techniques, such as user interviews, surveys, and usability testing.)

Understanding Expectations

The client company's appetite for user research can vary immensely, based on the importance placed on it by the project team or the project sponsor. The fact that you're talking to a project sponsor about UX design before a project starts shows that someone on the client team knows it's a priority to ensure that user needs are represented. But as those who have worked on their share of computer-based projects know, introducing research can also introduce anxiety among project team members—sparked by concerns that user research will create a bottleneck, increase risk (What if we find something wrong, and need to make big changes to fix it?), or disprove the value of a particular idea that has gained a lot of momentum. The expectations for user research can vary between business stakeholders and the project team, so be sure to clarify expectations for the role with both groups.

The client may also expect the user researcher to provide insights based on site analytics—tools and reports that communicate patterns of use on the site, such as frequently visited pages and common points where users leave the site. Some of the most common analytics tools are from Google (www. google.com/analytics), WebTrends (www.webtrends.com), and Omniture (www.omniture.com/en/products/web_analytics).

You may find yourself taking on all three of these roles: information architect, interaction designer, and user researcher. Can you balance all three, or are you biting off more than you can chew? In part that depends on the size and timeline of the project, but the type of project also has an impact on how much involvement each role is likely to have. Table 2.1 describes how UX design roles can vary by project type.

Surfing

Need to make the case for UX design? These articles offer approaches that can help:

"User Experience as Corporate Imperative," by Mir Haynes: www.hesketh.com/publications/user_experience.pdf

"Evangelizing User Experience Design on Ten Dollars a Day," by Louis Rosenfeld: http://louisrosenfeld.com/home/bloug_archive/000131.html

TABLE 2.1 Common Responsibilities of the UX Design Role

	BRAND PRESENCE	MARKETING CAMPAIGN	CONTENT SOURCE	TASK-BASED APPLICATION
Information Architect	Medium involvement. The greater the content challenge, the more like a content source the project will become.	Low involvement for smaller sites (like a single landing page). Medium involvement if working with larger microsites.	Very high involvement. Content sources require an information architecture that has an appropriate balance of structure and flexibility, to give users a solid base to stand on and allow for planned growth.	Medium to high involvement, mainly focused on creating the navigational framework, unless there are larger content areas that need to be referenced during some workflows.
Interaction Design	Medium involvement. The greater the number of tasks, the more like a task-based application the project will become.	Low involvement for smaller sites, medium to high involvement for larger microsites or *advergames* (sponsored online games meant to generate play and buzz).	Medium to high involvement. Search, tagging, and filtering features cross the line between information architecture and interaction design. Content sources may also have workflows involving content creation and management.	Very high involvement. This kind of project often requires the heaviest lifting, as interaction design deliverables (such as user process flows and wireframes) are key to communicating requirements visually.
User Researcher *Involvement will vary based on budget and access to users. Listed here are common techniques for each project type. For more on each of these techniques, see Chapter 6.*	Research efforts may focus on understanding needs of priority user groups (through surveys or interviews) or design research testing the effectiveness of a particular visual design in conveying the right brand message.	Due to the often temporary nature of campaigns, user involvement is often light. More permanent solutions may use research similar to brand presence sites. It's also common to use analytics tools to present two or more variations of a particular page to see which one leads to the most conversions. This is called *A/B testing*.	Field research such as contextual inquiry can help the team understand how different users currently work with information. Card sorting is an excellent way to understand how your users may group information and common patterns and mental models. Once a framework has been set, usability testing can validate the structure.	Field research such as contextual inquiry can be done to understand tasks as users are currently completing them. The most frequently used and best understood technique for involving users in the design of a task-based application, however, is usability testing.

Other Roles You May Play or May Need

Several roles don't typically fall under the role of UX designer, but their responsibilities often overlap with the UX design role—especially if you're working on a project where no one is officially playing the role and you have skills to bring to the table.

Some of the more common overlapping roles include:

▶ Brand strategist or steward

▶ Business analyst

▶ Content strategist

▶ Copywriter

▶ Visual designer

▶ Front-end developer

The following sections look at each of these roles in more detail and discuss how they may vary depending on the type of site being designed.

Brand Strategist and Brand Steward

A *brand strategist* is responsible for building a relationship with key markets through the definition and consistent representation of the company's branding elements, which can include anything from brand values (such as "responsiveness") to guidelines for copy and messaging to specifications for logo treatments, colors, and layout. This role often entails creating or representing branding guidelines and understanding how they apply to different projects. It may also involve knowing or defining the target audiences of importance on the project you're working on. For the most part, you'll probably work with a brand strategist but won't be taking the responsibility on yourself.

The *brand steward* doesn't necessarily set the guidelines but is responsible for ensuring that they are followed appropriately during the project. This responsibility may be given to the UX designer or visual designer on a project.

If the company's brand attributes, values, and guidelines have already been well defined and the site is expected to follow them, your role as the project's brand steward will mainly be to ensure the result is in line with those guidelines. Your touchpoint outside the project would most likely be a member of the marketing department who is available on a consultative or review basis but is not on the team full time.

The brand steward role may be more active if the site is meant to extend the brand somehow—targeting a new market, for example. It's most involved when a completely new brand presence is being created or when the company is making a dramatic change in its brand, effectively rebranding itself. For example, CellularOne rebranded itself completely to become Cingular, a major effort for an established company. In that situation you should either be very experienced in brand development or establish a clear and close relationship with the person at the company who is.

Key questions that will help you understand expectations around a brand-related role are these:

▶ Do brand guidelines exist already?

▶ If so, how closely do they need to be adhered to for this project?

▶ Who is responsible for setting or maintaining brand messaging, brand look-and-feel, and tone of content (such as casual or professional)?

▶ Are new audiences going to be targeted that aren't covered by previous brand definitions? If so, who is responsible for ensuring the brand guide-lines are still appropriate to those audiences?

▶ Will there be naming or renaming activities? If so, how should I plan to be involved? (An example would be creating a name for a new tool that will be heavily promoted.)

For projects that don't have a large potential impact on customers' perception of the brand, such as the development of an internal application, brand steward involvement may be as light as an occasional check-in to ensure the brand is being well represented.

Business Analyst

A *business analyst* (sometimes referred to as a business *systems* analyst on IT projects) is responsible for identifying key business stakeholders, driving the requirements-gathering process (see Chapter 5), and serving as the primary liaison between business stakeholders and the technology team. He or she is also the primary owner of detailed requirements documentation, such as functional specifications and use cases, if needed.

The role of business analyst or product manager may not exist on your project at all or it may be one of the most important roles through the design process. Task-based applications and content sources often have this kind of role; brand presence projects and marketing campaigns may not. A task-based application is most likely to need this role. The more features and the greater the complexity of the project, the greater the needs will be for a dedicated person and for documentation of functionality.

Although a business analyst is not typically considered a member of the UX team, small UX teams are often asked to fill the role, so it's important to understand where these responsibilities lie. Business analysts drive the capture of business requirements, serving as the liaison between the technology team and the key business stakeholders. If there is a business analyst on a project, that person and the interaction designer are often joined at the hip. If it's the same role, the person responsible may have a lot of documentation to keep up with!

To understand expectations in this area, ask who will be responsible for outlining the scope of the project, facilitating the discussions around requirements, and documenting requirements throughout the project. For small projects or those that are not heavy in functionality, the project manager sometimes will take on these responsibilities. Either way, if it's not you, you'll still know who you need to stay close to in order to ensure your deliverables are in sync.

Content Strategist

A content strategist is responsible for understanding business and user requirements for content in various media (articles, documents, photos, and video), identifying gaps in existing content, and facilitating the workflow and development of new content.

Content-related efforts are often underestimated. A client may have a large amount of content that's wonderful in one medium (such as print brochures or videos), but that content may not be appropriate for the project you're working on. Also, there are sometimes unspoken expectations that people within the client organization will generate content—expectations that may come as a surprise to those people when the time comes to populate your product with descriptions, news, and help topics! If high-quality content is a key business driver in your project, make sure you know who is responsible for the following:

▶ Setting content guidelines for the new product (type of content, tone, amount).

▶ Assessing the appropriateness of existing content against those guidelines.

▶ Developing new content. This will vary based on general project type. For task-based applications, it may include instructional copy, error messages, and help topics. For content sources, it may include articles, news items, and blog posts.

▶ Serving as the stakeholder–technical team liaison to communicate the limitations and possibilities of the content management system.

▶ Defining different content types as well as each one's *metadata* (the information that ultimately makes searching and cross-referencing more effective).

▶ Planning for the *migration* of content, which involves creating templates for different content types and making sure content is tagged and loaded properly when it's moved into the site's content management system. (This is another area where the effort required is often underestimated.)

Copywriter

A *copywriter* is responsible for writing the text on the site that frames the overall experience. In some cases, this copy remains fairly unchanged from day to day. It typically includes site and page introductions or in-page instructions. A copywriter may also be involved in the ongoing creation of dynamic content, such as news stories or copy for marketing campaigns.

Copywriting is one of those gray areas that often falls to a UX designer, especially if wireframes are being created (see Chapter 11). You may initially put in sample text to serve as placeholder for copy such as a site description or in-page instructions, but someone eventually needs to populate it with the final text that will be seen by users—and because many projects don't have a dedicated copywriter, this task may default to you.

You're less likely to be asked to take on the copywriter role for high-profile areas of brand presence sites or marketing campaigns; in those situations each word may be given close scrutiny. But if you're working on a task-based application that needs short instructional messages, error messages, or other types of information that don't necessarily fall into a clear content bucket, you may end up inheriting that writing task (or it will fall to the developer by default). Ask upfront if a copywriter will be available, and ask again when you're wireframing if one hasn't been found. If the job does fall to you, be sure to include that effort when you're planning your activities during the project. And be forewarned: This is a responsibility that's often left out or underestimated.

Visual Designer

A *visual designer* is responsible for the elements of the site or application that the user sees. This effort includes designing a look and feel that creates an emotional connection with the user that's in line with the brand guide-lines. For example, a banking site often needs to appear stable, trustworthy, and accessible. The visual design can give this assurance through visual ele-ments such as colors and imagery. That promise will then be kept (or broken) by the interaction design of the site and other touchpoints with the company (such as a call center).

Let's be frank: A lot of people out there call themselves visual designers, Web designers, or graphic designers, and a lot of sites have poor or only pass-able visual designs. There is a big difference between creating an effective, immersive, and emotional visual design and just getting by. Sometimes get-ting by is enough to meet the project objectives, and sometimes it leads to project frustrations and delays when the project sponsor is unhappy, or early users are not engaged with the design.

On the other hand, it can also be easy to focus too strongly on creating an impact with the visual design, allowing the usability of the design to suffer. If you're being asked to take on this role and are unsure of your abilities to create the right impact for the client, take a look at the company's current site and the sites or products the clients admire from a visual standpoint to assess your comfort level.

Visual designers often take a very central role in brand presence projects and marketing campaigns, having the primary role responsible for communicat-ing the company's brand effectively.

For content source projects, they may focus on creating content templates that can be applied to many pages (for example, a template for an article). For task-based applications, they may provide a style guide that can be applied to common interaction elements, such as navigation areas and tools (which calls for a high degree of collaboration with the interaction designer).

Front-End Developer

A *front-end developer* is responsible for building the technical structure behind the page designs and flows, as well as interactive elements within the site, such as rollover menus, expandable areas of content, interactions with multimedia elements like video. This work often uses technologies such as XHTML, CSS, Flash, JavaScript, Ajax, and Silverlight. Front-end development focuses on the elements of the site that tie directly to what the user sees, as opposed to the systems on the back end that provide the underlying platform (such as databases, content management systems, and the code needed to build the functionality behind complex features).

If you or members of your team are taking on the role of front-end developer, close collaboration with the rest of development team is important to understanding expectations and responsibilities. Other important questions include which back-end systems will need to be integrated with, the method used for generating HTML, the need for flexibility in page structure to accommodate customized "skins," and the expectations concerning technologies such as Flash. If a prototype is being planned (see Chapter 12), ask who is responsible for developing the prototype and what level of functionality is expected. A prototype meant to simply communicate possibilities can be created quickly in an application such as Flash, but a fully functioning prototype that needs to pull real data (for example the account information a user just entered in a form) will need to be done in close collaboration with members of the back-end development team.

Worried about taking on all these roles? Unless you're working on a very small project—or at a very small company—you most likely won't be taking them all on yourself. The key is to understand which of the roles you are able and willing to take on, as needed, for the particular project you're working on. For the rest, you can get the support you need on the project team by building a network within the client company or by recommending additional people to fill the needs. Let's take a moment to talk about ways you can do this.

Building a Network of User Advocacy

For those areas that you're not sure you can or want to take on, it's time to start looking for help. There are three main ways you can go about doing this:

▶ Recommend additional team members be added, if the need is apparent enough.

▶ Educate yourself in key areas where there are gaps—if the new responsibilities are manageable and you have the time to dedicate to them.

▶ Build a support network within the company to help you at key junctures.

Let's take a closer look at how you can build a support network.

There are most likely some key resources in other departments within the company that can help you be successful. You'll need to gauge how much time you can rely on from these people, because requesting outsiders' time can be a tricky request with projects that are primarily owned by one department. If you don't want to ask for a large amount of their time out of the gate, just ask if you can partner with (or consult with) them to ensure the best result for the major responsibilities for that role. Once you've done some partnering you'll have a better understanding of the amount of interaction you may need and whether you need to make a more formal request for his or her time.

Each company will have a different structure and different names for its departments, but here are some common places to look for partners:

▶ For the brand strategist role, ask if there's anyone within the marketing department who can serve as your touchpoint. This may also be a source for visual designers and content strategists.

▶ Visual design and content strategy partners may be also be found in program or product management or in the research and development, operations, or corporate strategy department, where you can often find business analysts and product managers.

▶ The IT or engineering department is often your best bet for front-end developers and others who can help you get access to and insight into tools for site analytics.

If you have recently been hired by a new company and expect to be working across departments, one of the best things you can do out of the gate is to identify key people who could be partners and schedule some interview time with them to understand their roles and experience. It starts you off with a network that you can often rely on for a long time and gives you the opportunity to explain your responsibilities (and user experience design in general). You can also ask a great question at the end of the interview: "Who else do you think I should talk to?" The answer can help you find people who may not be apparent to your main project manager or client contact.

If you've been at a company for a while, you can still initiate an interview schedule like this. In that situation it's best to tie it to a particular milestone (such as the start of a new project) or a corporate objective that has some urgency behind it, to ensure high participation.

Make sure that your manager knows what you're doing to avoid looking like you're going around him or her. Good communication is key to understanding expectations about roles and building trust.

Another key to gaining trust within the company is to understand its *culture*, the often unspoken expectations of how a company works, such as those created by past project experiences (positive or negative), etiquette regarding organizational hierarchy, and acceptable work logistics (such as working from home).

Understand the Company Culture

Culture is a little like dropping an Alka-Seltzer into a glass—you don't see it, but somehow it does something.

—Hans Magnus Enzensberger

A company's culture may not be consistent across all of its regions, business units, or departments, but you can usually identify key characteristics that will affect you and the project or projects you're undertaking. The following are some aspects that are good to keep in mind as you scope projects and navigate potentially tricky political situations.

History

We all know the quote that those who cannot remember the past are condemned to repeat it, and project work is no exception. Understanding how a project or team has gotten to its current state of need can help you understand the challenges you may face during the project.

Let's cover some of the questions you can ask to understand the history that may affect a project. Although some of the answers to these questions may seem dire, keep in mind that something has triggered the need to bring you in on the project, so a project can have a rocky history and still be successful. Perhaps you'll be a key component of that success! However, if many of the problems discussed below seem to apply, and you don't feel you'll be able to help address them, it may be a red flag. In that case, consider an overall evaluation of whether this project is positioned to succeed.

▶ **What is an example of a past project that seems to have been considered a success, and what seems to have made it so? What is a past project that seems to have been a failure (or particularly painful), and why did it fail?**

Asking these questions (either directly or in a more subtle, conversational manner) can help you understand a couple of things: how the person answering defines success, potential risks to your project, and any biases or expectations that will be carried through to this project, as well as approaches that worked well.

▶ **Has the company worked with and released a designer on the same project or team?**

If so, try to find out what didn't seem to be working and how the client expects your approach to be different. If you can ask more than one person at the company this question, it will help you understand a lot about unspoken expectations. If you get two very different answers, it could mean the designer's responsibilities weren't well defined and you may need to ensure there's a lot of communication about your responsibilities throughout the project.

▶ **Has the project team been working on the project (or related materials) for what seems like an unusually long time without finishing?**

If so, this could be a sign that key client stakeholders are not on the same page or are not being involved at appropriate times, causing multiple stalls, direction changes, or lost time due to multiple iterations. It may also mean there is not a clear leader, someone who can say no (or at least effectively prioritize) to keep the focus on business objectives. If you're in a position to influence the communication on the project, it may help to create guidelines for participation to help move the project forward.

▶ **Has the company created designs without the previous participation of a UX designer?**

This can be a mixed blessing. On one hand, you're dealing with a team that understands the need for design and has attempted to fill the gap. On the other, you may be given a design that you feel does not meet the project goals for the user experience. This can be a delicate situation to navigate. It's often best to approach the creator of those designs with the tone of a respectful mentor or helpful consultant, pointing out the good aspects of the design first, then discussing user experience goals and how they may be better achieved with a different approach. The creator is likely to be a valuable member of your support network, so it's important not to burn the bridge here, but to redefine your roles in a collaborative way to keep the enthusiasm alive.

▶ **Does the main sponsor or project manager seem particularly anxious about the project?**

There are many reasons this could occur, especially if some of the factors above are in play. Anxiety could also be due to market pressures that it would be helpful for you to understand. For example, has the company stock price been dropping? Has a particular competitor made recent alarming strides? Is the business operating in the red? Again, these situations do not necessarily mean you shouldn't take the project on; after all, they're the kind of situations that often get a project funded in the first place. But if you have a significant concern that the company won't be able to pay its invoices, that's a risk you'll want to weigh.

Hierarchy

Geert Hofstede has an excellent model outlining differences in culture, what he calls "cultural dimensions," that often affect the way people interact and communicate. One of them is the concept of *power distance*, which is the extent to which members of a society (in our case, a company) understand and accept the distance between people of different levels of power. For example, if members of a company's executive team are viewed as particularly powerful and potentially unapproachable, a company may have a large power distance and its employees may be more focused on the hierarchy. If the company encourages a democratic sharing of ideas and questioning of vision, it may have a relatively small power distance.

Power Distance Is

"... the extent to which the less powerful members of organizations and institutions (like the family) accept and expect that power is distributed unequally. This represents inequality (more versus less), but defined from below, not from above. It suggests that a society's level of inequality is endorsed by the followers as much as by the leaders."

Geert Hofstede
Cultural Dimensions
www.geert-hofstede.com

Neither extreme can be considered good or bad in itself, although generally in the United States most employees seem to prefer the appearance of a small power distance in their workplace. What's interesting to note is that this isn't necessarily an indicator of how successful a company is. Apple has a relatively large power distance (if you consider the aura around Steve Jobs), and Google has a relatively small power distance as part of its culture, but both companies are known for being innovative leaders.

What is important to note is that the power distance within the client company will have an impact on how you successfully navigate the political waters during the project. This aspect will become particularly important at key points in the project: during requirements gathering (discussed in Chapter 5) and at key milestones such as sign-off points (discussed in Chapter 4). If you're working at a company with a large power distance, take some extra time to understand reporting relationships before scheduling meetings such as stakeholder interviews and reviews, and consider involving more people at intermediate levels during your communications.

Logistics

In addition to the larger aspects of culture mentioned above, it's also helpful to understand some of the elements that are more logistical in nature, so you can better integrate with current work methods or introduce change in a thoughtful way.

For example, it's helpful to understand the general pace expected within the company, including key release dates or deadlines that will affect the project (creating a software application on a yearly release schedule would probably have a different pace than a microsite supporting a seasonal campaign, for instance). Will your team be expected to work late hours to meet looming deadlines?

Expectations regarding remote work versus on-site work are good to understand as well. If heavy on-site time is expected, you'll need to plan for travel and resource setup there. If remote work is acceptable (or encouraged, which is common when working with global companies), it's important to understand methods and tools of communication. For example, Is use of instant messaging applications acceptable? What Web conferencing tools are in use? Are there methods of including international stakeholders that have proven effective in the past?

It's also interesting to understand the "paper culture" at a company. Some companies favor electronic media for most things, in which case a good projector and a consistent Ethernet connection is important. Others are very paper-centric, in which case you'll need to make sure you bring enough copies to a meeting to make it productive. You may be able to change the culture of the project if you think another way is more effective. But it's good to know that you're asking people to change so that you can smooth the transition—and potentially understand why a particular approach isn't working as you expected.

Pulling It Together

Now that you've explored the terrain of the project, you should have a better understanding of the project ecosystem: the environment you're working within (the company culture), the general type of work you will all be engaged in (such as the types of sites you're designing), and the people who you'll be interacting with (including their roles and responsibilities).

This information will be valuable as you outline your role in the project and get ready to begin in earnest. If you're working as a freelancer or subcontractor, it will provide a base for writing a proposal covering your work on the project (see the next chapter, which discusses UX proposals). If you're working as a member of a larger team and are not directly involved in writing the proposal, you can take your new knowledge into the project kickoff—the first meeting of your team. For a basic guide to running a good meeting, see the online chapter, "A Brief Guide to Meetings," or if you want to get straight into the kinds of questions to ask when the project gets started, see Chapter 4, "Project Objectives and Approach."

3 Proposals for Consultants and Freelancers

A Guide for Those in the Business Who Also Manage Their Own Business

It can be challenging enough to manage projects and client expectations, but if you don't have an appropriate agreement in place, you can find yourself on the losing end of any project you take on. Proposals and statements of work are essential to protecting your business—and yourself—from financial and legal troubles. After you accept a project and shake hands, make sure you spend the right amount of time composing an agreement that details the terms of your relationship and the payment schedule for your client.

Russ Unger

Proposals

There is an old saying that "no good deed goes unpunished," and the same generally goes for getting invited to pitch a potential client on a new project—the high-fives and feel-good moments are quickly replaced with "Oh, crap! It's time to write the proposal!"

The biggest challenge in writing the proposal is writing your very first one. It's nearly impossible to know where to begin if you've never had to author one yourself, and that's where this chapter should come in handy.

Every type of project you encounter will have varying flavors that will keep you on your toes when it comes time to author the proposal. Fortunately, there's something of a core that is common to all proposals and can be reused from project to project. (For a detailed discussion of project types, see Chapter 2.)

When should you write a proposal? Always.

Why should you write a proposal? Throughout the history of working on projects, the ones that have put people in the most uncomfortable situations have been those where there was no agreement in place between the client and the vendor.

You may be very tempted to skip this step when you make the first connection with a potential client and things seem to click. Even though you have an apparent understanding about the client's needs and are able to articulate it in way that they understand, you really are not quite yet ready to start working.

In fact, this is exactly the point where you need to slow down and take a breath.

Instead of getting right to work, take the time to define your professional relationship and the rules of engagement with your new client. Jean Marc Favreau of the law firm Peer, Gan & Gisler, LLP, in Washington D.C., says,

> All too often contractors and their clients believe there is a meeting of the minds at the beginning of their relationship, when in fact ambiguities are just lying in wait. While it is almost impossible to prepare for all possible contingencies, a comprehensive written contract is your best defense and the smartest way to ensure that you do not later find yourself in a courtroom arguing about the terms of your relationship. The more clearly you define the terms and parameters of your relationship with a client in a written contract up front, the less likely you will end up fighting over each party's obligations down the line.

New projects and new people are exciting. There is often a desire not to "kill the deal" by throwing a proposal into the mix, but, as in any relationship, the honeymoon feeling can eventually subside.

Promises can be broken on both sides of the relationship.

A client can fail to provide you with timely access to content. (I know that this is almost unheard of, but believe it or not, it happens! That's sarcasm, in case you missed it.) Funding that was once available for the project may be shifted elsewhere—and then you, the one who is engaged in the work, may be left holding the bag.

Companies also realize that they are taking risks working with external vendors—especially those who are very small businesses or independent contractors. Well-written proposals provide clients with a sense of stability and protection, which can help alleviate many of the concerns that might arise.

A proposal also allows you to define terms that protect both sides in the event that something changes. If the client does not provide you with timely access to their resources, your timeline may slip; you need to make them aware of their obligations to the project's success. If a client loses funding and kills the project—and you do not have a proposal or other form of contract in place—then you may run the risk of not getting paid for work you have already completed.

The point should be crystal clear: Always write a proposal.

Creating the Proposal

After you land the project, it's time to get the proposal done. The sooner a proposal is approved and signed, the sooner you can begin work and—most importantly—begin to get paid for the work.

The core components of a good proposal are

▶ Title page

▶ Revision history

▶ Project overview

▶ Project approach

- Scope of work
- Assumptions
- Deliverables
- Ownership and rights
- Additional costs and fees
- Project pricing
- Payment schedule
- Acknowledgement and sign-off

Let's take a deeper dive into each part of the proposal.

Title Page

The title page is the simple page that introduces your document. Title pages are an interesting beast: there are a number of ways you can create them from a style and information perspective. How you do it is up to you.

A typical title page consists of the following elements:

- Client company name
- Client company logo (if you have permission to use it)
- Project title
- Document type (proposal)
- Version of proposal
- Submission date
- Your company name
- Proposal authors
- Project reference number
- Cost
- Confidentiality

For your first proposal include everything—except the client's company logo, the cost, and (potentially) the project reference number.

Why not include these elements on the title page?

Your client knows who they are. It's probably not worth the time and effort to request permission to use the company logo, nor is it worth the possible unpleasantness if you inadvertently misuse it. The cost is best placed after you have identified the various components of the project in the body, and the cost information leads nicely into the payment schedule. The project reference number is something to be aware of. A lot of companies will not use one at all; however, some government agencies are known to rely upon this particular item, and if it is not found on your title page, your proposal may be rejected.

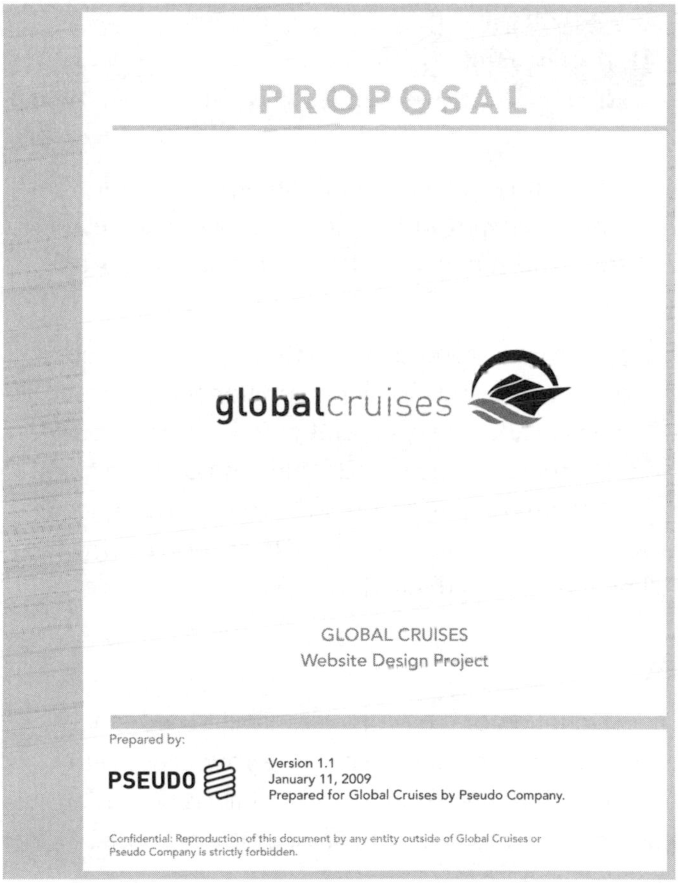

PROPOSAL

globalcruises

GLOBAL CRUISES
Website Design Project

Prepared by:

PSEUDO

Version 1.1
January 11, 2009
Prepared for Global Cruises by Pseudo Company.

Confidential: Reproduction of this document by any entity outside of Global Cruises or Pseudo Company is strictly forbidden.

Figure 3.1 *Sample proposal title page*

In Figure 3.1, the (fictional) client logo was used. In the event that permission was not given or a relationship was not established, it is best not to display the logo of the client company.

Revision History

The revision history is its own section of the proposal and is used to identify how many times you have updated the proposal since the original version. In general, it is best to provide the version number, date, author, and any comments associated with the version, such as what was modified, in order to provide the reader with context as to the modifications (Table 3.1).

TABLE 3.1	Sample Revision History Table			
REVISION	SECTION	DESCRIPTION	EDITOR	DATE
1.0		Original Document	REU	8-Jan-09
1.1	Assumptions	Updated to reflect software requirements	REU	11-Jan-09

Occasionally, clients will sign off on a proposal and then ask you for further revisions. If you choose to move forward with the client and make these changes, you should take the opportunity to update your document from version 1.x to 2.0.

In essence, when a client approves a proposal and both parties agree upon the terms, you are ready to begin working. So when additional modifications are requested, you need to review them very carefully. This ensures your costs still make sense and that there is a clear understanding on both sides about the modifications and at what stage the project is restarting (if necessary). You should also always provide an appropriate explanation of why the revision constitutes a full new version in the revision history.

Project Overview

The overview section is a description of the project you will be working on—in your own words. This description should provide your client with a clear picture of what you envision their product will entail, as well as an explanation of what they can expect to find in the rest of the proposal.

Here is an example of the beginning of an overview:

> [Client Company Name] is seeking to create a new online Web presence. This Web presence provides [Client Company Name] customers with an ability to research and purchase products online, as well as other services and benefits available through the company. The goals of the online Web presence are to...

You should be able to give a solid overview in one or two paragraphs, providing a very high-level amount of detail as to what the client should expect from you. It is a good idea to conclude the overview with a sound explanation of your recommendations and proposed approach to completing the project:

> This proposal will detail [Your Company Name]'s recommendations and approach for the design and development of [Client Company Name]'s online Web presence. Given the deadline of [deadline date], it is proposed that...

Project Approach

The approach to the project will vary depending on what type of project you are undertaking. This is your opportunity identify to your client how you plan on working on the project with them. You get to define your rules of engagement and set expectations for the work that is ahead of you.

Many individuals and companies operate with very similar methodologies—but use different names or clever acronyms that dovetail with their overall branding.

Once upon a time, a mythological methodology was created to show to (potential) clients, and it found its way into many proposals. The process was called The PURITE Process™ (pronounced "purity"), and in sharing this with you, a mythological being has just died a little on the inside, so please take care to read this as a piece of fiction. The name of the process is slightly cheesy, and the process is clearly somewhat incomplete. Post-launch analysis was omitted from this methodology (an oversight), but it should be included for all clients, of course. Without further delay, here's the PURITE approach:

> [Your Company Name] has identified a standard process for project success with our clients. Although each of these phases may not be applicable to [Project Title], the entire process is defined as follows:
>
> **The PURITE Process™** is [Your Company Name]'s in-house methodology for ensuring success across the board for all initiatives. By utilizing PURITE, [Your Company Name] has a proven set of guidelines for working closely with clients and users/audiences to reliably maintain and exceed delivery expectations.
>
> **P – Prepare.** We dedicate a portion of every initiative to understanding your industry and your competitors and how they do business in order to be as informed as possible prior to beginning requirements gathering.
>
> **U – Understand.** We work closely with your subject matter experts and/or users to define the requirements for building the project correctly.

R – Render. Through the Render phase we create and develop all the pieces of the project/product. In our experience, any development phase requires a lot of heads-down, focused work effort but also timely, open communication with your team(s). It also requires that we...

I – Iterate. The Iterate phase is repeated throughout the entire lifecycle of the project. We move as quickly as possible to bring the project to life, and this often requires creating multiple iterations in rapid timelines. This requires direct and timely involvement from you and your dedicated resources. The end result is the product you've specified—and helped to create.

T – Test. We test every project throughout the course of our Render phase; however, we also require an extra set of eyes—from our own testing team and from your designated user group/audience group to perform goal-based testing. This additional round of testing helps ensure that as few stones as possible are left unturned in order to deliver a project that has been rigorously evaluated from multiple levels.

E – Enable. Upon successful completion of the five previous phases and your signed approval, we will enable the solution and take it live.

The PURITE Process™ doesn't end there. After project completion, we regularly communicate with our clients. We will continue to gauge your satisfaction levels, understand your changing goals or project enhancements, and assist you in defining the best approach for the future development of your project.

You are welcome to use as little or as much of this as is applicable or useful to you. The mythological author who created the process does not mind if you do not credit the source, either.

Defining your process can be as detailed as above or as simple as the following:

Plan, Define, Develop, Extend

▶ Plan the overall strategy

▶ Define the detailed project requirements

▶ Develop, test, refine, and launch the work product

▶ Extend the project by recommending enhancements and improvements based on information learned during development, testing, and post-launch

After you define your process, you have the opportunity to detail the various efforts that will take place in each phase of your approach, as well as what each of those efforts means to you and your client.

The approach section of your proposal will vary in length depending upon the project, your process, and the activities that take place within each step of your process. Try to keep it to two to three pages maximum, though, and ensure that you include only the outputs that you will be able to deliver to your client—to prevent further updating of the document or revisiting the project pricing.

Scope of Work

The scope of work section is where you identify the division of labor for the project. That is, you identify which components of the project you are responsible for and which the client is responsible for.

Reread that. Think about it for a moment. Let it sink in. There we go.

That's right. This is the part of the proposal where you tell the client, in writing, *we* are going to do this and *you* are going to do that. Then later, when the client signs your proposal, they are agreeing to this arrangement, and you have a paper trail to back you up in the event of any misunderstandings.

The intention here is to clearly identify who is going to be handling what aspects of the project, as well as what aspects of the project are included within your proposal and for the price that you have estimated.

If you can find no other really compelling reason to write a proposal, this should be reason enough.

Here is a very brief example of a scope of work:

> We were approached by [Client Company Name] to provide all services required to build [Project Type].
>
> [Your Company Name] will focus solely on the [User Experience Design Aspect(s)] of the [Client Company Name]'s website.
>
> [Client Company Name] will provide detailed feedback on all aspects of [Project Type] in accordance to the Project Plan.
>
> [Client Company Name] will provide any required assets for use in the project, including fonts, color schemes, brand standards, etc.

Assumptions

The assumptions section of the proposal is a good place to spell out, without leaving room for debate, what is needed from your client to ensure your success. That is, these are the things that you are assuming—and communicating to the client—that you will have access to or that will be delivered to you to make the project a success.

What you're calling *assumptions* in this section are really *expectations*. It's just a lot more polite to assume.

You can create as many project plans as you would like, but if neither you nor the client commit to meeting milestones and objectives, both sides are committing to certain project failure. In general, the assumptions are an expectation of resources and assets, as well as timely (translation: prompt, immediate) access to both of these.

Here is an example of how to write assumptions:

Assumptions

It is necessary that [Client Company Name] provide the following assets and resources. An inability to provide these assets and resources in a timely and complete manner may contribute to the unsuccessful or delayed delivery of this project.

The following assets and resources are expected:

Timely access to all required [Client Company Name] employees.

Timely access to all required assets of the [Project] in current state, including any source files, if available.

Content, as required and including but not limited to copy, imagery, audio, etc. for any aspect of [Project].

Deliverables

Deliverables are the work product that you will create and turn over to the client. This section is your opportunity to detail to the client what type of work product they can expect from you during the course of the project. It is recommended that you handle status reporting separately, closer to the end of the project, but feel free to add it to this part of the project.

Do provide descriptions of any work product that you might include, even if the work product does not get produced. This might seem as if it could be overkill or has the potential to open the "I read about [deliverable type] in the proposal, but I don't see it here" can of worms, but one little word, *may*, can make the difference.

Deliverables

[Your Company Name] provides a variety of deliverables throughout the course of a project. For [Client Company Name], we have identified the following deliverables:

Creative Brief

The Creative Brief is the first step of the project. This document will help us to create a quick and effective, high-level overview of the project. The purpose of the Creative Brief is to clarify the goals and needs of the users and to define any of the special resources and/or constraints related to the project.

And so on…

Ownership and Rights

It is important to consider the extent to which you will allow your client to use the work product that you produce. These rights can be defined in many different ways, but the majority of your work will fall into two categories:

▶ Work for hire

▶ Licensed work

Work for hire (known in the legal world as "work made for hire") projects are considered to be created by and under copyright by the party who pays for the work—not the party responsible for doing the actual work.

This means that when performing work on a project that is work for hire, you have absolutely no rights to the work and everything you create related to the project is owned by the client. This situation is difficult for many companies and individuals to contend with: It often means there is no downstream "maintenance" work (with its additional revenue), as clients may decide to maintain the project on their own once it has been completed.

Do not be swayed from a project where a client forces the stipulation; it is not uncommon. When you put work for hire projects in the context of full-time employment with a company, this is pretty standard for an employer-employee relationship. It is also an opportunity to visit your pricing model—many projects are billed at a somewhat increased rate to compensate for the potentially lost revenue in the future.

Remember, this all depends upon the relationship you have with your client and how you choose to do business. Time and experience will help you make the right determination for the types of work you do and the pricing models you choose.

Licensed work projects enable you to retain the copyright to the work but grant other parties the right to copy and/or distribute it. You can build any number of stipulations into the licensing agreement. You will most likely take advantage of licensing your work when you retain ownership of all of the source material of your work and deliver only limited-use work product to your clients (such as PDFs instead of original, editable Word, Visio, Axure, OmniGraffle, or other documents).

You can take many different approaches to licensing your work, including licensing work to be used without modification, noncommercially, or a number of other ways that may fit your situation.

Creative Commons (http://creativecommons.org/about/licenses) provides easy-to-understand explanations of a variety of license types that you might make use of, but those are only a small subset of the licensing world. If you find yourself in a situation where you are getting into very detailed and specific needs, it is always best to contact a copyright attorney to assist you in creating the best possible solution.

Additional Costs and Fees

It is important that your client understand whether the project pricing you will provide for them does (or does not) account for external resources.

For example, some projects may require the purchase of stock photography from a vendor. You can either purchase the imagery (with the appropriate usage rights) and include that as a part of your fee, or you can clearly identify the purchase of imagery as an additional cost that will be passed along to your client.

You may also offer services that you want to make your client aware of—this is a good opportunity to promote those services.

Here is an example of how to explain how additional costs and fees will be handled:

Additional Costs and Fees

In the event that outside resources are required (such as content, imagery, fonts, etc.), these shall be identified, approved by and billed to [Client Company Name].

In addition, [Your Company Name] can provide hosting services to our clients with very low overhead. We provide hosting services—including configurable, Web-based e-mail—starting as low as $25 per month, with a $25 setup fee. In the event that [Client Company Name] would like to purchase a "maintenance" package, [Your Company Name] will work to create a package that is mutually agreeable and beneficial to both parties.

Project Pricing

After you document the details of how you're going to perform the work for the project, it's a pretty good idea to let the client know the cost.

How you arrive at the price is largely up to you, but here's a tip: Estimate how long you think it will take *you* to do the project—including a specific number of revisions, estimate a reasonable amount of time for project management, which could be around 25 percent; then determine the hourly billable rate you want to charge, and calculate it all out. There are a variety of formulas to help you with this, such as applying degrees of difficulty to each portion of the project, to help you come up with a cost range to provide to your client.

In most cases, experience is going to be the key to helping you appropriately estimate your projects—from a time-and-materials perspective.

How do you determine your billing rate? Research what others are charging, for comparison, by locating salary surveys and contractor rates. For example, organizations such as the Information Architecture Institute (www.iainstitute.org), AIGA (www.aiga.com), Coroflot (www.coroflot.com), and the talent agency Aquent (www.aquent.com) perform salary and contractor rate surveys. You can get a decent idea of the rates you could charge by taking into account your experience, what others in your market are charging, and what you feel is somewhat fair.

Remember: You can always lower your rate. It's a lot more difficult to ask your client to pay you more money once they've seen numbers on a page!

There are many different ways to structure the pricing for your project. Depending on the nature of your project, you may want or need to provide multiple estimates that allow for a variety of pricing options. Suppose, for example, you provide a client with two options: a static HTML Web site and a Web site with a content management system (CMS) that would allow for dynamic content (which the client could then administer without dedicated resources). Here's how you could phrase the project estimates:

Project Estimate

[Your Company Name] has proposed multiple estimates for [Client Company Name], in order to provide the best possible options for your immediate and/or future needs. [Your Company Name] makes the assumption that all content will be provided by [Client Company Name]. In the event that [Your Company Name] is requested to provide content services, the estimates will need to be redefined.

[Your Company Name]'s estimates allow for flexibility from a cost and needs perspective. The estimates are as follows:

Estimate 1

[Your Company Name] estimates that the [Project] for [Client Company Name], without any interactive content...

Remember, there is no real wrong way to put together your project estimate—unless you put yourself into a negative cash flow position!

Payment Schedule

There is a myth floating around that all freelance projects are paid 50 percent up front, before the work begins, and 50 percent upon completion, when the project ends.

This myth needs to be dispelled—*right now*! This is no way to do business, and it is no way to ensure timely, consistent income while you perform the work. You don't want to put yourself in a position where you have to make change after change for a client simply because you want to get the project done and get paid, instead of working through a change order process.

You can price projects a number of ways—from submitted invoices in a predetermined time frame to milestone-based payments. A wiser approach is to steer your projects to a recurring payment schedule with regular, detailed invoices. This approach should also provide clients with a clear understanding of what has been accomplished and what work is remaining on the project.

The following example is one way to structure payments for your work:

Payment Schedule

[Your Company Name] typical payment schedule is to receive a retainer fee of XX% of the total estimated price of the project prior to commencement.

[Your Company Name] shall submit invoices on the 1st and 15th of every month; payment is due in full within 14 days.

Upon completion of the project, [Your Company Name] shall deliver all work product to [Client Company Name]. Once the materials are satisfactorily approved, [Your Company Name] shall refund any payment excess remaining from the retainer or [Your Company Name] shall submit a final invoice for amounts not covered by the retainer.

Note: If [Project] is placed on hold for a period of more than 14 days with no work progress made, [Your Company Name] shall submit a final invoice for any fees not covered by the retainer and shall be provided with the right of first refusal in the event that the project is reopened.

Although it's not required, it is helpful to include a note about how the project will be handled if it is put on hold for an extensive period of time. This stipulation can help you keep your project on track and moving forward— and it gives you a discussion point with your clients. If you will not be doing additional work for them for a long time, you want to be able to move on and look for work to fill the void.

Acknowledgment and Sign-Off

While it is very important to ensure that you have a proposal in place, but by itself it's not enough. The proposal really doesn't mean much until the right person at your client company has approved and signed it.

It's vital to make sure that everyone has a clear understanding of what is going to be taking place and how much is expected from each side. It is equally important that you protect yourself from the "iteration superhighway" and reduce your risk of allowing a client to engage you in "feature creep": continually requesting "just one more thing" that needs to be included.

Sign-offs are pretty simple and clear. Once you have created the proposal document, you will provide your client with an acknowledgment and sign-off that will approve the agreement between your two companies. Always prepare two copies—one for each party—and ensure that both copies are signed.

Here is an example of an acknowledgment you can use:

Acknowledgment

This proposal is acknowledged and agreed in its entirety by [Client Company Name]. This proposal must be signed and dated by an authorized representative of [Client Company Name] in order to be in effect. Alternately, a signed purchase order referencing this proposal will constitute acceptance in place of this signed document (provided, however, that any preprinted terms on such purchase order shall be considered null and void and of no effect).

This proposal constitutes the entire agreement between the parties with respect to the subject matter of this proposal. This proposal merges and supersedes all prior oral or written agreements, discussions, negotiations, commitments, writings, or understandings. This includes without limitation any representations contained in any sales literature, brochures, or other written descriptive or advertising material and is the complete and exclusive statement of the terms of the parties' agreement. Each of the parties acknowledges and agrees that in executing this proposal it has not relied upon, and it expressly disclaims any reliance upon, any representation or statement not set forth herein or in the Agreement.

Accepted by the authorized representatives of:

[Your Company Name]   [Client Company Name]

By: _____   By: _____

Name: _____   Name: _____

Title: _____   Title: _____

Date: _____   Date: _____

Make all checks payable to: [Your Company Name]

Statements of Work

A statement of work (SOW) is a high-level definition of your project objectives that you should be able to put together in a two- to three-page document (not including cover). The SOW is typically written before you get into detailed requirements, although depending upon your client and your project needs, you may choose to create a hybrid document that best suits your needs.

In general, SOWs should be used to build consensus between your team and your client's stakeholders early on. The SOW will define the inputs and outputs of the project, as well as assumptions and limitations.

At this point, it is not uncommon for clients to ask you to provide a "ballpark figure" for the work you will be doing for them. It can be a little risky to answer that at this point. It is recommended that you do your best to avoid specifics or commitments without defining the details. It's just not possible to know how much a project is going to cost when you haven't yet written the proposal and/or requirements document.

That said, you have to make a judgment call at this point. If you are working on a project such as a basic Web site, and you have successfully completed several similar projects before and/or have worked with the same client before, then you have some wiggle room. Remember, erring on the side of caution is always better than an uncomfortable situation later on in the project.

A statement of work should be approximately two to three pages and, at minimum, contain the following:

- ► Title page
- ► Revision history
- ► Project reference number
- ► Project summary
- ► Start date
- ► End date
- ► Rate/price
- ► Project explanation
- ► Activities and deliverables
- ► Itemized costs and payment schedule
- ► Acknowledgement and sign-off

Do the elements look familiar? They should—you can put together an SOW utilizing a trimmed-down version of the proposal.

You have now learned how to put together two types of documentation that will allow you to identify the work you are performing for a client. These documents should be the foundation of any project work you do for any client and will give you and your clients a well-defined set of marching orders for your projects.

4 Project Objectives and Approach

Know Which Star to Navigate By

One of the keys to a good project is to start the team out with clear project objectives and a well-understood approach. Ideally, the project leadership will have this defined for you—but how do you know if they don't?

This chapter talks about forming project objectives and offers some questions that will help you solidify those goals. We'll also discuss some common project approaches (or *methodologies*) and how they may influence the way you work.

Carolyn Chandler

You're in the project kickoff, with the full team for the first time. The project manager hands out some materials and gives you an overview of the project. By the end of the meeting, ideally, you should have the following information:

▶ Why is the project important to the company?

▶ How will stakeholders determine if the project was a success?

▶ What approach or methodology will the project follow?

▶ What are the major dates or *milestones* for key points, such as getting approval from business stakeholders?

All of these questions concern the expectations that stakeholders have for the project: *what* the project will accomplish and *how* they will be involved in it. The first two questions pertain to the project's objectives and the last two to the project's approach.

A *project objective* is a statement of a measurable goal for the project. Let's talk about objectives in more detail.

Solidify Project Objectives

Objectives are an important focusing lens that you'll use throughout the project. They should spring from the client company's overall business strategy, so the project objectives should be in line with the strategic initiatives within the company. For example, if there is a strategic initiative to appeal to a new group of prospective customers (called a *market*), the site or application you're creating may be an effort to provide that market with online access to products and services relevant to them. The objective for that project would then be focused on reaching and engaging that market.

A clear objective resonates throughout a project. It helps you

▶ Ask the right questions as you gather ideas from business stakeholders

▶ Plan research with users and focus your analysis of the results

▶ Detail the ideas gathered from stakeholders and users and convert them into a consolidated list of project requirements

▶ Prioritize those project requirements based on their value to the company

- Create effective interaction designs
- Manage requests for changes to the design once development begins
- Focus efforts during deployment activities (such as training and communications to users about the new site or application before and during its launch)
- Determine whether you've met the needs of the client company, once the project is launched

When you start a new project, you probably have project objectives from the project's sponsor (the business stakeholder who has direct responsibility for the success of the project), as well as a set of project-related requests coming from business stakeholders and from customers, but they all may be a bit fuzzy (Figure 4.1). Your goal is to clarify these into solid statements that you can use as a yardstick for the project's success.

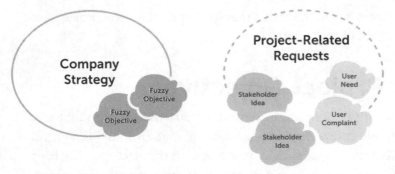

Figure 4.1 *Fuzzy objectives, ideas, and needs*

A solid objective is

- **Easy to understand.** Avoid insider terminology.
- **Distinct.** Avoid vague statements; instead, use wording that seems like it will be useful when you're prioritizing requirements.
- **Measurable.** Make concrete statements that you can set an independent measurement against to determine your success.

As you define a fuzzy objective, making it clear and measurable, it becomes a solid objective that you can base decisions on.

Figure 4.2 *Objectives being solidified*

You'll hear many statements that could be considered objectives. Analyzing fuzzy ones such as those below will help you solidify your objectives and communicate more effectively within the project team.

 Business Advocate **"Our objective is to become the market leader in industry x."**

This is an objective for the entire company, but is too broad for a specific project. Multiple initiatives at the company need to come together to make this happen; any one site or application may *help* with this but will be very unlikely to be able to handle the entire burden—unless the entire company is about this one site or application and it ends up being wildly successful.

 Business Advocate **"Our objective is to generate excitement among our customer base."**

This one is better, because a site or application could have an impact on this, but it's still too vague. Why is it important to generate excitement? How does that excitement translate into meeting a business need? And how can you tell if you've been successful?

 Business Advocate **"Our objective is to increase the amount of traffic on our Web site."**

Now we're getting there. This one is easy to measure, but it's too focused on an intermediate step. Suppose you do generate more traffic: It may not help you if people don't perform the actions you want once they get there.

Fuzzy objectives can give you a sense of a client's desires and larger goals. From these you can craft more solid project objectives, such as

▶ Increase the revenue from online sales by 10 percent.

▶ Increase the revenue from online advertising by 20 percent.

▶ Increase the number of current and potential customers in our customer database to at least 20,000.

▶ Deliver highly rated and highly referenced content to our primary users. (Note that this one requires some work to decide how to measure "highly rated" and "highly referenced," but the elements are there to build from.)

Each of these can be measured and affected by your project. They can also map pretty closely to your designs and the features offered. For example, it's very common to offer an online newsletter as a way to meet an objective of growing the customer database: To deliver the newsletter you'll need to capture customer e-mail addresses, which will be added to the database. Objectives may also bring out new requirements. For example, if you're measuring success by the average rating given to articles on your site, you'll need a feature that allows users to give ratings. In these ways, objectives help you focus as you gather ideas for the site, and these may later become project requirements.

If there are multiple objectives, be sure to create a prioritized list with your business sponsor and project team. Objectives sometimes conflict with each other during design, and the team will need to know what takes precedence. The final prioritized list of objectives should come from your project sponsor, but you can be a key part of the discussion. Let's talk about how.

How Can a UX Designer Help?

If you find the project objectives are unclear at the beginning of a project, you can bring your facilitation skills to bear. Help the project team understand the business-related context of the project by holding a workshop with key stakeholders (see the next chapter for more on identifying the right stakeholders). Your goal in this session, which usually lasts two to four hours, is to bring out information on the company's strengths, weaknesses, opportunities, and threats. Called a *SWOT analysis*, this is a common business analysis technique and one way to discuss a company's position in the market. You can also use this time to discuss the company's competition.

Understand Strengths and Weaknesses

The *SW* in a SWOT analysis are the company's current strengths and weaknesses as they pertain to the project. Strengths and weaknesses could include internal processes as well as external perceptions—and often they influence each other. For example, a company with a large research and development (R&D) department could have access to a large source of original research that is published (a strength), but there may be no one to help make that content more accessible to the average user, leading to the perception that the company is "too academic" (a weakness).

Identify Opportunities and Threats

The *OT* is the future-facing half of the SWOT. Considering the things that differentiate the company from its competitors, what future initiatives could it pursue that will open up a new niche or strengthen a current one? What situations could threaten those plans?

For example, our R&D company may decide to hire writers to publish more accessible feature articles around its original research (an opportunity), but if the current site toolset doesn't have robust content-management features, the publishing process may be prohibitively slow. That could give competitors a chance to respond more quickly (a threat).

Compare Competitors

What is the company's main competition? Who are the competitors for the site being developed? They can be different, especially for large companies or brand new sites.

Are there sites that aren't direct competitors but that represent interesting models to consider? You can learn a lot from reviewing other e-commerce sites to see whether and how they sell what you're selling.

Pull It Together

The SWOT and competitor discussions are good topics to discuss at the same time because they interact with each other. It's hard to talk about future threats without knowing who your competitors are—and once you start talking about future opportunities, new competitors may come to mind.

Once you have a full picture here of the company's competitors and SWOT, your project objectives—as well as the overall fit of your project within the company strategy—should become easier to define, and the priorities among them should become clear.

Solidifying project objectives helps you understand expectations of what the project is going to accomplish. Next, let's talk about expectations concerning how the project will be run. Understanding the project approach will help you collaborate effectively and involve the right people at the right time.

Understand the Project Approach

Knowing the overall approach, or *methodology*, of a project is an important part of understanding when and how you'll be involved and how you should be involving others, such as your project team and business stakeholders.

Sometimes there seem to be as many project approaches as there are projects. How to choose the right approach for a project is a large topic in itself. The methodology you choose can depend on many things, including the structure and location of the project team, the technologies being used on the project, and the degree to which collaboration is a part of the company's culture. For the purposes of this book, we're assuming that you've joined a project where the approach has largely been determined by those responsible for the project's success, such as the project sponsor and project manager. In this situation, your main goal will be to understand the approach and help make it effective for the business stakeholders and your users.

Here we'll focus on two of the most common types of approach, as well as a third that shows a possible variation you might encounter on a project. The important thing to note is that most approaches involve the same steps:

▶ **Plan** the overall strategy, approach, and team structure.

▶ **Define** the project requirements.

▶ **Design** interaction and visual concepts and evolve them into detailed specifications.

▶ **Develop**, test, and refine the solution.

▶ **Deploy** the solution via messaging, training, and a planned launch.

▶ **Extend** the project by making recommendations for improvements.

The names for these steps may vary, as may the degree to which they overlap and the way information is documented. But the general activities in each step are common to most projects and to all three models presented here.

Waterfall Approach

A *waterfall approach* involves treating the steps of a project as separate, distinct *phases,* where approval of one phase is needed before the next phase begins. For example, the Design phase does not begin in earnest until requirements have been approved by business stakeholders, who sign off on one or more requirements documents at the end of the Define phase.

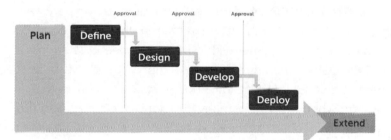

Figure 4.3 *Example of a waterfall approach, where each phase "falls" into the next*

The problem with a pure waterfall approach is that it assumes that each phase can be completed with minimal changes to the phase before it. So if you come up with new requirements in the Design phase, which is common, you must suggest changes to documents that were approved at the end of the Define phase, which can throw off the plan and the schedule.

Agile Approaches

Because change is constant, project teams are continually looking for more flexible approaches than the waterfall model. Many methodologies follow a more fluid approach, with some steps happening alongside each other; for example, versions of the Web site could be released on a rapid, iterative schedule using an *agile* or *rapid development* approach. An agile approach generally has a greater focus on rapid collaboration and a reduced focus on detailed documentation and formal sign-off.

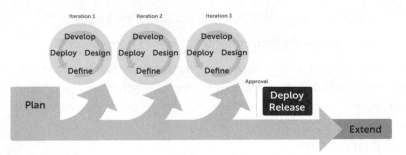

Figure 4.4 *Example of an agile approach*

A true agile approach (following the best practices developed by members of the Agile Alliance, for example) calls for small teams whose members are located next to each other physically, with little focus on defining formal roles between team members. Working this way allows a very high degree of collaboration, which reduces the need for heavy documentation between the stages of design, development, and testing. A team member can pose a question, come to the answer together with other team members during a quick whiteboarding session, and implement a solution without the delay of detailed documentation and approval. Stakeholder reviews occur with a fully functioning system when one of the many iterations is released, and the resulting input is taken into account as the next iteration is planned. (*Iterations* are draft versions of a particular site or application.)

When an agile approach is working as it's designed to, it's a beautiful thing. At most companies and within most consulting engagements, however, teams rarely follow a pure agile approach. In part, this is because companies are increasingly using distributed teams and remote workers, which makes it difficult to maintain the high degree of collaboration needed to take best advantage of the pure agile approach.

Modified Approaches

Most projects try to follow an approach that marries the best of both worlds, with enough structure and documentation to reduce the risks posed by distributed teams and turnover of team members, but enough collaboration and iteration to respond to changes in a relatively nimble way. For example, a project may follow a waterfall model but include an overlap in phases so that there are key collaboration points from team to team. This allows potential changes to surface earlier in each phase. This may also include an early release (such as a beta release to a particular user group) with a shorter iteration cycle. Feedback from that release can then be incorporated before the full deployment of the new site.

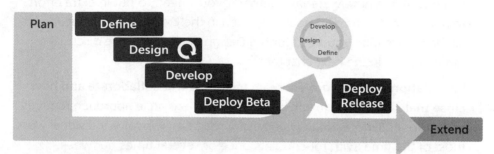

Figure 4.5 *Modified waterfall with beta release*

Notice the smaller iterations within the Design phase in the Figure 4.5. That's one of the greatest values you bring to your team as a UX designer. Tools such as wireframes (Chapter 11) and prototypes (Chapter 12) allow you to gather feedback on quick iterations of ideas, before a lot of development time has been put in.

A modified waterfall approach like the one in Figure 4.5 is among the most commonly used methodologies, so it's the approach that forms the framework of this book. However, many of the topics covered here will apply to your project regardless of the specifics of your approach, because the basic activities behind them—defining and designing, for example—are still necessary.

 Deep Diving

If your project is using an agile approach, you'll have unique needs during requirements gathering, such as the writing of "user stories" as a way to capture requirements. We recommend *User Stories Applied: For Agile Software Development* by Mike Cohn (Addison-Wesley Professional, 2004).

How Does the Approach Affect Me?

Knowing your approach helps you understand a number of things:

▶ **What questions you should be asking, and when.** For example, if you're working with a pure waterfall approach, you'll need to put in extra effort to make sure the requirements captured in the Define phase contain all the information you need for the Design phase. (We'll be discussing requirements in the next chapter.)

▶ **Expectations on how project team members will collaborate and how close that collaboration will be.** For example, an agile approach requires very close collaboration. A waterfall approach may involve individual work most of the time, with touchpoints once or several times per week.

▶ **The level of detail needed in your documentation and the level of formality.** Documents submitted at sign-off points need to be formal, almost like legal contracts. Typically, you'll need more formal documents in a waterfall approach, where sign-off is required before you move on to the next phase. However, you may also have some formal sign-off documents when using an agile approach—for example, to capture information at major decision points, such as when a particular iteration is prepared for full release and deployment.

▶ **Important milestones that involve approval from stakeholders and deployment to different groups.** The approach will determine what different audiences need to provide at various points in the project, including approvals from stakeholders at sign-off points and feedback from potential users during a beta release.

Now that you've solidified your project objectives and gained an understanding of the project approach, in the next chapter we'll start with the primary work in the Define phase: gathering requirements.

5 Business Requirements

Know the Problem Before You Create the Solution

By the time the project team gets together you'll probably have heard, or have come up with, a lot of ideas about what needs to be done. There may already be lists of features provided by some prominent members of the company (your business stakeholders), along with their opinions about which features are most important. These are *elements* of the business requirements for the project, and they're a good start. To make sure you have a complete solution at the end of the project, you'll need to generate and clarify requirements from multiple viewpoints. In this chapter we'll focus on gathering and detailing requirements from your business stakeholders.

Carolyn Chandler

C hapter 4 covered fuzzy objectives and discussed some ways you can help clarify them for yourself and the project team. In the early stages of a project, you're also likely to have a set of requests that are relatively fuzzy. These may be ideas from stakeholders, user complaints, or user requests. To make these useful and trackable components of your project, you'll need to coalesce these ideas into *requirements*.

Requirements are statements defining what the site or application needs to do. Ideally, a business requirement

▶ Provides insight into the overall need that must be addressed

▶ Represents and consolidates needs provided by different stakeholders

▶ Gives direction for design, without being too specific about how it will be accomplished

▶ Serves as a distinct unit of work for purposes of prioritization and tracking

Here's an example of an idea for a feature on an e-commerce Web site. You could receive this same idea from a couple of different business stakeholders early in the Define phase:

"Customers can track their orders online."

This is a good base for a requirement, but it's fuzzy. Start asking questions that get to the details of the requirement, such as

▶ Why is it important to the business that customers be able to track their orders online? For example, is it to cut down on the number of calls to customer support?

▶ Does the company currently have the capability to track packages online? If not, new requirements will need to be captured for the tracking features, or the company may need to partner with a third party.

▶ How accurate does the tracking have to be? What kind of information should be included in the tracking details? For example, does the site have to provide an updated estimate for delivery time?

Asking these sorts of questions will help you coalesce fuzzy ideas into solid requirements. It will also make it apparent that the same statement can mean different things to different people.

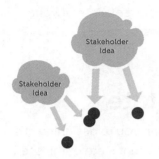

For example, one stakeholder may think tracking packages involves receiving a confirmation e-mail with a tracking number, which can be entered on UPS.com or another site so that the customer can see the latest stop the package has reached. Another stakeholder may think the company needs to push the envelope on package tracking and invest in developing the ability for customers to track packages via GPS, seeing the exact location in real time using an online map. As you can imagine, there's a significant difference here in user experience and scope!

It's important to outline these differences early in the project. Otherwise, you'll end up developing a solution that misses the intent of the business stakeholder—and potentially misses the project objectives. That leads to unhappy stakeholders and, if the feature needs to be redesigned, lost time and money.

So, clear and detailed requirements are a key part of your overall project. Getting to a consolidated list of project requirements involves the following steps:

1. Understand the current state of the site or its competitors.
2. Gather needs and ideas from business stakeholders as well as current and potential users. (See Chapter 6 for details on working with users.)
3. Coalesce ideas into requirements.
4. Prioritize requirements based on project objectives. (See Chapter 9 for suggestions on setting priorities.)

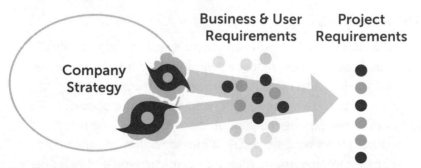

Figure 5.1 *Coalesce ideas from business stakeholders into business requirements, and ideas from research with users into user requirements. Then, use project objectives to focus prioritization efforts and create a consolidated list of project requirements.*

First, let's talk about gaining an understanding of the current state of your site so that you have a context for the ideas that will be coming your way during requirements gathering.

Understand the Current State

When diving into the specifics of the site or application you're designing, it's important to ground yourself by understanding the current state of the site (if you're redesigning one that already exists) or by understanding key competitors more thoroughly (if you're designing a new site or application).

You can learn a great deal about the current state through stakeholder interviews (more on this in a few pages). You can also gain a lot of understanding on your own, and this can serve as a strong base for stakeholder interviews and user research efforts. A great way to gain background information and generate ideas that could become requirements is to conduct a heuristic analysis.

By Any Other Name...

The word *heuristic* means a rule of thumb or best practice. A heuristic analysis has come to mean a review of a product against a set of rules (heuristics) for usable design, usually conducted by a UX designer. User-friendly sites will follow most or all of the heuristics you use in your analysis.

You may also hear this technique called a *heuristic evaluation*, *expert review*, or some combination of these terms.

Heuristic Analysis

A *heuristic analysis* is a technique you can use to evaluate the usability of an existing design, based on best practices within the user experience field. You can conduct such an analysis on the current site at the beginning of a redesign project or analyze competing sites to understand opportunities for offering a better user experience than other companies. The result is a document describing the strengths and weaknesses of the site, including recommendations for improvement. After it's complete, you'll have a deeper understanding of the site analyzed and a list of ideas to contribute to the requirements for the new site.

For example, a commonly used heuristic is this one, from Jakob Nielsen's list of ten usability heuristics (view the complete list on Jakob Nielsen's site, at www.useit.com/papers/heuristic/heuristic_list.html):

Visibility of system status. The system should always keep users informed about what's happening, through appropriate feedback within reasonable time.

There are many situations on a site where this heuristic may not be followed. For example, let's say the user clicks on a Download button and gets no message that his file is being downloaded. The system has not informed the user that the file is in the process of being downloaded, even though the download has started. So the user may click the button again, thinking that he missed the button the first time...and then click again....

This can lead to multiple downloads—potentially causing problems for both the performance of the site and the user, who now has multiple downloads in progress without realizing it.

During the heuristic analysis, you can note this as a problem area, describe it, and rate its impact. You may also share an idea that might address the problem, which could be added to the requirements list.

Why Conduct a Heuristic Analysis?

Conducting this kind of analysis is a relatively quick and inexpensive way of obtaining feedback on a design. A heuristic analysis can provide a general understanding of the design quality and help identify any potential design issues.

Keep in mind that this activity does not directly involve end users and shouldn't be a replacement for true user research. For example, it's possible that only 50 percent of your heuristic findings may actually be validated by later research. The analysis does, however, give the team a good handle on likely areas of concern. If you're working on redesigning an existing product or site, it can also be good for identifying obvious quick fixes that can lead to immediate improvements as the redesign efforts continue behind the scenes.

How Do I Do It?

The specific heuristics you use may vary from project to project, but the process for conducting the analysis will generally remain the same:

1. Gather product and project background knowledge.

   Make sure you have the objectives of the site, a list of the main user groups that need to be supported, information on the kind of environment users are likely to be working in, and a basic understanding of any specialized knowledge your users are likely to have. (Your analysis will be different for a site built for general consumers than a site built for pharmacists, for example.) If you need help with the last one, visiting a variety of competitive sites or applications can help you understand the most common terminology and areas of interest.

2. Choose the heuristics to use.

   There are many heuristics out there to reference. In addition to Jakob Nielsen's list, many UX designers refer to Bruce Tognazzini's list of design principles: www.asktog.com/basics/firstPrinciples.html. Once you're familiar with the subject matter of the site, you may want to add a few of your own—especially if you're analyzing more than one site. Be sure to keep your list to a manageable size (say, 8 to 12); too many heuristics can make the technique unwieldy for you and your readers.

3. Walk through prioritized areas of the site, identifying areas where the heuristics are followed well or missed.

   Each observation you make should have the following information:

   The general observation. A short statement summing up the finding. Ideally these will be numbered so that you can reference them quickly as you walk people through the report.

   A short description. A paragraph or two describing the context of the observation—for example, the point in a particular process where you noticed a problem.

   An impact ranking. This rating can be high, medium, or low for observations of issues, or it can be a note of a positive finding if you're sharing something that the site did well. In general, high-impact issues are those that you believe will cause many users to fail a particular task or permanently lose information (for example, an issue that causes a user to lose changes to a document she's been working on). Medium-impact issues are those that cause frustration and errors but don't cause irreversible issues. Low-impact issues are minor problems that may cause some confusion but don't typically lead to lost time or frustration.

Recommendations. These are next steps or ideas that you share, which may serve as a remedy to the problem you encountered.

Figure 5.2 shows an example of these elements together, as they might appear in your heuristic analysis.

| Observation #4 | HIGH |
| The search function does not appear to be bringing back all possible results. | Concern |

A sample test of the search function yielded mixed results. Searches using a name in a relatively new post, featuring a less commonly covered topic, occasionally returned no results. It also appears that primary search returns links to new stories only, not videos.

Recommendations
1. Ensure newly added content is indexed and searchable before, or very shortly after, being publicly available.
2. Consider surfacing related content when search results are brought back—for example, stories in similar categories or with similar tags—so users who are exploring have more threads to follow.
3. Consider universal search that presents results organized by category.
4. Use search term logs to understand commonly searched items. This may also provide insight into items that users are having trouble finding.

Figure 5.2 *A sample observation in a heuristic analysis report*

4. Present your findings to the project team and primary stakeholders.

Walk them through your observations and recommendations. Discuss why you gave the ratings you did. (This is also a great time to have a prepared recommendation on how to validate your findings, using one of the techniques discussed in Chapter 6.)

How Does a Heuristic Analysis Help with Requirements Gathering?

Once you've completed your heuristic analysis, you'll have a deeper understanding of the current state of the site (or its competitors), and a list of ideas that can contribute to requirements gathering. You'll also have some ideas on how to structure the topics you'll need to cover during requirements-gathering sessions—which leads us to the next step of that process.

Gather Ideas from Stakeholders

As we saw in our example at the beginning of this chapter, if you don't get context for an idea, such as "Customers can track their orders online," you risk missing the differences in expectations between stakeholders, like those of our friend who wants packages to be tracked by GPS. One of the most common mistakes made on a project is to seize on a feature and call it a requirement without first understanding the problem and the expectations around a solution.

So why does the requirements-gathering process get shortened so often?

Gathering ideas—and coalescing them into requirements—can take quite a bit of time. It's easy to underestimate the number of questions you need to ask to outline requirements so that they can be prioritized. And if the process isn't well structured or participation is incomplete, there can be a lot of churn that can last throughout the project. (*Churn* is time wasted in extra meetings and work iterations caused by lack of communication and involvement. These are different from the more productive work iterations that are part of designing and testing valid solutions in an effort to find the best one.)

So how do you encourage a well-balanced requirements process that's focused on business needs but avoids being a churning time-suck? Here are some steps for an efficient process:

1. **Outline roles and responsibilities.** Make sure project team members understand the roles that they should be filling as requirements are gathered.

2. **Gather the right stakeholders**, in the right groups, to ensure time is used in the best way during requirements-focused interviews or meetings.

3. **Create a plan for the meetings**, including topics to be covered and questions to be asked during meetings.

4. **Run the meetings efficiently**, capturing ideas and getting clarification. Investigate ideas to dig down to the needs behind each one.

When your meetings are finished, don't forget to thank the stakeholders involved and keep them updated on progress once you move to a consolidated, prioritized list.

Let's examine each of these steps in more detail.

Outline Responsibilities

The act of gathering business requirements generally involves members of the project team interviewing key business stakeholders to gather ideas.

Business stakeholders are those within the company who have a business-oriented stake in the success of the project or have subject matter expertise to contribute, or both. These folks aren't on the project full time, but they need to be involved at key points in the process, and requirements gathering is one of those points. Keep in mind that they also have day jobs (so to speak), so their time is valuable and often hard to get, unless you plan ahead.

The **project sponsor** (or sponsors) is the business stakeholder who also has direct responsibility for the success of the project, often at a relatively high level in the company, such as director. He or she won't be on the project on a day-to-day basis for the whole project lifecycle but will likely be actively involved in requirements gathering and ensuring a high level of participation by business stakeholders. The sponsor may also sit in on some or all sessions.

The **project team** includes people officially assigned to the project as ongoing resources. They may be involved as the project manager, UX designer, business analyst, technical lead, visual designer, quality assurance lead, and so on. Depending on the size of the project, this may be their primary job.

Within the project team itself, responsibilities during requirements gathering are often unclear. Taking time to define responsibilities early on will help ensure an efficient gathering process.

Here are some questions to ask as you determine the specific responsibilities each team member will shoulder during requirements gathering:

▶ Who is primarily responsible for gathering and scheduling the right business stakeholders in the most productive groups? This could include both internal and external stakeholders (such as partners, vendors, and so on).

▶ Who creates the structure of topics and questions for the business stakeholder meetings? This is a great collaborative exercise for the team, if time permits. The main facilitator can then arrange them in a structure that flows well in a meeting.

▶ Who facilitates the meetings?

▶ Who takes notes, and how are they shared?

- Who follows up with whom afterwards?

- Will someone from the technology team be present at all the meetings? If so, how is that person involved (are they listening, providing input, or something else)?

As a UX designer, whether or not you're primarily responsible for one or more of these areas, you have important skills to bring to the process. Creating a structure for topics and questions requires a knack for clear categorization (which sounds like a good crossover with information architecture), and of course facilitation skills are important for keeping the meeting on topic, with participation from all attendees.

Gather the Right Stakeholders

The main purpose of interviewing stakeholders is to gain an understanding of relevant project-related ideas, needs, knowledge, and frustrations from various points of view, which can then feed into the project requirements.

There's also the sometimes-unstated benefit of involving many different groups so that each one feels like it's had its say in the project—and as a result will buy into the final solution. Although involving people to get their buy-in may seem more political than practical, it's often a key step that puts you in touch with a network that will support you throughout the project. It may also help you avoid eleventh-hour changes, which can occur when someone you didn't talk to raises an issue late in the process. So involving a large variety of people is frequently a good idea.

On the other hand, schedules and budgets must be kept in mind. Involving a large number of people takes time, from their standpoint and from yours, for the meetings alone—not to mention the time sorting through notes to identify trends and consolidate redundancies. For efficiency and your own sanity, it makes sense to prioritize the groups to talk to and to choose key people from those groups to serve as thought leaders for their team.

Who are possible stakeholders you could involve? These groups are often good sources for ideas:

- Groups with initiatives that depend on the site (for example, those with marketing campaigns that need to have information presented on the site)

- ▶ Groups that need to support the processes directly behind the site or application, such as providing content, entering and managing data, and responding immediately to information gathered
- ▶ The front line of customer service, such as phone or online support or anyone who deals with customers face-to-face (for example, at a retail location or via deliveries)
- ▶ Sales, product management, or consulting services, to represent the products and services being presented
- ▶ Human resources, for meeting recruiting objectives
- ▶ Public relations, for presenting information to investors and the media
- ▶ Any groups responsible for other relationships that need to be developed as part of the project and that will influence its design, such as relationships with partners or vendors

When choosing the individuals who should be included, get help from your project sponsor and any project team members who are familiar with the groups involved to pick the right people.

Create groups that will get a good discussion going. There's no one right way to do this, but one common way is to group stakeholders by department, like this:

- ▶ Marketing (five people)
- ▶ Product management (four people)
- ▶ Customer support (two people)
- ▶ Sales (four people)

A smaller project might include one person from each of these groups, in a series of two or more collaborative work sessions where everyone meets together.

Once you have your stakeholders in mind, as well as a general structure for the meetings (discussed in the next section), you can start scheduling the meetings. Try to start scheduling at least a couple of weeks beforehand; it can be hard to get everyone in a room together.

Create a Plan for the Meetings

In parallel with your effort to choose the right stakeholders, pull together a list of topics to cover and questions that need to be asked (this will also help you refine your list of stakeholders). You should have a different plan for each group you meet with, although several of your questions may be the same from group to group.

You'll also need to decide on the level of detail you're aiming for in the meetings. If you're meeting with a large number of people only once (for example, members of various departments, as suggested above), you'll want to gather ideas, but you probably don't want to spend too much time diving into the gritty details during the meeting. In that case, if one of your stakeholders gives you the idea "Customers can track their orders online," you may want to simply ask why this function is important and if the stakeholder can think offhand of a site that does this well. These questions should help bring up the major differences among stakeholder expectations of the feature without spending the whole meeting on one statement. You can then work out the specific details of the idea with the project team, circling back with the stakeholder to make sure the requirements that you generated still represent his or her original idea.

Let's say you're redesigning an e-commerce site and you're meeting with a large variety of stakeholders, holding one meeting with each group. Here's an example of a plan for meeting with a group from a sales department.

Sales: Requirements-Gathering Meeting

Participants

Inside Sales: Jenny Bee, Tracy Kim, Joseph Arnold

Lead Management: Kevin Abernathy, Cat Parnell

Time frame: 2 hours

Objective: Understand the current sales process and identify issues and opportunities for how the Web could better support that process.

Background: We have reviewed a PowerPoint presentation on the purchasing process, which provided a good background on how purchasing decisions are made. We also plan to talk to the Customer Service team.

Sales: Requirements-Gathering Meeting *continued*

Questions

Sales process:

▶ How is the sales process different for different product lines?

▶ Are there regional differences?

▶ Are some differences based on customer size (e.g., small companies versus large companies)?

▶ How has this process evolved over the last two years and how is it antici-pated to evolve over the next three to five years?

▶ How does a potential customer understand all the things that need to be purchased and how they work together?

Overall impression:

▶ Who do you believe are the primary visitors to the current site? Why? What are they like? What are they trying to accomplish on the site?

▶ How does the Web contribute to the sales process and/or the sales closure rate today?

▶ What information do customers need to make a purchasing decision? Is that information available on the site today? Is it easy to find? Is it accurate?

▶ How hard is it to maintain content on the site today?

▶ What metrics do you get from the site? What additional metrics would you find valuable? Why?

Envisioning the future:

▶ As you think about a future Web site, what could we do to better support the sales process?

▶ What current functions and features on the site are critical for sales?

▶ What is not necessary?

▶ What is missing?

Summary:

▶ Are there any other thoughts, suggestions, or concerns that we haven't addressed?

▶ What Web sites do you think do an excellent job of supporting sales?

▶ What is the number one thing the company could do to improve customer satisfaction?

Run the Meetings Effectively

Here are some practices that will help you with requirements-gathering meetings.

Ensure a Shared Vocabulary Is Used

A lot of confusion can be avoided if the team gathering requirements agrees on a common list of terms and definitions. For example, are the people using the system going to be called *users, customers,* or *clients*? Are people more familiar with the term *interaction designer* or *information architect*?

To avoid confusion, take some time at the beginning of each meeting to state which term is being used and what it means. You may also benefit from creating some visual elements that help explain relationships between different terms or roles (see Figure 5.3).

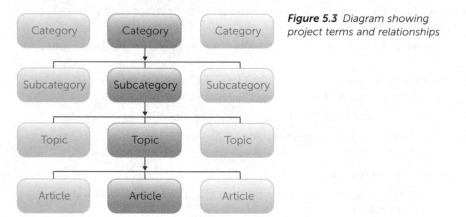

Figure 5.3 *Diagram showing project terms and relationships*

A common vocabulary for the deliverables that will be used in the project will also help stakeholders understand the process and the type of output they can expect to see. This can build trust that their time and effort isn't going to go into a black hole of ideas.

Generally, if you find yourself defining the same words more than once or twice (especially if you find the definitions are changing subtly each time), consider putting them into a project glossary and sharing it with the project team. Other examples of terminology that is good to clear up at the beginning of the project include

- Roles that will be interacting (for example, *job seeker* versus *client* or *content producer* versus *editor*)

- Primary deliverables that will be widely referenced (*functional specification, wireframes, site map*) and a brief description of how they differ

- Distinctions between different levels of information (such as our category information in Figure 5.3)

- Distinctions between *needs* and *ideas*

Listen to Ideas and Dig Down to Needs

Stakeholders may make statements that appear to be needs. Consider an example.

 Business Advocate   **"We need a blog on the site."**

This is really an idea, not a need. If blog functionality is then fully designed and implemented, it becomes a solution, but it is not necessarily the solution that best meets the core need of the stakeholders requesting it.

By asking why a blog is important, you may get a wide range of need statements, such as

"**We need to appear relevant and in touch**. Everyone is talking about blogs, and I feel like we'll be behind the times if we don't include them."

"**We need a way to get people to come to the site repeatedly** to generate more ad revenue, and blogs mean freshly posted content with a following."

"**We need to position ourselves as thought leaders**, and blogs are a more personal way to show our expertise."

"**We need to have a better way to communicate and innovate with our customers**, and blogs get us comments so we can hear their thoughts."

Each of these statements describes valid needs. By bringing them out, you'll learn about the drivers behind requests for particular feature, which will help you build consensus as you consolidate and prioritize requirements.

Coalescing Requirements

When the meetings are over, take the ideas you've gathered and sort them into general areas of functionality. You'll start noticing a lot of overlaps; this is a good sign that a particular idea has a lot of buy-in from your stakeholders. Remove redundancies and try to consolidate a list of ideas that efficiently captures the intent of your stakeholders.

To turn the ideas you've gathered into useful and trackable components of your project, you'll need to coalesce these ideas into requirements. Think of raindrops forming from a cloud: You're moving from one large and undefined cloud to a larger number of well-defined raindrops.

So when you get an idea cloud such as "Customers can track their orders online," you'll need to convert it into distinct statements defining what the system needs to do. The resulting requirements should

▶ Provide insight into the overall need that must be addressed

▶ Represent and consolidate needs provided by different stakeholders

▶ Give direction for design, without being too specific about how it will be accomplished

▶ Serve as a distinct unit of work for purposes of prioritization and tracking

As you start moving from ideas to requirements, make sure your technical lead (or another person who can represent the development team on your project) is involved to ask the questions that will help estimate the effort required when you're prioritizing later. If you have a dedicated quality assurance team member, that person can also provide some great detailed questions to help coalesce requirements.

To detail the tracking idea into requirements, ask questions such as

▶ How accurate does the tracking have to be?

▶ What kind of information should be included in the tracking details; for example, do we have to provide an updated estimate for delivery time?

These kinds of questions can be asked and detailed with the stakeholders who gave you the original idea, if they have a large amount of time dedicated to the project. If you don't have that much access to those stakeholders, you can work out the details yourself by having project team discussions and then reviewing the requirements with your project sponsor to ensure that your choices make sense for the business.

Table 5.1 lists the kinds of requirements that might coalesce from the tracking idea and how you could capture them.

TABLE 5.1 An Example of Business Requirements

ID	AREA	REQUIREMENT	BUSINESS NEED
1	Order Tracking	Orders can be tracked by entering a tracking code online	Encourage self-service during delivery (Support benefit)
2	Order Tracking	Users can track their package by GPS, following trucks or airplanes	Show innovation in efficient delivery (Competitive benefit)
3	Order Tracking	Users can view all past orders made in the last 365 days	Encourage reordering and self-service (Sales, Support benefit)

Notice that in some cases the requirements overlap with each other, as in the case of the first two requirements in the table—both are methods of tracking. They can live together in the same system because you can enter a code to find your package through the GPS view. They're separated, however, because the GPS-related requirement is probably a larger effort and should be prioritized independently of the other features.

As you consolidate the statements, note the business requirements that you think could come in *conflict* with user needs. For example, a business requirement could be to gather personal information from prospective customers, such as their e-mail addresses. But customers may have reservations about providing information. After all, it takes time to fill in forms, security and privacy is a concern, and this step may be interrupting the larger task they're trying to accomplish.

As you identify conflicts like these, they'll start to give you ideas that could help you meet both business and user needs. For the tracking example, you may suggest using a "Send to a Friend" feature to capture the e-mail address and provide a convenience to the user. This means Send to a Friend may become a requirement you put in the mix for prioritization. Ideas like this one can help meet both business and user requirements, so they're great to capture. They also live in that overlapping area between the Define and Design phases (see Chapter 4), because you're starting to think of design solutions to business problems.

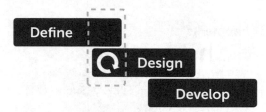

Potential conflicts between business and user needs are excellent things to explore during user research, which we'll discuss in the next chapter. User research will also allow you to extend Table 5.1 into a full set of potential requirements, which will be prioritized into a list of project requirements (shown in Figure 5.1, and discussed further in Chapter 9). Remember, the gathering of business requirements usually occurs in parallel with the exploration of technical possibilities and the gathering of user requirements.

Next up: time to talk about users!

6 User Research
Get to Know the Guests You're Inviting to the Party

There are many user research techniques that can be used throughout the project lifecycle, either to better understand your users or to test out their behavior on versions of a site. This chapter will focus on some of the methods that are most commonly used in the beginning stages of the project.

These techniques will help you define the user groups that should be of highest priority during the project, put their needs and frustrations in context, and assess the performance of the current site (if one exists) using best practices in the field of user experience design.

Carolyn Chandler

Basic Steps of User Research

1. **Define your primary user groups.** This involves creating a framework that describes the main types of users you're designing for—allowing you to focus your efforts in recruiting users for research.

2. **Plan for user involvement.** This includes choosing one or more techniques for involving user groups in research, based on the needs of your project.

3. **Conduct the research.** We'll cover the basic techniques here, such as interviews and surveys, and provide tips on how to go about them.

4. **Validate your user group definitions**. Using what you learned from the research, you can solidify your user groups model. This model will then serve as a platform for the development of more detailed tools, such as personas (discussed in Chapter 7).

5. **Generate user requirements**. These are statements of the features and functions that the site may include. You'll add these statements to your business requirements (discussed in Chapter 5) and prioritize them to become project requirements (discussed in Chapter 9).

This chapter will cover the first three steps, starting with the first: defining your user groups.

Define Your User Groups

Planning for user research at the beginning of a project can feel like a chicken-or-egg dilemma (which comes first?). How do you make sure you're talking to the right people, if you don't know yet who those people need to be?

One way to get started is to create an initial or provisional definition of the users you'll be designing for. This describes your site's primary user groups, which can help you focus your research efforts for the right roles, demographics, or other variables that may have an impact on how users will experience your site. User group definitions can be high level (a list defining each of your target user groups) or detailed and visual (a diagram showing multiple types of users, as well as how they interact with each other).

A high-level definition for a company's primary .com site might include the following user groups: potential purchasers, current purchasers, partners, and job seekers

As you begin defining groups for user research, you'll start prioritizing user groups in more detail.

Your initial definitions are based on the collective knowledge of business stakeholders and project team members regarding the potential types of users who may be interacting with the site. Those definitions can be built by collecting some of the goals and attributes that different user groups may have. Here are the basic steps for defining your user groups:

1. Create a list of attributes that will help you define the different users of your site (the next section will cover some of the most common).

2. Discuss the attributes with those at the company who have contact with relevant types of users (for example, customers).

3. Prioritize the attributes that seem to have the largest impact on why and how a potential user would use your site or application.

4. Define the user groups that you will focus on in research and design.

The next sections take a closer look at some brainstorming techniques to help you collect these attributes and how to prioritize and model them (creating representations of the different user types that will help you focus your research efforts).

Create a List of Attributes

A good start for your attribute list is to gather and absorb any research or other documentation the organization has that could provide direction with regard to users. Here are some potential sources:

▶ Documents explaining company strategies, such as company goals, competitive information, marketing strategies, and business plans

▶ Market segmentations of current customers and other demographic data gathered by the marketing department

▶ Previously conducted user research (see Table 6.1 for some examples)

- ▶ Surveys, such as user satisfaction surveys and feedback forms

- ▶ Customer service reports covering frequently occurring issues

Next, identify people within the organization who have some insight into current or prospective users. The number and variety of people you should include depends on the type of project and its scope and timeline. If you know the initial definition of your user groups may have a short lifespan (for example, it's in use for only a month or two while user research is being planned), you may include just two or three participants. If you think the initial definition may need to hold you through a good portion of the design process (for example, if you only have this one to work with until you conduct usability testing, after some design has been done), include more participants and ensure you have a cross section of perspectives.

Some possible participants include marketing staff who are responsible for brand representation, segmentation, and campaigns; sales staff; product managers; customer service or support representatives; and trainers.

It's also good to include project team leadership and other business stakeholders in this exercise.

Ask the group to think of the different types of potential users they tend to interact with. Then ask them to list some of the common attributes they've encountered. Here are some examples of what could vary:

- ▶ **Primary goals**, as they relate to the subject matter of your site. Why are users coming to it and what are they trying to accomplish? For example, purchasing an item, trading a stock, or getting a specific question answered are common goals.

- ▶ **Roles.** This can be defined in many ways, but one way is to tie roles to the user's primary goal: job seeker, support seeker, potential client, and so on. Once you have more user information, roles can be subdivided by different needs or styles; for example, on an e-commerce site shoppers could include bargain-hunters and connoisseurs.

- ▶ **Demographics,** including age, sex, family (single, married, children), income level, and region.

- ▶ **Experience** including level of education, level of familiarity with relevant technologies (often referred to as *technical savvy*), level of subject matter expertise, and frequency of usage (one-off, occasional, frequent).

▶ **Organizational attributes,** including the size of the company users work for, their department, type of job (entry level, freelancer, middle management, executive), tenure (long-term or high turnover?), and work patterns (remote work, amount of travel).

Once you have a list of some of the attributes that come up most often when stakeholders are describing potential users, you can start to prioritize them by their level of importance and then use that hierarchy to begin defining and modeling user groups.

Prioritize and Define

Which of the attributes listed above do you think have the greatest influence on how and why different user groups might use the site? Focus on the ones that you think will have the greatest impact on a user's goals or behavior. Prioritize those attributes, and remember the objectives you created in Chapter 4—they will help drive your choices as well.

An example best illustrates how to prioritize attributes. Say you're working with a company that provides tools for online trading of stocks, options, and futures. This particular company has determined that part of its strategy will be to engage *nonprofessionals* who are trading stocks on their own, online, and to encourage them to try trading new types of products such as options and futures. The company plans to do this by providing trading tools that are easy to use and targeted to those who want hands-on learning in a safe environment.

In discussing attributes with business stakeholders, you may find that the following ones seem to have the biggest impact on how individuals might use these tools:

▶ **Current frequency of trading**, specifically, frequency of direct online trading (for example, once a quarter, once a day, several times a day). Those who just dabble in trading (say, once a month) may not be serious about trying something new, while those who are already trading full time may not find much value in tools targeted to newer traders. But those who are active part-time traders could have a strong interest in the company's tools.

▶ **Number of product types traded:** just stocks or stocks, options, and futures. Those who are already trading all types of products may already have a preference for their own tools, but those who only trade one type may be ready to branch out to others.

▶ **Level of subject-matter expertise** (for example, familiarity with trading terms). This will help determine how much help they'll need along the way, with tutorials and glossaries.

▶ **Level of technical savvy** (for example, familiarity with making purchases online and online banking and trading). This will influence how much reassurance they'll need about information privacy and how advanced or simple the online interface needs to be.

You can prioritize these attributes because they may affect the user types you'll be targeting for research. If where traders live doesn't seem to have a real impact on how or why they trade, the Region attribute can drop off the list as a consideration for research participants. On the other hand, if the importance of a particular attribute sparks a lot of discussion it may be a good subject for a survey question or interview question (we'll be discussing surveys later in this chapter).

Comparing two or more attributes can help you prioritize as well. For example, if you make a chart using two attributes for online traders, you can start to see how groups fall within some of the ranges. Figure 6.1 is an example of a rough user model you could make using the two attributes of Frequency of Direct Trading and Number of Product Types Traded; it also shows the resulting user groups that might form out of the discussion.

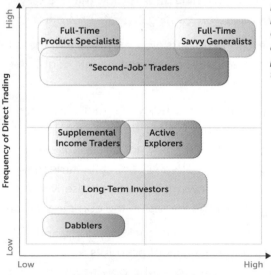

Figure 6.1 A chart of two attributes, representing a rough user model. Creating this model collaboratively can facilitate discussion about potential differences in user motivations and experience.

This user model provides a high-level way to discuss different user types. It's not meant to be the final model, and it doesn't label user groups exclusively (a user could be a long-term investor in stocks and also be actively exploring other possibilities in options or futures). But it does begin to express your understanding of different user groups and how they may be motivated to use your site.

This discussion concerning important attributes also helps you discover which ones that you'll want to focus on when recruiting users for research. If you determine that Frequency of Trading is important, and that the priority will be to engage those who currently have a medium level of frequency, you'll want to define what *medium frequency* means (one to three times a week, for example) and recruit your research participants accordingly.

Speaking of research, let's talk about techniques you can use to involve users in your project.

Can You Design from User Models Alone?

There's debate within the user experience field about creating user models before research is conducted, because doing so can color your thinking before you have real user data, and because your project team or project sponsor may see the model as a replacement for user research. Using an unvalidated model does introduce more risk that your assumptions will be incorrect. In projects where you'll have no contact with users at all, however, a well-thought-out model (verified with sources outside the project team, such as a customer service group or training group) is better than having no model to use during design.

Choosing Research Techniques

Now that you have a rough idea of the user groups you want to include, it's time to plan the next step: your recommendations for the amount and type of user research activities to conduct during the project.

Table 6.1 presents some information on the most commonly used research techniques and when they are often most useful. Use this table as a reference to help you choose which ones best apply to your project. The next section describes each technique in more detail.

TABLE 6.1 Common User-Research Techniques

ACTIVITY	WHAT IT IS	WHEN IT'S USEFUL	CHALLENGES	TYPICAL TIME FRAME *
User Interviews	A one-on-one conversation with a participant who belongs to one of the site's primary user groups.	There is access to users but type of access (in person, by phone, etc.) varies. You want to gain context but can't go to the user.	Getting straight-forward opinions. It can be hard to gather information about attitudes and context, especially if interviews are conducted remotely.	2–4 weeks for 12 interviews: Up to a week to plan, 1–2 weeks to interview, and up to a week to compile results.
Contextual Inquiry	An on-site visit with participants to observe and learn about how they work in their normal, everyday environment.	The project team has little information on target users. Users work in a unique environment (e.g., a hospital). Users are working with fairly complex tasks or workflows.	Gaining access to participants. Going to users' environment may raise concerns about security, intellectual property, and intrusiveness. For business applications, it can be easier to visit on a workday.	3–4 weeks for 12 inquiries: 1 week to plan, 1–2 weeks to observe, 1 week to analyze and report results.
Surveys	A series of questions consisting of mainly closed-end answers (multiple choice) used to identify patterns among a large number of people.	You want to state results in more quantitative terms (e.g., "80% of the target user group said they never purchase cars online"). You're more interested in gathering information about preference than actual performance.	Getting an appropriate sample. Making sure questions are well-written so that you get accurate answers without leading respondents to a particular answer.	3–4 weeks for a short-run survey: 1 week to plan and write the survey, 1–2 weeks to run the survey, 1 week to analyze and report results.

TABLE 6.1 Common User-Research Techniques (*continued*)

ACTIVITY	WHAT IT IS	WHEN IT'S USEFUL	CHALLENGES	TYPICAL TIME FRAME *
Focus Groups	A group discussion where a moderator leads participants through questions on a specific topic. Focuses on uncovering participants' feelings, attitudes, and ideas about the topic.	The team believes that users' attitudes will strongly influence their use of the solution (e.g., if there have been problems with it historically).	Understanding how to target your questions to get the right information out. Facilitating the group effectively.	3–4 weeks: 1 week to plan and write questions, 1–2 weeks to conduct focus groups, 1–2 weeks to analyze and report results.
Card Sorting	Participants are given items (such as topics) on cards and are asked to sort them into groups that are meaningful to them.	You're working on a content source site with many items and want an effective structure for your user groups.	Determining which topics would be best to include.	3–4 weeks: 1 week to plan and prepare, 1 week to conduct research, 1–2 weeks to analyze and report results.
Usability Testing	Users try to perform typical tasks on a site or application while a facilitator observes and, in some cases, asks questions to understand users' behavior.	An existing solution is being improved. Competitive solutions are available to test. You have a prototype that lets users complete (or simulate) tasks.	Choosing the appropriate tasks to focus on. Determining how formal to make the test.	3–4 weeks for 10 users and medium formality: 1 week to plan and write the tasks, 1 week to run the tests, 1–2 weeks to analyze and report results.

* Typical Time Frame represents the time often needed from the point users are scheduled. Two groups of six to eight users are assumed (except for surveys, where the number of users should be larger). This does not include time for recruiting, which can take one to two weeks after creation of the screening questionnaire.

How Many Research Activities Can I Include?

Before you choose among the activities, ask yourself how much money and time the team can dedicate to user research. Consider the following situations to understand how much appetite your client company has for user research.

If project leadership and the project sponsors are comfortable with user research and are interested in using it for known goals, such as ensuring the site meets specific project objectives, then you're likely to have more leeway in planning for two or more activities, or for one activity that you conduct multiple times (for example, testing a design, changing it based on your results, and retesting the new design).

If no one at the organization is familiar with user research and there's some resistance to it altogether, you may be better off proposing one round of research and picking the technique that you think will bring the most value to you, the project team, and the business stakeholders. Once you have the results of the research, the project team will have a better idea of what's involved and how the project can benefit. You'll then have a strong case for including more research later, if needed.

If you have room for at least two rounds of research, a good approach is to include one round during the Define phase, or early in the Design phase, to better understand the users. Then include one more round before development starts, to validate the design. For example, for a task-based application you might conduct user interviews before designing and then perform usability testing on a prototype later in the process. Or for a content source you might start with contextual inquiry and then include a card sorting exercise.

Considerations When Planning Research

When planning for any research techniques, consider the following:

▶ Why you're conducting the research: what you want to learn from it

▶ Who you're including: the primary user groups you outlined above

▶ How you'll get participants: recruiting people to participate and screening them (that is, asking questions to make sure they fall into the user groups you're targeting)

▶ How you'll compensate participants

▶ What space and equipment you'll need

▶ What you're covering: the primary topics

▶ How you're capturing information: the number of people involved and the tools they're using

Chapter 13 will cover each of these considerations as part of a detailed look at one of the most common techniques used by UX designers: usability testing.

Note *See Chapter 2 for more on task-based applications and content sources.*

Surfing

Steve Baty wrote an article describing different methods and how to choose among them based on the phase of development, your information needs, and the flexibility you have to incorporate user research. It's titled "Bite-Sized UX Research," by Steve Baty, UXmatters: http://uxmatters.com/MT/archives/000287.php.

Let's take a closer look at each of these techniques and the ways they're commonly used.

User Interviews

User interviews are structured conversations with current or potential users of your site. These can be conducted over the phone, in person in a neutral location (such as a conference room), or, ideally, in the environment in which the user is likely to use the site. (This last situation is also great for conducting a contextual inquiry, covered below.)

Interviews help you understand participant preferences and attitudes, but they should not be used to make formal statements about actual performance. If you're looking for specific information on how people interact with a site, it's better to observe them using it (for example, in a contextual inquiry) or ask them to perform tasks on the site (during usability testing). Site analytics can also give you some insights into some performance information that can be particularly strong when paired with interviews or inquiries that provide context for the data.

The Basic Process

For user interviews, the UX designer creates a list of questions aimed at eliciting information such as the following:

▶ Relevant experience with the site or with the subject matter

- ▶ The company's brand, as experienced by the participant

- ▶ Attitudes, for example, toward the subject categories covered (for a content source), the process being designed (for a task-based application), or methods of marketing (for a marketing campaign)

- ▶ Common goals or needs that drive users to your site or that of a competitor

- ▶ Common next steps users take after visiting the company's site

- ▶ Other people who are involved in the experience. For example, does a user tend to collaborate with someone else as part of the larger goal they're trying to achieve? Are they likely to share information or ask opinions of others along the way?

- ▶ Any other information that will help you validate the assumptions you've made about user groups up to this point—for example, whether the variables you discussed when creating a provisional user model really seem to influence the way users are experiencing your site

If more than one person is conducting interviews, it's a good idea to have a set list of questions and a scripted introduction that can be used to maintain consistency across interviews.

Choose ahead of time how structured you want the interviews to be. If you're going for a formal report, you'll probably want a high degree of structure, where question order doesn't vary much and every question is asked, with few additions. If richness of data is more important than consistency, you may decide to opt for semistructured interviews, where you start with a list of questions but allow the conversation to follow a natural path, with the interviewer asking questions to further explore interesting comments (called *probing*).

The length of your interview can vary; 45 to 60 minutes is often the best range to shoot for. It gives you enough time to build a rapport and cover a wide range of questions without fatiguing your participant.

User interviews provide a rich set of data that you can use to write personas, which are covered in Chapter 7.

Interviewing Tips

The quality of the information you get out of an interview has a lot to do with the quality of the questions you ask.

Focus on participants' personal experiences. Don't ask them to speculate on what they may do in the future or on what others may do. This kind of information rarely predicts what they actually will do.

Don't ask questions that imply a specific answer or lead a participant in a positive or negative direction. Ideally, questions are simple, neutral, and open ended. Some examples of leading questions are

▶ What do you like about PseudoCorporation.com?

   This assumes the user likes using the site. Use this question only if you also ask what they dislike about it.

▶ Does PseudoCorporation.com meet your expectations?

   This can be answered with a simple yes or no, which doesn't give you much detail to help with your design efforts.

▶ Would you rather use PseudoCorporation.com or CompetitorVille.com and, if the latter, why do you think they are better than Pseudo?

   This has a couple of problems: It's asking two questions in one statement, and it forces an implied opinion on the participant.

Better questions to ask are these:

▶ Tell me about your last visit to PseudoCorporation.com. Why did you go there?

▶ What do you remember about your visit?

If you're doing a large-scale, more formal set of interviews, you may want to include some multiple-choice questions. For the most part though, these don't give you very rich information. They can be hard for participants to follow when asked verbally, and they don't allow users to elaborate. In general, save that type of question for screeners or for surveys.

Perform a test run with someone, perhaps someone within the organization who isn't a member of the core team. This will help you discover questions that may not be clear and will also help you refine the timing and flow.

If it's possible, and the participant consents to it, record the interview so that others can benefit from hearing answers straight from the participant's mouth.

Contextual Inquiry

Contextual inquiry combines user observation with interviewing techniques. The UX designer goes to participants, ideally to the environments in which they're likely to use the site. For example, for an office application contextual inquiry would involve sitting at the participant's desk.

This method gives you rich information about the context a participant works within, including

▶ The real-life problems users are facing

▶ The kind of equipment they're working with

▶ The space they're working within—in particular, the amount of space they have, how much (or little) privacy, how often they are interrupted, and how they use the phone and paper (pay special attention to printouts they've posted or notes they keep handy).

▶ Their preference in using a mouse versus keyboard. This can greatly affect your design choices, especially if you're designing a tool that requires a lot of data entry.

▶ How they're working with others, in terms of both collaboration and sharing resources. If more than one person is using the same computer, for example, it will affect how you design login and security features.

▶ Other tools they're using, both online and off. How people use paper is especially interesting—for some tasks, it can be hard to design an online solution that competes with paper!

Inquiries combine observation time and interviewing time. They can last anywhere from a few hours to several days.

If participants can't dedicate at least 2 hours, you should consider just performing an interview. During an observation, it takes some time for the participant to adjust to your presence and act somewhat naturally, and this doesn't happen after just 15 minutes.

The Basic Process

Prepare a 10- to 15-minute introduction you can use with each participant. It should include the purpose of the inquiry, a high-level description of what you'll be doing together (the observation and interview), and how the information will be used. This is also a good time to get signatures on consent forms and to assure participants that what they share will be kept confidential.

Begin with some high-level questions about the participant's typical processes, especially ones that are relevant to the design of the site.

Let the participant know when you're ready to stop talking and start observing. Observation can range from active to passive. With *active observing*, a common approach is to have the participant take the role of the master while you take on the role of the apprentice. The master explains what he is doing as if teaching you his process. Active observing often gives you more background on the reasons for the participant's behavior, but it may affect how the participant works.

In *passive observing*, you encourage the participant to act as if you're not even there. Your goal is to observe behavior that is as natural as possible. For example, if a participant is talking to you, she may be less likely to take a call or go ask someone a question on a problem she's trying to solve, but if you're observing passively, you're more likely to see this happen. You can then follow up during the interview portion to ask about the reasons behind some of the behaviors you observed.

Either approach can work well. Generally, if you don't have a lot of time with participants (let's say, only 2 to 4 hours each) you may decide to use active observation to ensure you get the depth of information you need. If you have a full day or more, passive observation offers a good balance of natural behavior and discussion.

Once you have information from your inquiries, you'll have a lot of rich data to sort through! So how do you identify patterns or trends in your results?

One way that's helpful is a technique called *affinity diagramming*. There are many great resources available on this topic, but here's a short description.

A Quick Guide to Affinity Diagramming

Affinity diagramming is the technique of taking a number of distinct and separate items (like statements made by users or observations made by a researcher) and grouping them together to form patterns and trends. Here are the steps involved in a simple affinity diagramming session:

1. Gather the team that performed the inquiries, with their notes.

2. Give each person a pack of Post-it notes and ask them to write a statement on each one, along with a short code that will allow you to track that statement back to a participant, such as their initials. Focus on statements that seem to have relevance to the site design, either specifically (a feature statement) or in a more general way (a statement that represents as participant's attitude to the company or subject matter).

3. Have everyone put their Post-its up on the wall. You'll need a big blank wall if you're working on large study; try to get one that you'll have access to for at least a few days.

4. Once all the notes are up, start grouping similar statements next to each other. This portion of the exercise can include the larger team. It's a great way to start sharing results.

5. Once groups start to form naturally, start labeling the groups to provide further structure. If some Post-its belong to more than one group, you can write duplicates and place them in each appropriate group.

Note *This method works well for contextual inquiry but can be applied to many other situations. For example, it's a great way to collaboratively create categories for unsorted topics, so it can help you move card-sorting results into additional levels of structure.*

Patterns can emerge in many ways, so it's best to let them form on their own. However, here are examples of the kinds of categories that you might see, including the kind of statement you'd find in them:

▶ Goals: "I try to clear off all the open items here before I leave for the day."

▶ Mental models (includes statements that demonstrate how users are mapping external experiences to internal thinking): "I use this online tool as my briefcase, for things I reference a lot but don't want to carry around with me."

▶ Ideas and feature requests: "I wish this would allow me to undo. I keep moving the whole folder accidentally and it takes me forever to cancel out of it."

▶ Frustrations: "I'd ask the help desk about this, but half the time they don't know what the problem is either."

▶ Workarounds: "This takes so long to do here that I just end up printing out the list and working with it throughout the day. Then at the end of the day I enter in the results."

▶ Value statements: "This tool here saves me a lot of time, so if you're making changes don't take it away!"

Deep Diving

The quintessential resource on contextual inquiry is *Contextual Design*, by Hugh Beyer and Karen Holtzblatt (Morgan Kaufmann, 1997). The book also includes detailed information on interpreting results through techniques such as affinity diagramming.

For more information on mental models and how to understand them, take a look at *Mental Models: Aligning Design Strategy with User Behavior*, by Indi Young (Rosenfeld Media, 2008). This is especially helpful when you're working on the information architecture for a content source.

Surveys

Surveys involve a set collection of well-defined questions distributed to a large audience. They most often consist of closed-ended questions (such as multiple choice questions) that can be easily collected with a tool that can display patterns among responses.

Surveys are good tools when you want to be able to state results in more quantitative ways (for example, "Of those surveyed, 82 percent of those who work from home state they have some form of high-speed Internet connection") than you would get with the kinds of open-ended questions that are used in interviews. However, you can gather qualitative information from them as well, about user habits and attitudes.

In the user experience field, surveys are often used to measure user satisfaction (with existing sites or applications) or to build or validate user models like segmentations or personas.

The Basic Process

As with user interviews, you don't want to ask questions that require users to speculate. Don't ask "If you got Feature X, would you use it?"

Unlike with interviews, in surveys multiple choice or Yes/No, True/False questions are best and easiest to analyze afterwards. They're also quicker for participants to answer.

Use surveys when you have questions that are factual requests for demographic data, such as these:

Of the devices listed below, which do you personally own? Choose all that apply.

_____ Computer

_____ Mobile phone

_____ Game system, such as Xbox, Playstation, or Wii

or for questions that are attitudinal with a set range of distinct choices:

Read the following statements and select the degree to which you agree or disagree with each of them.

The Customer Service at Pseudo Corporation is responsive to my needs.

_____ Strongly Agree

_____ Agree

_____ Neither Agree nor Disagree

_____ Disagree

_____ Strongly Disagree

In particular, questions like the second example are often used to supplement usability testing tasks. You can use this type as a follow-up question to find out if participants were frustrated when completing a task. Participants don't always like to state a negative opinion out loud, but they are often willing to express one when faced with a ranking system.

This brings out another point: Surveys are an excellent supplement to other forms of research you may be doing, such as user interviews or contextual inquiry. Combining two research methods provides a richer picture of the user than one method can provide on its own.

Surfing

If you want a high degree of confidence in your results and have the budget for it, there are formal tools available for measuring user satisfaction with regard to ease of use. These tools include questions that have been tested to ensure they are not leading or confusing to a broad audience. Some of the most commonly used are

ACSI (American Customer Satisfaction Index): www.theacsi.org/

WAMMI (Website Analysis and MeasureMent Inventory): www.wammi.com

SUMI (Software Usability Measurement Inventory): http://sumi.ucc.ie

When planning a survey, consider the following:

▶ Who are you targeting?

Use your provisional model to determine this. It'll make a difference in how you answer the rest of the questions here.

▶ What method for distributing the survey will give you the best results?

If your primary user groups tend to congregate in a particular location, you may get more results if you go there and set up a table for people to fill out the survey on paper. If your user groups are active Internet users, having an online survey could be the best choice for a large number of participants. Or you may decide your user group will be best found with phone surveys using a list of current customers.

▶ How much time will participants probably be willing to spend filling out the survey?

If you're providing some kind of compensation or they get some other benefit from filling it out, you can usually create a longer questionnaire—one that takes maybe a half-hour to complete. If not, you'll need to keep it short to help ensure people complete it—think 5 to 10 minutes. Either way, make sure participants are given an estimate of how long it will take and update them on their progress as they go through it (use page numbers like "2 of 4," for example, or show the percentage completed).

▶ How will you know when to start analyzing the data?

You may choose to run the survey until you reach a certain number of participants or until you hit a certain deadline, whichever takes priority.

▶ What tool will you use to collect and analyze the data?

If you're running the survey online, the tool you use to collect the data may have options for viewing and analyzing the results. If not, you'll need a method to enter the data into your tool of choice. For paper-based surveys this means a lot of data entry, so be sure you're planning for that time.

Focus Groups

Focus groups involve bringing together a variety of people within a target audience and facilitating a discussion with them. Common goals are to elicit opinions on topics relevant to the organization or its brand, such as past experiences, related needs, feelings, attitudes, and ideas for improvement.

A focus group is a good technique for several purposes:

▶ **Hearing a variety of user stories.** Open discussion is a great way to bring out the storyteller in all of us. When a focus group is going well, individuals build off each other's stories and ideas and remember situations they might not in a more structured one-on-one interview. The group format and energy can give people the time they need to recall these stories and share them.

▶ **Understanding relevant differences in experiences.** Most people are natural information sharers and want to compare favorite tools with others in their interest group. Often you can learn of competitive sites or services, or you'll hear tips for workarounds, resources, and support.

▶ **Generating ideas.** Although you don't want to make the group itself the designer, you often get some excellent ideas for new features or designs either directly from the group or from hearing about their work processes or frustrations. As with stakeholder ideas, be sure to trace these back to the core need (see Chapter 4) so you can be sure it's being addressed.

▶ **Understanding multiple points of a collaborative process.** If you're designing a process that involves multiple related roles and collaboration, groups can be a great way for you to fill in the gaps in your understanding of how people are interacting. For example, if you're working with a content source like an intranet, it can be helpful to gather a mix of those generating the content, editing the content, and consuming the content to identify the points where the process could be improved.

There's a lot of debate about the use of focus groups in UX research. It's not a good technique for testing usability (since users most often work individually, rather than in groups), and sometimes the group setting can unduly influence participants' statements. If planned and facilitated well, however, focus groups can bring out many insights that will be valuable to you as you're designing. Chapter 13 discusses this further in the context of concept testing.

The Basic Process

When writing questions for focus groups consider the same tips you would use for writing user interview questions (covered earlier).

Begin with some of the easier questions, such as "Tell me about your last visit to PseudoCorporation.com. Why did you go there?" Save any questions focused on idea generation to the middle part of the group, when partici-pants are feeling comfortable with you, each other, and the topic.

Assign time blocks to each topic and keep to them; it's easy for discussions to really get going and for time to slip by! If you're worried about time, put your most important questions in the middle of the topics list, after people have warmed to the activity but before any potential time crunch that could occur near the end.

Many of the logistics for focus groups will be the same as those for usability testing. (Chapter 13 offers suggestions on screening, recruiting, and sched-uling.) The primary difference with focus groups is that you'll need a larger room with a table allowing participants to interact with each other easily. Shoot for six to eight people per 1- to 2-hour group session.

Give each person a nametag or a place card at their seat, so everyone can address each other by name.

The format of the discussion itself should include an introduction, which often hits these key points:

▶ Your role as moderator, and what you're expecting to get out of the dis-cussion (for example, some of the points above).

- Why attendees were chosen to participate (for example, "You are all current users of the Pseudo Corporation site, and we've brought you together to find out about your experiences").

- How this information will be used—both in the design and from the standpoint of confidentiality.

- That as the moderator, you're there to hear about their opinions and experiences. You want them to feel they can share honestly, so ask individuals to be straightforward but also respectful of others in the group.

- That there are many topics to cover, so at some point you will end a discussion on one topic to be sure you can cover all of them.

This can then go into a round of introductions for group members, often including some kind of icebreaker question.

Your goal is to get everyone to talk on the first question, even if they just tell a short story. You can either start with one person and work around the table or let people answer naturally and then call on the people who haven't answered yet by name. Often you'll end up going around the table for the first few questions and then, when you feel the group is ready, with body language you can open up the questions to everyone.

Snorkeling: Body Language

A good understanding of body language can be an amazing tool when moderating focus groups or any user research conducted in person. It can help you understand when someone is feeling frustrated, excited, angry, or threatened, so you can identify when you should try to make someone more comfortable or probe on a particular comment.

The following book on the subject may take more than a weekend to read completely, but it's designed to be easy to flip through: *The Definitive Book of Body Language*, by Allan Pease and Barbara Pease (Bantam, 2006).

When you call on someone who hasn't answered yet, be sure to repeat the question in case they didn't understand it or weren't listening to the last few statements in the discussion. Also, avoid making a difference in opinion seem like a disagreement between two individuals.

Don't say, "Bob, we haven't heard from you yet. What do you think about what Chris just said?" but rather (looking at Bob), "How about you, Bob? What kinds of experiences have you had with Pseudo Corporation's customer service?"

As moderator, you control the flow of the discussion and you pass the virtual microphone around. You keep control using eye contact, volume of speech, arm movements, and orientation of your body. Most people will be very aware of your body language, and these cues can be useful signals if someone is dominating the conversation. If an overly vocal participant doesn't get those hints, use a gentle but firm statement such as "OK, great, I'd like to open that thought up to others. Has anyone else encountered some of the same issues that Theresa has?"

When moving on to a new larger topic, give verbal notice that the previous discussion has finished and that a new one is beginning, so that people can clear their minds for the next topic.

Finally, when the activity is nearing its end, a simple look at your watch and shift in your body orientation can signal that the conversation should be wrapped up. As with any other activity, be sure to thank the group for their time.

Sharing results with your team typically takes one of two forms: findings are either shared according to the main topics being covered or are grouped into relevant categories much as they are for contextual inquiry. Affinity diagramming can be another effective way to bring together various trends and attitudes for illustration to the project team.

Card Sorting

In a *card sorting* activity, participants (working either individually or in small groups) are given items printed on cards and are asked to put them into groups that make sense to them. Either they group them into categories that are provided beforehand (called a *closed sort*) or they make their own groups and title each group themselves (called an *open sort*). At the end of the round of card sorting you should begin to see common patterns emerge in how people are sorting the items, as well as common areas of confusion or disagreement.

A common reason for doing this is to create a site map for a Web site or to create a hierarchy of content, categories, and subcategories containing items such as articles, documents, videos, or photos. This makes card sorting an excellent technique if you're working on a content source.

Note *See Chapter 2 for more on content sources.*

Say you're working on a common type of content source: the company intranet. Many intranets tend to categorize their information by the department that owns it, with navigation to human resources, operations, legal, marketing, and so on. For longtime employees this may not present an obvious problem, because they have probably learned the lines of responsibility of each department and built an understanding of where to find information.

But for new employees, or for those who need information that they don't usually reference, it can be difficult to locate information that could fall within more than one department (or doesn't seem to fall into any). For example, where would you go to find a policy on signing of contracts with newly hired employees? It could fall under legal, or it could fall under human resources.

With card sorting, you can find common patterns in how potential users would categorize information, regardless of departmental lines.

The Basic Process

Collect the items you'd like to include in the card sort; 40 to 60 is usually a good range. You need enough to allow for a potentially large number of card groups to be created, but not so many as to overwhelm the participants with options (or to overwhelm *you* when you need to analyze the results).

Choose items that you think will be easy to understand and free from unnecessary jargon. You can include some subject-matter terms that you believe your user groups are likely to know, but avoid including too many "insider" terms. If you include too many company-specific terms or acronyms (such as "the SUCCEED campaign" for growing sales), you'll be testing the effectiveness of the company's marketing and communications, rather than building a common information hierarchy.

For the intranet example, you might include the vacation policy, 401(k) plan information, new-hire contract, vendor contract, nondisclosure agreement, new-employee orientation, health insurance information, and computer security policy.

This list represents a mix of clearly worded items that could be categorized in multiple ways. You could have one participant who groups new employee orientation and vacation policy together under human resources, and you could have another who groups new employee orientation and new hire contract together and names it "employee onboarding."

Once you have your list of items, put them onto cards that can be easily grouped and ungrouped. You can print labels and stick them onto index cards or print directly onto sheets of card stock that are perforated to separate into individual cards.

Perform a test run by asking someone to sort the cards into groups and give the groups names—for example, by putting a Post-it on the stack and writing the name on it with a pen. Ideally, your test participant is someone unfamiliar with the items and the activity. This will help you get a rough idea of how long the activity might take. If the test run takes over an hour, you may need to cut out some cards!

Once you have a finalized deck, you can bring in a real participant and give these basic instructions:

1. Arrange these cards in whatever groups make sense to you.

2. Try to have at least two cards in a group. If a card seems to belong to no group, you can place it to the side.

3. At any time as you're sorting, you can name a group. By the end of the activity, please name as many groups as you can.

Some trends will become obvious simply by observing the sessions. Others may take a little more analysis to bring out. There are several tools for entering and analyzing the results of card sorts; many of them come with tools that allow you to run card sorts remotely (see the "Variations on the Card Sort" section below for more on this).

In particular, OptimalSort (www.optimalsort.com/pages/default.html) and WebSort (http://websort.net) provide both remote sorting capabilities and helpful analysis tools. Or, if you want to do your own sorting in a more manual fashion, take a look at Donna Spencer's excellent spreadsheet, complete with instructions, available at www.rosenfeldmedia.com/books/cardsorting/blog/card_sort_analysis_spreadsheet.

Variations on the Card Sort

The discussion so far has focused on a card sort carried out with an individual, in person, where the participant is asked to name the categories he created. This is an open sort, meaning that the main categories have not been given to the participant—instead they are *open* to being named. This is a good approach when you're determining a new navigational structure or making significant changes to an existing one. For other situations, you might consider these common card sorting variations:

► **Closed sorts.** In a closed sort, you provide the high-level categories and participants add to them. The results are relatively easy to analyze, because you have a small set of possible categories and can focus on understanding which items fell most often into which categories. If you're adding large amounts of content to an existing information architecture or you're validating an existing site map, a closed sort can provide quick and actionable information to help with your categorization decisions.

► **Group sorts.** Rather than having an individual sort items into groups, you can have card sorting be a part of a focus group activity, where participants work together to sort items. Although the results don't necessarily reflect how any one individual would group the items, you can get a lot of insight into how people think about the items and their organization by hearing them work through the activity together, debating the rationale for each placement.

► **Remote sorts.** Sorting with physical cards can be a fun activity, especially for group sorts. But there are many great tools for performing sorts online with individuals. This also allows you to reach a greater number of participants or particular participants that may be difficult to meet with physically. OptimalSort and WebSort, mentioned above, are two of the tools that make this type of online sorting easy.

Usability Testing

Usability testing involves asking participants to perform specific tests on a site or application (or a prototype of it) to uncover potential usability issues and gather ideas to address them.

You can perform usability testing during the Define phase if you want to gather information on how the current site can be improved. Or you can perform it on similar sites (such as competitive sites) to understand some of the potential opportunities for a more user-friendly solution.

Most often, usability testing is conducted as part of the Design phase, ideally in iterative rounds (where a design is created, tested, refined, and tested again). We'll discuss usability testing again in full detail in Chapter 13, "Design Testing with Users"; that chapter includes tips for recruiting and planning that can help you conduct the activities discussed earlier in this chapter as well.

After the Research

Once you've completed one or more of these user research activities, it's time to revisit the assumptions you originally made about your user groups. Put those assumptions away for a moment, and ask yourself what user groups you would create now that you have more information. If some of your earlier assumptions weren't valid, consider any gaps you may have in your user research because a key group wasn't included. If this gap is identified early enough in your research activity, you may have time to adjust and add another set of participants to research in progress, to ensure you're getting a full picture.

With your new knowledge, you can revise your user definitions to more accurately reflect the groups that should be the focus. This will help you create more detailed tools like personas (discussed in Chapter 7) and will help you create user requirements for the list we began in Chapter 5.

In that chapter, we discussed the process of taking statements from business stakeholders and refining them into requirements. You'll follow a similar process with users—your work doesn't stop when you capture the idea or request. Dig down to root needs and goals to make sure you understand them. This will ultimately help you design a solution that best meets that need for all relevant user groups.

In the next chapter, you'll learn how to use the insight you gain in conducting user research to create tools that can bring focus to your user groups throughout design and development: personas.

7 Personas

Find the Best Way to Put Your Team— or Your Client—in Your Users' Shoes

Personas are often a topic of debate among user experience practitioners. Opinions range from how much content is needed to how much research is needed to whether they provide any value to projects. Some people question whether or not they belong in the process at all. Regardless of where you position yourself, personas may be used to help your project team and your client empathize with their users. Personas can deliver a gut check to many parts of your project—business requirements, visual design, or quality assurance—by providing insight into who your audience is and what their expectations and behaviors are.

Russ Unger

What Are Personas?

Personas are documents that describe typical target users. They can be useful to your project team, stakeholders, and clients. With appropriate research and descriptions, personas can paint a very clear picture of who is using the site or application, and potentially even how they are using it.

User experience designers often see creating personas as a great exercise in empathy. Well-crafted personas are often used as a touch point whenever a question or concern arises about how aspects of the project should be designed. You can take out your personas and ask, How would *<this user>* perform *<this task>*? or What is *<this user>* going to look for in *<this situation>*? Although this process may not be as accurate as testing functionality and design with actual users, it can help move your project along until you are able perform more extensive tests.

Josh Seiden (www.joshuaseiden.com) points out that there are two distinct types of personas:

▶ Marketing-targeted personas that model purchase motivations

▶ Interactive personas that are modeled toward usage behaviors

This chapter focuses on interactive personas.

Why Would I Create Personas?

In the user experience design process, personas help you focus on representative users. By providing insights into "real" behaviors of "real" users, personas can help resolve conflicts that arise when making design and development decisions, so you and your team can continue to make progress.

How real do personas need to be? The answer varies widely. A single persona document may be enough for one team, while another may create full "living spaces" for the user personas to deeply understand how they "live." You could even go to the extreme of creating individual online presences that can be interacted with to provide insights into online behaviors. However you choose to extend your personas is up to you.

Personas can be constant reminders of your users. A useful technique is for your team members to keep personas in their workspaces; this way they are continually reminded of who their users are. When you share a cube with "Nicolle," the 34-year-old certified hand therapist from West Chicago, Illinois, for a while, you begin to find yourself compelled to provide an experience that works well for her.

If it helps you, feel free to keep printed copies with you while you sleep and let the osmosis fairy impart empathy from the pages through the pillow and into your slumbering subconscious. The purpose of personas is to help you, your team, and/or your clients remove some of the confusion that can crop up when you reach a decision-making crossroads.

Finding Information for Personas

Effective personas must accurately depict a number of specific users of your product or Web site. To achieve that goal, personas must be supported by research. Chapter 6 presents techniques for researching and modeling your potential users to provide a firm foundation for your personas. Don't look for one method to be the answer, however; it's best to find as much data as you can *and* mix it with a blend of observational and interview data—this can also include utilizing online surveys and analyzing behaviors in social networks.

It's a common theme to creating personas: Get real data, but make the personas into real people on the pages. To learn how one company accomplishes this, see the sidebar "Case Study: Messagefirst Personas."

Creating Personas

Once you identify your audience and accumulate data to support your personas, your next step is to put pencil to paper and start to bring them to life. How many personas you need to create varies. In general, the minimum is three, but upwards of seven is not uncommon. Rather than aim for a specific count, consider the number of target segments you have and what you feel is the best way to get a fair representation of them.

Case Study: Messagefirst Personas

To create effective, data-driven personas, Messagefirst (www.messagefirst.com) uses no less than three different data input sources, drawing from the following:

- **Stakeholders.** We interview them to find out who they think the personas are and what they think their behaviors are. This is *always* included.

- **Customer advocate.** We interview people in the company who speak directly with customers, which typically means Sales/Marketing and Customer Service. Each of these has their bias, which we make sure we keep in mind as we document our findings. For example, the people who most commonly contact Customer Service are those with too much time on their hands (often retired or unemployed), or someone who's so upset about a product or service that they'll actually take time to contact you.

- **Customers.** We talk directly to the actual people who are going to use or currently use the product or service. This is included whenever possible.

- **Customer data sources.** We review any available Weblog traffic, surveys, and e-mails that are available to us.

- **Someone we know.** We pick someone we know who fits the initial profile of the persona. This helps keep us grounded, ensuring the persona is believable and realistic, and provides a real person to contact should we have additional questions. This is very important for validation, and *always* included.

Because each data input source we use has a particular bias, we use multiple sources to normalize the data. What's important for data-driven personas is not to go in with an expectation of how many personas you will have, but to let the data reveal how many personas there should be. When analyzing the data, I look for gaps in the behaviors and activities. These gaps reveal the individual personas.

Todd Zaki Warfel, President, Messagefirst

This chapter's example persona is Nicolle, a 34-year-old Certified Hand Therapist from West Chicago, Illinois. She happens to be a nondriving commuter who spends 2 to 3 hours per day traveling to and from her job. The fictional client is a company called ACMEblue, a manufacturer of Bluetooth headsets for Apple's not-so-fictional iPhone.

That brief bit paragraph tells you a lot about Nicolle, but as you can see in Figure 7.1, the actual persona contains a much more thorough story about Nicolle. Note that the content is written *about* Nicolle, not "by" Nicolle. It's best to write your personas from the third-party perspective and not contend with writing in their distinct voices, especially when you're just getting started. As you expand your experience, you should naturally explore and find the style that fits you best and provides the most value.

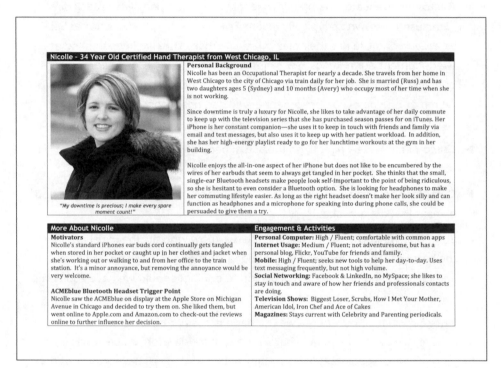

Figure 7.1 *Persona for fictional client ACMEblue*

What kind of information goes into personas? The kind of information that your audience will find relevant and believable, that's what kind.

Based on the research data you've gathered, you should be able to ascertain what is important to the client, brand, and project.

The majority of the personas you create will share a common set of required content mixed with any amount of data, statistics, and other relevant information that can be considered optional, because it will vary from client to client, if not project to project.

Minimum Content Requirements

When creating personas, you need to provide enough information to draw people in and make them relate to the person they are reading about on the page. To help your audience understand how your persona behaves and thinks, be sure to include six key pieces of information: photo, name, age, location, occupation, and biography. The next sections take a closer look at filling in the details for each item.

Photo

A photo is the first (and the real) step to putting a face to your persona. When choosing a photo for your persona, try to make sure that the picture doesn't look too posed or polished.

Photos that appear to be posed do not have the same effect as those that are in more natural settings. Personas seem to be more effective with photos taken in more natural settings, such as the photo on the right in Figure 7.2, where the subject is standing outside in her winter coat, conceivably during her commute. Make sure the photo fits the lifestyle of the persona!

Posed

Natural

Figure 7.2
Natural-looking photos are more effective.

There are a variety of online photo resources. Some of the better options are iStockphoto (www.istockphoto.com), Getty Images (www.gettyimages.com), and Stock.XCHNG (www.sxc.hu).

Finding the right photo can be a complete time suck if you're not careful. If all else fails (or you have the time and budget), take your own!

Name

Simply put, you've got to put a name to the face. The photo you use will humanize the mix of research data and personality traits, and the name will be how everyone refers to your persona during discussions. Not only does Nicolle sound better than "Mid-30s Blonde Professional Mom," but it's a lot easier to remember and associate with a specific persona.

Try to keep the names you use for different personas on a project from sounding too similar. Nicolle and Noelle could be easily confused, for example, so look for distinct names. And, although it may be tempting to use the names of coworkers or clients, don't. When you use names that are like or the same as those of people involved in the project, it is easy for them to try to identify themselves in your personas. Choosing different names avoids any uncomfortable situations or hurt feelings. If you find yourself having difficulty choosing names, some online resources can help you with this: baby-naming Web sites!

▶ BabyNames.com: www.babynames.com

▶ Babyhold: www.babyhold.com

▶ Social Security Administration's Popular Baby Names: www.ssa.gov/OACT/babynames

▶ Random Name Generator: www.kleimo.com/random/name.cfm

One last thing about names: Make sure your name is believable for the persona. Nicolle works just fine for a Midwestern mother, but Nicola or Natalia may be a much better name for an Italian mother. Also, names that appear to be a little more fun or lively, such as Bob the Builder, aren't. They tend to make your personas look silly and can detract from their value.

Age

Although your research should identify the age range of your consumers, providing a specific age for your persona helps to add authenticity to the biography that you write. Behaviors of a 21-year-old college student and a 34-year-old professional mother are significantly different!

Location

At first, location may not appear to be vital information; however, it is important to remember that cultural and behavioral shifts can occur from location to location. In Italy, for example, different dialects are spoken in different regions of the country. In the United States, a person who lives in Chicago would most likely have a different cost of living than a person in Savannah, Georgia.

Occupation

Knowing what your persona does for a living helps you to identify with them by relating to the patterns of their day-to-day lives. A persona who works in therapy meets with many people on a daily basis, whereas a drawbridge operator may not interact much with others.

Biography

The biography is the compelling story that makes the persona real. This is where you provide details that you derive from your research data and infuse it with a bit of "real people." That is, the data is *very* important to the persona, but you do not want to simply quote that information in choppy sentences. Instead, you want to weave data, anecdote, and observation into a story that your audience can relate to.

It may seem a bit strange, but the biography needs to be believable, and it's certainly not cheating to bring aspects of a real person into your persona. Nicolle, for example, is based upon both statistical data and the very real behaviors of a person who shares similar activities, beliefs, and desires.

Depending upon your project, you may need to delve fairly deeply into the biography—sometimes the more details you have, the better. Don't feel as if you have to squeeze your persona onto a single sheet of paper. Go with what works best to make your persona true to life and as meaningful as possible to the project you are working on.

Optional Content

As you work with personas, you will find that different projects will require different sets of information to make the personas more applicable. The minimum content requirements might also be considered the least common denominators from most of the personas you will create. In most cases, you will blend some of these optional content elements with the core of your personas.

Optional content that may add value to your personas includes

▶ **Education level.** Knowing how educated a person is can provide a bit more insight into some of their habits. A person with a high school diploma *may* have substantially different purchasing habits and brand perceptions than a person with a master's degree, and this information can influence how your persona is perceived.

▶ **Salary or salary range.** Money talks, and in many cases, the amount of income a person has substantially affects their standard of living and their disposable income. This information can provide significant insight when you are targeting certain levels of affluence.

▶ **Personal quote.** What would be the motto that your persona would claim as their own? Sometimes this can give a quick overview into the core of your persona's way of thinking.

▶ **Online activities.** This can get tricky; there are a lot of ways people spend their time online. Some people pay their bills, some people are heavily into blogging and social networking activities, and some people simply use their computer as an appliance that gets turned on when they need to perform a task. Given that so many projects have some online component, this element is a bit of a judgment call. You'll need to lean on your research to help paint the picture.

▶ **Offline activities.** Does your persona have a hobby? Is there additional information about what the life of your persona is like when they're not online? This element can be every bit as tricky as online activities, and can be every bit as important in influencing your persona.

▶ **Key entry or trigger point to client, brand, or project.** Often it is important to understand how a persona interacts with the client, brand, or project. Does the persona hear about it via word of mouth, online reviews, a billboard, television or radio, or from an online pop-up ad? Is your persona looking to solve a problem that can be addressed through the client, brand, or project? Using your statistical data to understand this point, and writing it into your persona, can help ground your approach to engaging users.

▶ **Technical comfort level.** Does your persona use a PC or a Mac? Does she own a computer at all? Does she use instant messaging, Flickr, or write a blog? Is she very comfortable with that activity, or is she confused by it? Would she be helped by a very simple solution directed toward a novice? Does she have an MP3 player or other portable device? Does she use a DVR or AppleTV or on-demand programming to watch television? The list can go on and on. And on. Depending upon your client, brand, or project, these notions—and a variety of others—may be important to identify.

▶ **Social comfort level.** Given the growth of social media and social networking, it may be important to identify very specifically how your persona engages in that particular space. Does she have a Twitter account? If so, how many followers does she have? How active is she? Is she a leader? Does she use MySpace, Facebook, LinkedIn, or other aggregators or online communities?

▶ **Mobile comfort level.** As the usage of mobile devices becomes more prevalent, it is important to consider including how your personas find themselves in the mobile space—if at all.

▶ **Motivations to use client, brand, or project.** In some cases you may want to include the reasons the persona would want to use the client, brand, or project. If she is continually getting the wire for her headphones tangled in her coat and yanking them off her head, that may be a good reason for her to consider new headphones. Real scenarios based upon research data can help uncover key motivators to include in your personas.

▶ **User goals.** You may also want to identify what the persona is hoping to accomplish by using the client, brand, or project. This can help provide insights into the persona's drivers for using it.

These are just data points to get you started. You can structure your personas and present them in an infinite variety of ways. If you are interested in taking a deep dive into the world of personas, a great place to start is *The User Is Always Right: A Practical Guide to Creating and Using Personas for the Web*, by Steve Mulder with Ziv Yaar (New Riders, 2006).

Advanced Personas

Once you have an understanding of the basics of creating personas, there are infinitely many ways you can extend your documents. A simple persona often can meet most of your needs, especially when your project team is just trying to get an empathetic understanding of your users.

Things tend to get more interesting when you present personas to your clients. In those cases, you'll often find that you need to provide much more than the information that you put together for the basic persona. Figures 7.3 through 7.7 illustrate some of the ways you can extend personas.

Feel free to borrow from these examples, remix and mash them up to create something even better for your project!

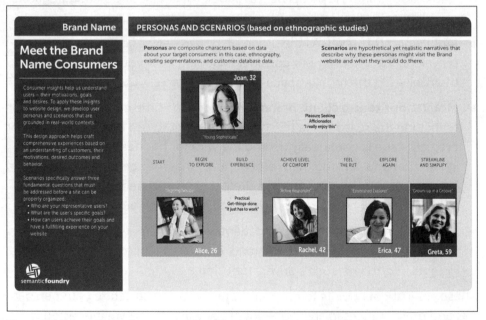

Figure 7.3 *Persona overview master sheet (landscape orientation). Provides an aggregated view of several personas, along with the segments they represent, in the context of a high-level organizational strategy. Courtesy of Will Evans.*

Figure 7.4 Target audience persona (landscape orientation). This detailed view of a persona incorporates a broader spectrum of data and provides a more comprehensive perspective of users' goals, needs, and behaviors—all set within a larger ecosystem. Courtesy of Will Evans.

Figure 7.5 Target overview and target audience persona (portrait orientation). The target overview at left provides high-level summary information and shows the brands the three personas interact with and relate to. The detailed description at right presents an overview and biography of a single persona, along with information about her behaviors and motivations.

Figure 7.6 *Target audience group persona. This persona presents an age-range target, drawn from research data. The information it contains is broad and speaks to audience grouping, not specific individuals. This approach can be useful when you are making a business pitch or when the client's budget doesn't permit detailed exploration of personas. Courtesy of Todd Zaki Warfel.*

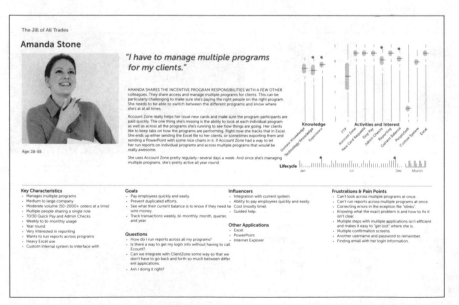

Figure 7.7 *Target audience individual persona. This persona is a heavily data-driven model. While the day-in-the-life story is a narrative, the rest is given in bullet points to serve as a design checklist. The diagram is used to communicate a significant amount of information in a small space. Courtesy of Todd Zaki Warfel.*

As you can see, you can combine data in many different ways to present personas, tailoring them to a variety of situations. Start with the basic persona and expand it to suit your needs.

Final Thoughts on Personas

Many practitioners in the user experience design world do not believe that personas do a good job of articulating the needs, goals, and attitudes of users. They believe that personas can hinder creativity, innovation, or good design for any number of reasons. Other practitioners believe that personas meet a specific need that influences the design process in a very positive way—when they are based on solid research data and mixed with a dose of personalized reality. Which side of the coin you land on is entirely up to you.

This chapter is not meant to influence your decision one way or the other. Plenty of articles on the topic are available online, and plenty of professionals are ready to give you their view. All of these resources can help you figure out how personas will work best for your projects, so seek them out. Jared Spool, CEO and founding principal of User Interface Engineering (www.uie.com), also offers some insight on the topic:

> That value comes when the team visits and observes their target audience, absorbs and discusses their observations, and reduces the chaos into patterns, which then become the personas.
>
> What's in the team's head, as they are designing, is what will make a difference in the final design. The persona descriptions are just there to remind everyone what happened.

Jared's point is simple: By watching your target audience, infusing what you learn with research data, and synthesizing all of this into segments, you should be able to create personas that trigger the kind of empathy that keeps your team on track and building the best possible application, Web site, or product.

Ultimately, however, your personas are going to be a lot like Santa Claus: They'll only be valuable as long as people believe in them.

8 User Experience Design and Search Engine Optimization

User Experience Design's Fundamental Role in Successful SEO

Search engines are the cornerstone of the interactive economy. Everything that we do as "interactivists" is ultimately connected to the world at large through Google, Yahoo, MSN, Ask, and the myriad minor engines that make up the infrastructure for finding things online. Information architecture is a critical component of how Web sites are interpreted by search engines. This chapter is designed to give you some basic understanding of why UX design is critical to search engine optimization and what you must take into account so that the environments you create will have a fighting chance on Google.

Jonathan Ashton

Introduction to SEO

Simply put, *search engine optimization* is the process of developing and maintaining a Web asset with the intention of gaining and keeping top placement on public search engines for specifically targeted keyword phrases. Search engine optimization (SEO) is like a martial art, a process of learning and doing that is never complete. Even a master can progress further using observed behavior or learned method. As long as there are search engines and Web sites interested in selling something to the people searching, there will be a role for search engine optimization.

SEO relies on three fundamental areas for improvement and influence:

▶ The critical group of things that the professional user experience designer can influence—site infrastructure, technology, and organizational principles

▶ Content and all the keyword issues that relate to optimized words which the search engines can see

▶ Links, or link popularity—the quantity and quality of links that point at your site from other sites, as well as the organizational structure of the links inside the site

We will take apart each of these three areas and examine them from the UX designer's perspective, to better equip you for the optimization challenges that lie ahead.

Why Is SEO Important?

It is interesting that even today we need to explain the relevance of search engine optimization. Clients tend to understand on some level that it is important for their Web sites to attract targeted visitors from the natural search results of the main search engines, but beyond that it is difficult for most interactive marketers to understand the impact SEO can have.

Data on global search volume is available from a variety of sources, but what is most important to understand is that, whatever the source, the numbers are simply huge, and the year-over-year increases are always in double digits. For the most part, every quarter the global volume of searches increases. When Google first launched in 1998, 10,000 searches a day was a huge volume and placed an incredible burden on the beta version of the system.

Hitwise (www.hitwise.com) reports that Google and its affiliates (including AOL and YouTube) own the lion's share of searches globally, with nearly 72 percent of U.S. searches performed in November 2008. Yahoo is a distant second, with nearly 18 percent, and MSN and Ask.com trail in at 4 percent and 3 percent, respectively. Internationally, Google is even more dominant: Its market share reaches more than 80 percent in many markets.

> **Note** For more background on Google's early days, see The Google Story, by David A. Vise and Mark Malseed (Delta, 2008).
>
> According to comScore (www.comscore.com), in 2008 there were easily more than 60 billion searches per month performed globally by 750 million people, with over 18 billion searches performed in the United States alone. To put it another way, 95 percent of Internet users use a search engine at least once a month, with a global average of more than 80 searches per month.

Aside from these remarkable volume numbers, what does this really mean on a practical level to interactive marketers? Simply put, if you are not reaching your target customers when they are searching for your products or services, your competition is getting the opportunity to sell to them.

Look at your site analytics and think of the issue this way: How much more revenue would the site generate if there was a 10 percent increase in strategically targeted traffic? What about a 100 percent increase? Or 1000 percent? If your site is not generating meaningful traffic through natural search, then SEO is a requirement.

A little investment in SEO can go a very long way, particularly if the interactive marketing effort to date has focused on purchasing clicks through sponsor listings. We have seen sites achieve a return on investment of 35 to 1 on monthly SEO expenditures. If you are paying the search engine companies for traffic from sponsored listings but you are not investing in natural traffic, you are really limiting yourself to about 10 percent of the opportunity. Think of your own search behavior: When was the last time you clicked through more than one or two of the paid sponsor listings in a search result?

Any discussion of why SEO is important and why it is here to stay could go on for chapters. Suffice it to say that Google is not going anywhere but up, and that effective interactive marketing must include search engine optimization as a core component of competent execution.

Important Basic Resources

Expertise emerges from a well-rounded education. The professional who simply focuses on his or her specialty loses perspective on everything else around. That is why it is imperative that every interactivist spend at least a few minutes learning about SEO. Although there is no official set of guidelines, Google has been kind enough to provide some very salient resources. If you're interested at all in getting better search engine performance from your efforts, check out these links:

▶ Webmasters/Site Owners Help: Search Engine Optimization: www.google.com/support/webmasters/bin/ answer.py?hl=en&answer=35291

▶ Webmasters/Site Owners Help: Webmaster Guidelines: Quality Guidelines: www.google.com/support/webmasters/bin/ answer.py?hl=en&answer=35769

▶ Search Engine Optimization Starter Guide: www.google.com/webmasters/docs/ search-engine-optimization-starter-guide.pdf

If that is not enough, drown yourself in newsletters and blogs. Start at SEOmoz.org and dig down. Just remember, as in all other things in life, If it sounds too good to be true, then it probably is.

Site Technology, Design, and Infrastructure

Search engines are essentially Web 1.0.5 technology that is firmly implanted in the Web 2.0+ world. The basic premise of the search engine has changed little since the World Wide Web Wanderer was launched in 1993 to crawl the Web and build the first Web search engine. Essentially every search engine has an application alternately called a *crawler*, *spider*, or *bot* that finds and follows links, sending back to the database a copy of the assets that it can see. The database is then analyzed according to the search engine's proprietary algorithm. Using these rules, a Web asset is indexed and then ranked according to how well it scores on that search engine's particular score card. In this rather straightforward process are a myriad of pitfalls for the UX designer.

Understanding these core relationships will enable you to see your site through the eyes of the search engines. An optimized Web site relies on a structure and technology that facilitates the movement of the search engine spiders. Likewise, many decisions about handling content determine how well the search engines ranks the resulting efforts. As a result, much of this is predetermined by the decisions that are made in wireframes and in the discussions that take place around how to style and manage content.

Flash, Ajax, JavaScript, and Other Scripted Content

Today's dynamic and interactive Web design relies on technologies that are not at all friendly to the needs of the search engines. There is a widening gap between what search engines can see and what designers can do. It is up to the UX designer to be sure that the strategic plans for dynamic, design-intensive sites are deployed so that both the search engines and the users get the best possible experiences.

Having a fundamental understanding of how search engines interact with this kind of content will help you to decide when to deploy it and where to compensate for its weaknesses. It is entirely possible to build an optimized site that relies heavily on scripted content if the appropriate compensations are in place at the beginning of the process. It is substantially more difficult to build static or indexable content once the site is built and live. So make a forceful argument for static content, on the grounds of usability and for the sake of the search engines' crawlers. It may seem like extra work up front, but the return on investment is exponential.

Flash

Flash content is technically "indexable." There have been some recent advances in the ability of the search engines to see into Flash files to find the text and links that are built into these assets. Although this content is indexed, have you ever seen an all-Flash asset win top placement in the search results? You probably haven't because it's risky for search engines to open themselves up to full compatibility with Flash. Let's assume that the search engines could completely see all of the links and text content that is embedded inside the SWFobject. What prevents an unethical (or "black hat") optimizer from putting apples in the text layers of the object while showing oranges to the human user viewing the fully compiled assets through a browser? How can you deep link into a Flash asset without it being fully compiled? These fundamental vulnerabilities will remain until the search engines can reach some level of artificial intelligence that can tell that an image is a picture of a horse without some associated text that says "this is a picture of a horse."

To architect a Flash Web site that is compatible with search engines, you must add a static layer of content that duplicates the Flash content. Leaving aside the needs of search engines for the moment, a static layer of content is a key for compliance with usability requirements. Think of the search engine as the person who is viewing Web content over a dial-up connection or is using a screen reader browser. These people may be the lowest common denominator, and it is possible that the strategy behind your Web development ment discounts this very small percentage of human users. But when you discount this handful of people, you also discount GoogleBot and Yahoo Slurp—the two most important visitors to your site, since they are the crawlers that will enable the major search engines to index your site. If no text words or spiderable links are visible to the search engines, your content will inevitably not be findable through meaningful search results.

A static layer can be accomplished in a number of ways. To comply with search engine requirements, the static layer of content needs to mirror the Flash content. *This is not an opportunity to show the search engines something different than what is deployed in the Flash*; if you do that you are violating the spirit of the game and standing squarely on the dark side.

The ideal way to embed Flash content into a static layer is to use SWFobject so that both the Flash and static content can live on the same URL. This will allow the search engine to find the static content and the Flash-enabled browser to display the animation instead of the static content. If at all possible, do not use redirecting so that you can conserve the popularity of the link that is pointing to the Flash content. Google Code provides a simple set of instructions for implementing this straightforward piece of JavaScript at http://code.google.com/p/swfobject.

There is another option that runs on the gray side of SEO. *Cloaking* can be a dirty word to SEO purists, but if you approach the following challenges from the right side you can have some cake and eat it too.

Cloaking takes advantage of user agent detection, detecting search engine crawlers as they visit a Web site and routing them to static pages to index. But when a human visitor sees the same page in search results and clicks the link, the Web site detects that the user agent is a human with a Flash-enabled browser and shows that person the dynamic experience on a completely separate URL. The crux of the issue remains the same as with the SWFobject method: You have to show the search engines the exact same things in your cloaked content as you do in your Flash content.

Ajax, JavaScript, and Other Scripted Content

A powerful driver of Web 2.0 content, Ajax provides Web developers with the ability to build pageless content. However, the problems that search engines have with Ajax are multifold and require good planning to avoid big mistakes.

Ajax stands for Asynchronous JavaScript And XML, which hints at the difficulties search engines have with this technology. Search engines essentially can't deal with JavaScript; the efficiencies that JavaScript brings to developers are the problems that search engines have with dynamic content. An additional problem search engines have with Ajax is the asynchronous nature of the technology. A search engine can only see the contents of the initial page load, and any content that is loaded through a script that takes place after the initial shell loads will not be visible for indexing. Because Google can't extend a session beyond the initial page load and doesn't have a mouse or external agent to activate a script, any pageless content that is activated by the user will be invisible unless the text content is included in the pre-loaded shell. It is up to the UX designer to be certain that the three-dimensional modeling necessary to structure pageless design also includes the requirement that text and links all preload in the page shell. Anything else, and your cool design is invisible.

Scripted Navigation

One of the most common problems that will hamper optimization is the use of JavaScript in the core of site navigation. This is a very common condition and is the result of the way many site development and content management tools work. The scripted navigation looks cooler, so people tend to be interested in using it. But if JavaScript is the technology that drives the site navigation, the result is that search engines can't properly build a model of the link relationships within the site: They simply can't see the link structure of the site. And if the search engines can't model the link relationships in the site, deep content will be invisible or will not be assigned the right link popularity.

Content Management Systems

Content management systems have been built for the convenience of humans—but many of these systems make it difficult for search engines to deal with their output. Following are some typical problems that need to be avoided, either by using work-arounds or choosing a content management system that is more search friendly:

▶ **Dynamic URLs.** Search engines don't understand a "page" of content; it understands the path to that content. A change in the path, or URL, leading to that content causes the search engines to accidentally clone the content multiple times. This condition substantially impairs the ability of a site to do well. If the content management system has a system that creates session IDs in URLs, you could be in real trouble. Track with mature analytics, not session IDs.

▶ **Multiple URL paths.** A typical problem with e-commerce content management is that as a product progresses through its lifecycle, it accrues multiple URLs. Again, since the search engine can only understand a page of content based on the URL where it finds the content, when a product appears in a category *and* is a part of a gift basket *and* is a weekly special (and on and on), pretty soon the search crawlers have followed a bunch of different links to find the same piece of content. Do whatever you can to ensure that each piece of content exists only on one URL and that multiple paths actually rely on one URL, regardless of where the links are deployed. Rely on mature analytics systems to parse channels.

▶ **Unintentional cloning.** When you come to the realization that a piece of content should only be accessible through a single URL path, it is easy to see other conditions in content management systems that cause content to be unintentionally cloned. Suffice it to say that the architecture must only have a single URL path to a single piece of content.

▶ **Infinite loops.** A corollary to the unintentional cloning issue is the infinite loop. Make sure that you do not put the search engine spiders into a potentially endless task of following "next" links in a calendar or some similar situation. If the search engine spider can traverse a next link onto the next day of a calendar where it can find another next link, it will follow that link to the next page, and on and on. Prevent this kind of situation by using a scripted link that the search engines can't follow so that the crawlers can spend their time on the content that you want to have indexed.

▶ **Old URL structures.** The first thing that many site redevelopment projects do is to replace the old URL structure. The trouble is that the search engines have probably already indexed the content at these old URLs, and as soon as you change all of them you are essentially sending your indexing back to square one. In addition, any deep links that the site has accrued over time are pointing at the old URL structure. At all costs, preserve as many of the old URLs as you can. It is probable that when you replace the content management system you will have to change all the URLs, so if this is inevitable, be sure to recommend that the old URLs are given a status code of "301 Moved Permanently" and redirected on a one-to-one basis from the old URLs to the new URLs. The 301 redirect is the only acceptable redirect for search engine purposes.

Domains, Directory, and URL Structure All Matter

If you are starting from scratch, and if the restrictions of branding issues allow, try to select a domain that contains a keyword or two. It is difficult these days to get a .com domain that has quality keywords, but if you do, separate those keywords with hyphens.

An important part of how UX affects SEO is in a site's directory structure. It has a critical influence on how link popularity is distributed throughout the site. Simple is better. Avoid having extraneous files in the directory structure at all costs. Some content management systems will automatically insert a subdirectory; prevent this if at all possible. This condition dilutes the relevance of the entire site. The search engines understand the hierarchy of the site based on the way the site directories are structured, so be sure that the most important directories are at the top of the architecture.

If your environment allows it, use keywords in the URL structure that are relevant to the section of the site. Separate keywords with a hyphen, and don't use too many keywords in one filename. Go for something like this: sitename.com/widget-catalog/aquatic-widgets/underwater-submersible.html.

In addition, be sure that you have redirects set up for http://site-in-question.com to 301 Moved Permanently redirect to http://www.site-in-question.com. If a site will resolve with and without the www, search engines (particularly Yahoo) will index content at both URLs, opening the entire site up for accidental duplication. This condition tends to propagate when a third party links to the site without the www and the site contains a dynamic link structure.

Content: The Once (and Current) and Future King

Although generating content is someone else's problem, the groundwork that is laid in site architecture has a lot to do with making the right content available to search engines.

As with all forms of keyword-driven search, you need to understand the actual search behavior of the people you want to view an asset. Search engines are still very "primitive," in that they rely on users typing in keywords to connect them with assets that are more or less relevant for these words. Picking the right phrases has everything to do with whether your site is relevant in the right context.

In a perfect world, your SEO partner will provide you with a set of keyword phrase targets before you begin and will collaborate with you throughout the wireframing process. If there is no such competent partner involved with your process, read up on the Google AdWords Keyword Research Tool (https://adwords.google.com/select/KeywordToolExternal) and do a bit of investigation into the actual search behavior of people exploring your category. Then spend some time with this input to figure out the phrases that potential customers are searching, and use those phrases as appropriate throughout the site. Search engines look for keywords in a number of places throughout their analysis of a site. Optimization relies on making sure that the right words are in the right places. By understanding the role of keywords in the UX design process, you will establish the framework necessary to enable future success.

So why is content king? It is the very core of what a Web site is designed to deliver. Search engines need text content that they can see and index. Site visitors need engaging content that is worthy of their attention. Bloggers and Webmasters need content that is linkworthy. Without the right content in the right places, search engines cannot connect the right visitors with your site.

Naming Conventions and the Battle Against Jargon

It is essential that keyword targets are reflected in the taxonomy developed for a site. Using keyword phrases in the main site structure makes the whole site more relevant for the things that you are selling. If you're selling widgets, don't call the online product list the Catalog, call it the Widget Catalog. Likewise, use your keyword research to make decisions against jargon. For example, use the words *laptops* as opposed to *notebooks* in your structure because people search for *laptops* 10,000+ percent more frequently than they search for *notebooks*.

Metadata, Headers, and Keywords

It is pretty remarkable that we have gotten this far into the chapter before digging back into basic issues of metadata. A myriad of meta tags are available, but only a handful really have much influence because all the others are susceptible to spamming. Relevant tags are these:

▶ **Page title.** Please note that this is not the <meta title> tag, but is the actual <title> tag in the page header. This tag contains the page's actual title, and it is the most important 65 characters on the page. Think of the title as the little tab sticking up in the old-fashioned library card catalog, which says "Clements, Samuel" and indicates that all the cards behind that tab are books by Mark Twain. Each page of the site must have a unique page title. Do not stuff keywords in the title, and be sure to front-load the title with the words that matter most.

▶ **Meta keywords.** This tag has virtually zero influence on the search engines because it is so vulnerable to spamming. The exceptions appear to be that Google AdSense syndication looks at the meta keywords tag and that Yahoo is influenced in a very tertiary way by it. Meta keywords need to match the content of the page, and this tag is actually a good place to insert potential misspellings. It should be different for each page.

▶ **Meta description.** As with the page title and meta keywords, be certain that the meta description is unique to each page. This description is just that: a summary of what is contained on the page in question. Tell it, don't sell it, in about 150 to 160 characters. This content is critical because it is probably what search engines will display under the link to your page. If the page does not contain a meta description, the search engine will look for a snippet of text or other content that contains the keywords searched and display that in its results. The meta description is more about usability than SEO, so be certain that each page is properly tagged.

▶ **"Noindex" meta tag.** If you have any pages you do not want to include in search engine results, use the noindex meta tag. Just be certain that pages you do want to be indexed do not inadvertently contain this tag.

▶ **Headers.** Search engines recognize the headers <h1>, <h2>, and so on as influencing factors so long as you are not spamming with them. Take care to allow for section headers that are both descriptive and contain the relevant keywords for that page.

▶ **Link anchor text.** Link anchor text is an important influencer of what search engines think about the page on the other side of the link. This is the factor that creates the "GoogleBomb." If enough links point at a page with the same link anchor text, Google interprets the destination as relevant for the phrase in the anchor text. For instance, if you search on Google for "click here," the Adobe site will show up in the top results. There are hundreds of thousands of links that point at Adobe and read "click here to download Adobe Reader" or something similar. Use this to your advantage; anchor text should not be "More" or "Click Here." Instead, it should contain keywords that are relevant to the destination page.

Split the Hairs

It is to your advantage to have separately indexed pages for both your left-handed corrugated widgets and your right-handed corrugated widgets. This level of granularity gives your pages a better chance to be an exact match for the legendary long-tail searches. A page that is all about one thing has a better chance of winning for that one thing than a page that is about multiple things (all other factors being equal of course). And who is interested in reading a page that is hundreds of words long anyway?

Use Site Maps

In recent years it has become popular to omit the classic site map page. This is a mistake for usability and a mistake for SEO. Find your way through to the fact that any site needs a site map. It may not be cool but it is necessary. Also, include site map files at /sitemap.xml and /sitemap.txt. Although this structure does not help the site rank better, it does help the search engines understand the directory structure and find new and updated content.

Keep Content Fresh

A key component to gaining and keeping top placement in search results is constantly refreshing the site content. This doesn't mean editing all the content in the site all the time; it means that the site must constantly grow. Build the directory structure so that adding content will be easy and intuitive, and anticipate that the site will grow over time.

Other Content Issues

A basic challenge in dealing with the UX of a content-rich site is to prevent cloning or duplicate content. Look out for creating duplicate pages with seemingly innocuous conveniences such as "printer friendly" content that is an exact duplicate of a page in a PDF or similar document type. Shield these kinds of pages with scripted links or use the rel="nofollow" link attribute.

Don't discount optimization for the wide array of digital assets that search engines can index. This topic would make almost another chapter in itself, but suffice it to say that PDFs, videos, images, and other non–Web page assets are clearly a part of natural search results. Structuring the wrappers around these assets is critical, because search engines need pointers to this kind of content. For example, search engines can't tell that an asset is a horse-race video unless there is a link pointing to the video with anchor text that reads "video of a horse race" placed near text about horse-racing videos in the page code.

Using alt attributes is another way to help identify nontext assets to the search engines and is always a good idea for the sake of usability.

Don't create dead-end content pages. Make sure that even the very bottom of the structure has links back into the main site, so the search engine spiders don't get stuck in a dead end. Breadcrumb links are a straightforward way to accomplish this if a page type does not contain the main site navigation.

Link Popularity Explained

If there is a Holy Grail of SEO, it is link popularity. It is the cornerstone of why Google worked so much better than the other search engines when it emerged on the scene. *Link popularity* is a determination of the quality and the quantity of links pointing at a Web asset from other Web pages. Google uses the term *PageRank,* and it is the über factor that can overcome many other deficiencies. Links are essentially votes for a Web asset, and it is generally assumed that something that is interesting or valuable to others will have links pointing at it from other trusted Web assets. Over time this concept has proven invaluable to overcome spamming efforts and is at its core a fundamental principle of quality search results. This principle is critical for the UX designer to comprehend because of the way that link popularity will distribute into the structure of a Web site.

Typical Link Popularity Distribution

Similar to the Richter scale used to measure the strength of seismic activity, Google's PageRank system (named by Larry Page for himself) is a logarithmic scale that ranges from 0 to 10. This means (in wildly general terms) that if one page has a PR of 4 and another has a PR of 5, the PR 5 page has 10 times the link popularity of the page with the 4.

It is important to understand this because PageRank distributes through a site based on the hierarchy of links and the structure of the directories. Generally speaking, if your home page has a page rank of 5, your primary section pages should have a PR of 4, the secondary pages PR 3, the tertiary pages PR 2, and so forth.

Pages with the most internal links pointing at them tend to have the greatest link popularity. The pages that are the most important to win need to have the most internal links pointing at them. This includes links in the main site navigation, site map, footer, and inline links embedded in text. Because link popularity is critical to ranking well in search results, you need to be as deliberate as possible in getting as much of it as you can into the pages that contain the "buying proposition."

Each page has a finite amount of link popularity that it can contribute to the other pages in the site. A page that has one link on it pointing at one other page is sending 100 percent of its available value to the recipient. A page that has a hundred links to a hundred other pages is sending 1 percent of its value to each of those hundred pages.

The home page tends to have the most link popularity, because the home page of a site tends to have the most links pointing at it from third-party Web sites. This means that the home page has the most value to contribute to other pages of the site. If there is a critical page that is a part of the "selling proposition," put in a direct link to it from the home page so that the search engines can understand how important this particular page is in comparison to the rest of the site. If possible, build a feature that can rotate links to deep content from the home page.

Footer Links

As we look for ways to marshal and control the distribution of link popularity throughout the site, remember that text links in the footer of each page are both a blessing and a curse, and they will have some bearing on the distribution of link popularity throughout the site. Typical footer links point at the privacy policy and other nontransactional pages, so if it is required that these links be in the footer, hide them behind some sort of scripting, or better yet, "nofollow" these links using the rel="nofollow" link attribute. This will prevent the link popularity of each page from leaking out to pages that do not really need to rank in search results. It is also better to prevent the passing of link popularity than to fully exclude the pages using robots.txt.

In-Content Cross-Linking

Search engines eat up links that are embedded in text. Just don't overdo it. Some schools of thought maintain that after the first few links in a block of text the search engines do not provide advantageous weighting. Put your most important links in the beginning of the text and use link anchor text that contains keywords that are related to the destination page.

Gaming the System

Who says that search engine optimization is all work and no fun? Search engines can contribute real dollars to Web site owners, and in certain environments, there is a real no-holds-barred approach to gaining top rankings at any cost. More than a few search engine optimizers have taken advantage of their clients, charging big bucks for spurious techniques that may have positive results in the short term but a devastating impact over time.

Over the years, a variety of optimization techniques have been employed by Webmasters looking for top results. One of the core evolutions in search engine technology has been work on engineering out the clever ways that have been found to game the system. From the search engines' perspective, their users' best interests are served by clean, highly relevant results at the top of any query. From the perspective of many search engine optimizers, all's fair in love and SEO.

White Hat Versus Black Hat

It is easy and fun to characterize SEO methods as being "white hat" or "black hat," but it's far more difficult to discern which is which. Many white hat optimizers are purists, saying in strong, declarative terms that certain technical management, content and link manipulation, and other approaches are simply off limits. The black hats look at the issue as a contest that has nothing to do with cheating: How can something be cheating if there is no specific written rule book or court of adjudication? Their approach is more along the lines of a game of cat and mouse where the cat holds all the cards and the mouse can stand to make some serious cash: Take a risk, get a win, and the payoff is big. But once the search engines catch up to you (and they nearly always do) be prepared for your site to be banned or at the very least unable to perform when the methods are revoked.

Spamming with Meta Keywords

Many of the "cheating" techniques have been based in the principles of UX. An early method to game the system was *meta keywords stuffing*—essentially filling the meta keywords tag with hundreds of occurrences of *apples* when the site content is all about oranges. At its root, the meta keywords approach was created to help with the taxonomy of the early Web. Today, because of all the keyword spamming, this piece of a Web page has virtually no influence on search placement. The search engines easily detected this technique and were quickly able to engineer around it. The next generation of spam was a bit more difficult to unravel, and also had its roots in UX issues.

Cloning and Doorway Pages

Both *cloning* and *doorway pages* are methods used to make a Web site look bigger or different to the search engines. By cloning a page over and over, Webmasters could essentially manufacture minutely targeted content that could quickly dominate for a specific search phrase. Because of this practice, it is important to be sure your architecture prevents inadvertent cloning, since search engines are sensitive to duplications, intentional or otherwise.

Doorway pages are another method for influencing search results that straddles the gray space between white hat and black hat methods. On the one hand, Google's quality guidelines for Webmasters say "doorway pages ... are in violation of our Webmaster guidelines" (www.google.com/support/ webmasters/bin/answer.py?answer=66355). The guidelines identify doorway pages as poor-quality pages that have been specifically optimized for a set of keywords that may not be relevant to the actual site or that are spammy.

On the other hand, how do you help search engines gain access to content that is trapped in a non-spiderable database or is obscured because of a technology that search engines don't like? In its positive definition, a doorway page is high-quality static content that search engines can see and understand while providing the visitor a door into dynamic content. Today's content management systems are getting better at the core issues that have necessitated this approach, but it can still be very useful to create extra pages for the express purpose of showing the search engines a static representation of content that they would otherwise be unable to deal with.

Link Spamming

Recent methods for gaming the system have centered on manipulation of link popularity, a concept that is core to the way that the modern Web search engines work. As discussed above, search engines determine the relevance of a particular Web asset by analyzing the quantity and quality of links pointing at that page from other places. Search engine optimizers have worked to manipulate this part of the puzzle through sneaky redirecting, overuse of subdomains, making every page of a site "/index.html," and a variety of other subtle machinations.

Some Final Thoughts

It is doubtful that this is your first exploration of search engine optimization issues. By now it is clear how much a site's architecture and related issues influence search engine performance. The current search environment is a quantum leap ahead of simple taxonomy or structure.

Thoughtful search engine optimization starts with quality UX. The architecting of a Web site is the critical point in its life cycle where it can either be destined for search engine success or set up for imminent failure. Search engine optimization is a strategy that never really ends, but quality SEO will never really get started without the careful attention of the UX designer.

Jonathan Ashton is vice president of SEO and web analytics for Agency.com and runs its Center of Excellence for SEO. His team provides SEO services for the entire company, ensuring that the process of designing and building rich interactive experiences results in sites that can be found on search engines. His monthly column, "Industrial Strength SEO," can be found at http://searchengineland.com/lands/columns/industrial-strength.php.

9 Transition: From Defining to Designing

Time to Visualize, Prioritize, and Plan

You now have a nice fat list of business requirements and user requirements. And you have information from your users to focus your discussions. So now what?

Unless you're on the Shangri-la of projects, you'll have a budget (tight), a timeline (crunched), or both that are telling you you'll need to focus and manage that list somehow. This chapter discusses some of the ways you can transition from definition to design, including tactics to help your team visualize the solution that needs to be designed, prioritize features to create a unified set of requirements, and plan the design activities that will follow in the next phase of the project.

Carolyn Chandler

Chapter 4 touched on different project approaches, or methodologies, and how they affect the way you collaborate with the project team and business stakeholders. It compared a waterfall approach, which has Define and Design phases separated by an approval step, with a modified waterfall approach that has some overlap in phases.

This chapter discusses the activities that can occur in the overlap between the Define and Design phases.

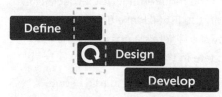

This point in the process is the right time to

▶ *Ideate* and *visualize* **features that did not emerge during stakeholder interviews or user research.** Doing this with the project team before prioritizing enables you to consider and plan for innovative features that meet both business and user needs.

▶ **Prioritize project requirements.** This involves taking the integrated list of business requirements, user requirements, and project team ideas and determining their relative importance in meeting the project objectives. At this point, you'll be working with the development team to understand the general level of effort required to meet each requirement.

▶ **Plan the activities and documentation you'll be using during design.** This planning determines how you'll work with other team members and what types of tools or documents they'll receive from you, such as site maps and wireframes (discussed in chapters 10 and 11).

This chapter covers each of these three areas, beginning with a method for ideation and visualization that is easy for a UX designer to use in collaboration with project team members.

Ideate and Visualize Features

UX designers have a unique set of skills that help bridge the mental gap between words (such as requirements) and images (such as site maps and wireframes). As much as people may talk about requirements and argue over language, often they won't really get onto the same page until they can see the concept represented visually.

On the other hand, if you go into specific visual details too quickly, you risk focusing the conversation on smaller details (say, whether a choice in a form should be a radio button or a drop-down option) before you resolve the big questions (such as whether your users should have to fill out that particular form in the first place).

There are many conceptual design techniques you can use throughout the process that help visualize context, flow, and story in a way that engages others before detailed design begins in earnest. These techniques will also bring out the need for features that can be added to your requirements document before prioritization occurs.

One such technique is the collaborative creation of *storyboards:* visualizations of particular user scenarios sketched on paper or a whiteboard during a brainstorming meeting. The UX designer then works from these sketches to add details.

The Basic Process of Storyboarding

Prepare for the storyboarding session by creating a list of scenarios that you'd like to explore. To build the scenario, consider the following questions and bring the answers to the session:

▶ **Who is the main user in this scenario? What role is he playing?** This is where your user model or your personas will come in handy. If you have them, bring them to the meeting—they will both focus the conversation and ensure your project team has a better understanding of how they can use user-modeling tools throughout the design phase.

▶ **Is the chosen user a first-time user of the site? If not, is he a sporadic user, or does he use it frequently?** This will affect the level of the features you'll discuss; a first-time user might be overwhelmed by the number of choices that a frequent user might like. You may want to talk through the scenario twice to reveal different features that could be needed for each group, such as in-context help for new users or customization features for frequent users.

▶ **What immediate need has led this user to the site? What is he trying to accomplish, and why?** You can generate thoughts on this by looking at the high-level tasks covered in your business or user requirements, such as "find product recommendations." Perhaps the user wants to find product recommendations because he needs a pair of snow boots and wants to make sure they won't leak and get his feet wet.

Gather your brainstorming team for the session. This team can be just you and one other person, or it can be a small group of three or four other people. (More is possible, but it can be difficult to gather everyone effectively around a whiteboard and keep them focused on the task at hand.)

Ideally, at least one person in the group will be responsible for representing the user viewpoint. Another should represent the business viewpoint (for example, a business stakeholder or a business analyst if that role is represented on the project). This doesn't mean you can't switch perspectives; you can, and should, consider both user and business needs as much as possible during the discussion. See the section "Maintain a Good Tension" for more on balancing user and business needs.

Once you have your team together, tell them the purposes of the activity: to understand some of the features that may be needed to meet business and user needs and to focus future design efforts. Present the answers to the questions listed above and the list of scenarios to be discussed. Then step up to the whiteboard (or put your pencil to the paper) and ask the group questions about the scenario, such as

▶ How is this user likely to get to the site? Consider online searches, banner ads, word of mouth, and other avenues.

▶ If online searches come to mind, do the requirements accurately reflect the types of features or activities (such as tagging for SEO needs) to support this search?

▶ Once on the site, what does the user see that will be relevant to their need?

▶ What path will the user take to complete the task? Sketch this out with high-level details.

▶ Are other people involved in the task? If so, how might they be involved (phone, e-mail, collaborative site features), and how might they influence the decisions or behaviors of the main user?

▶ Where is a user likely to need help along the way? How will he get it?

▶ What happens when the user finishes his task? A common design mistake is to think you're finished when the user's task is complete, but that's a great time to encourage the user to explore other areas of the site or consider purchasing related products.

Consider an example from a common business scenario: the need to post a new job to the company's .com site. For the sake of this scenario, say that you've conducted stakeholder interviews and found that the hiring process is primarily managed by one person, call him Jeff, in the human resources department, who works with those who need to hire.

Jeff is pretty familiar with the job descriptions that currently exist. When a new one is needed, he usually finds out when the potential manager for the new position asks him to post a job. It's then a collaborative process between Jeff and the manager (let's call her Emily) to write up and post the job description.

Figure 9.1 illustrates how the storyboard for this scenario might look.

The figure shows just one part of the storyboard you could create here. You might want to start earlier in the scenario to show the approval process Emily had to go through, or you might want to continue the storyboard to show a job hunter finding and applying for the job.

The important thing to note here is that a storyboard like this allows you and your project team to see the workflow as more than a series of pages. It brings in the human element and the context. And without the human element of a persona (Jeff), your team may not have thought to include the feature of pulling in an existing job description to start from—even though all of us have done this as a way to save time and ensure we're including everything we need.

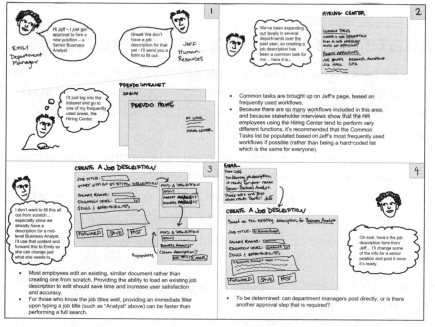

Figure 9.1 *A storyboard initially created on a whiteboard, then sketched out and detailed in Microsoft Visio using a Wacom tablet*

One thing to keep in mind when using storyboards and other types of sketches (such as user flows and conceptual wireframes) is that they are primarily meant to be brainstorming tools. Although some great ideas come out of the exercise, these sketches are not meant to be detailed designs. This fact may be apparent from their sketch form (as opposed to prototype form), but it is still an important point to make with business stakeholders, because seeing features visualized even in a sketch can sometimes lead to expectations that they'll exist in the final product.

Another risk here is that participants can get sidetracked in debates on user interface elements, such as whether something should be in the page or in a pop-up. It's very easy to get into those detailed discussions because those kinds of problems are often easier (or more familiar) to solve than the bigger problems that scenarios are meant to address. To keep things streamlined and use time efficiently, ask participants to save those kinds of discussions for the point where you're designing against your prioritized list of requirements.

And that takes us to the next step in the process: the often lively, sometimes painful process of prioritizing those beautiful requirements you've spent so much time collecting!

Facilitate the Prioritization Process

You've got your set of business requirements that have been fleshed out with features based on user requirements and your ideation work. Now comes one of the hardest parts: whittling it all down to a prioritized list of high-value requirements.

As you walk through the requirements that need to be prioritized, have the project objectives handy, as well as your user model, to help you focus the discussion on your target groups. In addition to you, in your role as *user advocate*, the prioritization process should also include:

▶ Someone who represents the viewpoint of the business (the *business advocate*).

▶ Someone who represents the viewpoint of the development team (the *development advocate*).

▶ Someone who represents the needs of the project (such as the *project manager*). This person may not need to be in the prioritization meetings but will set any constraints that affect prioritization (such as deadlines or budget) and ensure the final list fits within them.

The UX Designer's Role in Prioritization

It can be tempting to consider prioritization a shared responsibility between the project sponsor, the project manager, and the lead of the development team rather than an issue for a UX designer. There is nothing further from the truth.

Prioritization discussions are where successful solutions are made or broken. User experience designers have a *responsibility* to bring their skills to bear for these important conversations.

If you're already part of the prioritization process, this section will give you tips on participating. If you're not, do what you can to get yourself involved. This means you need to inform the project team of the skills you bring to the table—such as facilitation—and the balanced perspective you can bring. It's essential to demonstrate that you can understand different team members' perspectives and work together toward a unified understanding. See the section "Maintain a Good Tension" for more on how to achieve this balance.

The prioritization team walks through each of the requirements to answer the following questions:

▶ **What is its level of importance to the business?** How important is the requirement in achieving one or more project objectives? How great is the impact if this requirement is left out?

▶ **What is its level of importance to the user?** Does the requirement meet a common user need (or high-impact needs for priority user groups)? How does it affect the user experience if this is left out? Are there other requirements that are very similar and may compete?

For this last question, keep in mind that multiple solutions to the same problem can compete with each other and cause user confusion (as well as require more effort to support). For example, the *New York Times* may have a large enough development staff to support all the sharing features on nytimes.com (called out in blue in Figure 9.2), but some of its users may be confused about whether they should click Recommend, E-Mail, or Share to send the article to a friend. If your users may not be familiar with all the sharing options that have exploded over the past few years, you should probably start with a smaller set of features.

▶ **What is the technical feasibility of developing the requirement?** What kind of time is needed to develop it? If you're working with a relatively new technology, the time estimate will be higher here.

▶ **What is the resource feasibility of developing it?** Does the project team have the people, skills, and money required to develop the feature? (Consider the costs of purchasing and learning new technology tools.)

Figure 9.2 *A shot of www.nytimes.com, highlighting the many sharing features the online newspaper provides*

Create a worksheet that captures your decisions for each requirement. This could include a low, medium, or high rating based on the questions above, or you could use a numerical scale so that you can add up the numbers for sorting purposes. As you work down the list, you may find you'll need to consolidate similar requirements or break a large requirement into a number of smaller requirements that represent potentially independent units of work.

Keep in mind that this system is simply meant to help sort and prioritize; it isn't based on a scientific analysis of the requirement's feasibility. It is, however, very useful in managing a large list, inspiring discussion, and capturing relative importance.

Figure 9.3 shows an example of a prioritization worksheet that uses high-level categories of importance and feasibility (low, medium, and high) to assign relative values to each requirement.

Prioritization Worksheet

	Requirement	Description	Business Importance	User Importance	Technical Feasibility	Resource Feasibility
1	Contact Info Form	Users must provide contact information before seeing a list of distributors	High	Low	High	High
2	Email Confirmation	An email is sent to confirm an order has been made	High	High	High	High
3	Order History	Users can log in to see all past orders made in the last 365 days	High	High	High	Medium
4	Order Tracking	Orders can be tracked by entering a tracking code, given once an order has shipped	High	High	Medium	Medium
5	GPS Tracking	Users can track their package by GPS, following trucks or airplanes	Medium	Medium	Low	Low
6	Order Fulfillment Reviews	Users can read other customers' reviews of the company's fulfillment process	Low	Medium	High	Medium
7	Order Fulfillment Chat	Users can chat with other users about their order fulfillment experience	Low	Medium	Medium	Medium

Figure 9.3 *An example of a worksheet for requirements prioritization*

Assigning values to each of the categories will inspire a lot of conversations among the prioritization team. How can you help facilitate discussion and decision making?

Two of the most important things you can do are to understand (and sometimes represent) the different viewpoints that are key to defining a balanced solution, and to help resolve areas of conflict within the project team.

First, let's talk about representing the right set of viewpoints during prioritization. This involves creating and maintaining tension between user advocacy, business advocacy, and development advocacy—a good kind of tension, because it ensures a balanced solution that provides a good user experience, meets project constraints, and aligns with business objectives.

Maintain a Good Tension

As you gather requirements, and throughout the rest of the project as well, you may notice three roles pulling against each other during team discussions:

 Business advocate: The team member representing the business needs and requirements and ensuring they are captured and met as faithfully as possible. Primary concerns for the business advocate include meeting strategic objectives for company and department, ensuring the business vision doesn't get lost during the project, and setting and maintaining focus on project objectives.

 User advocate: The team member representing the needs and perspectives of the primary users who will experience the site. Primary concerns for the user advocate include ensuring the site meets expectations for usability, providing a satisfying and engaging experience, and encouraging behavior that supports the project objectives.

Development advocate: The team member representing the needs and constraints of technology and quality assurance teams. Primary concerns include ensuring the development team works efficiently and within scope and that it delivers a product that meets the quality standards expected by users and the business stakeholders.

Picture this as a three-way tug-of-war among the advocates. If tension is respectfully well-maintained among the three (meaning no one advocate dominates) then the three sides can work toward a well-balanced solution that meets project objectives.

Each team member should be aware that they have an interest in maintaining a balance throughout the project. If one side dominates, the other roles lose ground and the project risks missing its objectives—or achieving them at a much higher price than expected. See Figure 9.4 for examples of what can happen when the tension is not balanced.

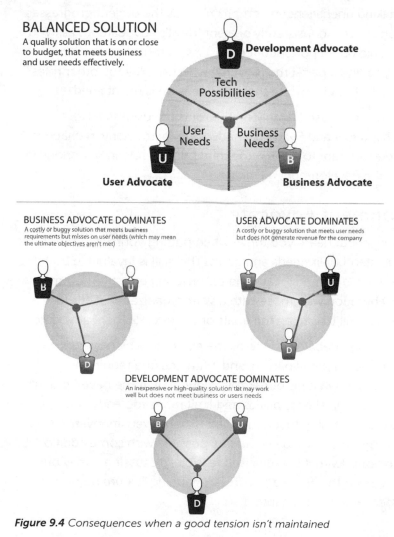

BALANCED SOLUTION
A quality solution that is on or close to budget, that meets business and user needs effectively.

Development Advocate

Tech Possibilities

User Needs

Business Needs

User Advocate

Business Advocate

BUSINESS ADVOCATE DOMINATES
A costly or buggy solution that meets business requirements but misses on user needs (which may mean the ultimate objectives aren't met)

USER ADVOCATE DOMINATES
A costly or buggy solution that meets user needs but does not generate revenue for the company

DEVELOPMENT ADVOCATE DOMINATES
An inexpensive or high-quality solution that may work well but does not meet business or users needs

Figure 9.4 *Consequences when a good tension isn't maintained*

Can you play more than one of these roles on a project? Absolutely! Ideally different team members have primary responsibility for each role, but that doesn't mean you can't switch places once in a while. In fact, you may switch roles from discussion to discussion—or even from topic to topic. As the UX designer you'll be playing the user advocate most often, but you need to understand the viewpoints of all three roles and ensure they are consistently represented in order to create successful designs.

Although switching roles from time to time is healthy, be wary of designating yourself the primary person responsible for more than one of these roles. You may start making unchallenged compromises as the project progresses because you won't have a consistently present "devil's advocate" to ask you those uncomfortable but important questions. If you must take on more than one role, try to find a part-time resource who can play the other roles for you occasionally, to help ensure that good tension is maintained.

Up to this point, we've focused largely on the roles of business advocate (particularly in chapters 4 and 5) and user advocate (particularly in chapters 1 and 6). Let's take a moment to discuss the third primary role in our prioritization discussions: the development advocate.

The Development Advocate

If you're a UX designer at heart, you thrive when putting yourself in the shoes of others to understand their needs and goals. This skill is invaluable both for performing your role as user advocate and for ensuring effective communication and collaboration with those within your organization. Let's take a moment to use that skill to outline the goals of the development advocate.

One of the great design debates concerns the extent to which the development advocate should participate in, and influence, the requirements-gathering process—and what his or her role is during it. If the development advocate presents technical possibilities and limitations too early, it may curtail some of the brainstorming that could lead to some very innovative solutions. After all, today's blue-sky idea could be possible with some additional technical explorations. Even if the idea isn't feasible, discussing it may bring out an underlying need that you can address. (Mapping feature requests to needs is addressed later in this chapter.)

These are the goals and related responsibilities of the development advocate:

▶ Meet the requirements on time and within budget

  ▶ Ensure team efficiency (avoiding redundant work, ensuring good communication)

  ▶ Make the best use of the tools and platforms available

  ▶ Select cost-effective additional tools

▶ Ensure future changes do not require a lot of extra work

  ▶ Make the solution scalable, to accommodate growth

  ▶ Make the solution modular, so that individual parts can be modified easily

  ▶ Make the solution as standardized as possible: The fewer modifications made to a purchased system, the less redevelopment work will be needed down the road

▶ Ensure that the development team functions well

  ▶ Limit turnover by providing relatively interesting and rewarding work

  ▶ Limit the burnout that can happen with last-minute pushes

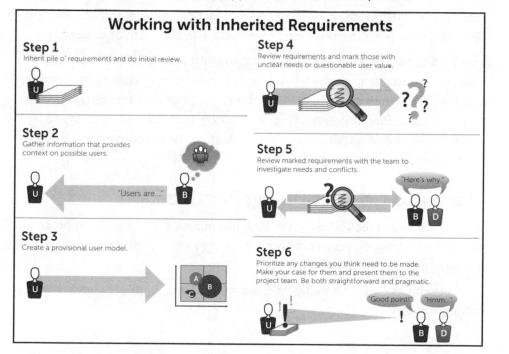

If the development advocate isn't involved early enough, however, the team may move far down the path of a certain option only to find that it's too expensive to include—or the development advocate ends up missing one or more of her own goals. And last but not least, the development advocate is a great source for bringing out some of the capabilities in the technology that could really make your solution sing, such as new technologies or underutilized functionality.

An effective approach is to plan key reviews with the development advocate once brainstorming is complete, high-level requirements have been captured, and the prioritization process is about to begin. This allows the development advocate to spend the initial part of the process exploring the selected tools to get more detail on what may or may not be possible, and then participate more heavily in the requirements process itself once certain themes and ideas have more weight.

If you feel some requirements-gathering sessions are key for the development advocate to attend, make sure you're both on the same page beforehand regarding his or her role in the meeting and how you'll be capturing any potential concerns the advocate may have after listening in. You could also record these kinds of sessions to review with the development advocate later. You may need them yourself when you're in the thick of designing!

This kind of clear communication and follow-up during information gathering is vital to building strong relationships between team members, which can make a big difference in how smoothly the prioritization step goes later in the process. But sometimes, despite your best efforts, conflicts arise as you try to prioritize requirements. Let's talk about how you can help the project team manage this conflict.

Managing Conflict During Prioritization

If there are large areas of disagreement, prioritization can be a long process. And if those disagreements aren't resolved, they will continue to surface during design and development.

These conflicts can have many different root causes; here are some of the most common:

- The team is not on the same page about the project objectives or underlying business strategies (either misunderstanding, forgetting, or disagreeing on them).

- Opposing team members are closely tied to a certain set of features. (Perhaps the features excite them, or they've promised them to a set of influential customers or stakeholders).

- There are conflicts between business needs and user needs that are not easily resolved.

- The technologies being used are relatively new to the development team, so they're uncomfortable making estimates.

Let's take a couple of the situations above and discuss how you, as a user experience designer, can be involved in resolving them.

Choosing Your Battles

During the prioritization process, some of your favorite features may be on the chopping block. It's easy to start feeling unhappy about this, especially if it seems that user requirements are the ones most often being dropped from the list.

If you passionately defend every requirement equally, you risk having prioritizing decisions made for you. Here are some questions to ask yourself as you decide when to push for a particular requirement and when to compromise:

- How does the requirement support project objectives?

- Does it significantly reduce a particular risk? For example, does it reduce users' exposure to spam, reducing negative opinions about the site?

- Do other proposed site requirements rely on this one to function properly?

- What is the impact if the feature is not included?

- Is the value of the feature worth the effort needed to develop it (even at the cost of other features you hold dear)?

If you have a strong answer for all of these, bring them to the prioritization table to make your case. If not, consider letting it go, but be sure to share your reasons so others see that you're compromising for the overall good of the project. That will demonstrate your ability to consider the larger business context and solidify your involvement in future prioritizing discussions and change requests.

Lack of Alignment on Project Direction

The team is not on the same page about the project objectives or underlying business strategies.

Let's separate this source of conflict into two areas: communication and consensus.

If communication of project objectives or business strategies is the issue, ask yourself how you personally can help improve communication. Is it a matter of posting the objectives or strategies where all team members will see them (such as in a war room or online collaboration area, or the top of every meeting agenda)? Or maybe what's needed is a visual representation of the objectives or strategies that will help bring them into focus for the team and get team members excited about the vision they're working toward. Remember the visualization skills discussed at the beginning of this chapter? Use them to create an image that can be easily printed and posted or quickly sketched out on a whiteboard to help focus conversations.

If consensus is the issue, ask yourself how you could help bring everyone together. Is the conflict caused by anxiety about the risk involved in releasing a very different feature set to users? Perhaps there's research you can conduct to help resolve some of the disagreements, such as surveys, interviews, or contextual inquiries (see Chapter 6). Or perhaps you can bring your facilitation skills to bear by holding a structured discussion about disagreements, working through issues point by point until they're resolved.

Conflict Over Favorite Features

Opposing team members are attached to their own sets of features.

Suppose the director of the training department wants integrated, topic-based tutorials and the head of sales wants one exciting demo to send out to generate interest. Meanwhile, you have ten other business stakeholders in various roles—and *they* all have urgent needs. How do you help build consensus?

One method is to apply a variation of a method you read about in Chapter 6: affinity diagramming. In this method, you can work from an existing set of requirements or have the stakeholders brainstorm their own requirements (especially useful if it's still early in the requirements-gathering process). If you're working from existing requirements, you can print them out on individual pages and tape them all to the wall. Otherwise, ask stakeholders to write their top-of-mind requirements on a set of Post-it notes.

What you'll need:

▶ A room large enough for your stakeholder group to move around in and that has one or more large blank walls you can apply Post-it notes to

▶ A pad of large Post-it notes, at least one for each stakeholder

▶ Sticker dots (you can find these in office supply stores; they come in various colors), one set of ten dots per stakeholder

Gather your primary stakeholders together in a room and ask each to take some time to write key requirements down, one to a note. Give them 15 to 20 minutes to do this. (No peeking!)

Ask everyone to put their requirements up on the wall. Then ask each person to walk up and describe what they posted. As you go around the room, start grouping similar requirements together (if the stakeholders agree they're similar).

Once the requirements are explained and grouped, hand out the sticker dots. Tell the stakeholders that they can indicate which requirements are of highest priority to them by allocating their dots among the Post-it notes. They can choose to place all ten of their dots on one requirement, for example, if they feel it's that important, or they could choose to place a dot on ten different requirements. You'll start to see some clear favorites form as people place their dots.

When they're done placing the dots, walk through the results together. When they are forced to choose this way, stakeholders will bring forth their own internal priorities, and the conversation will probably become a lot easier.

Surfing

For more on a variation of this technique to be used in prioritization, see this article "The KJ-Technique: A Group Process for Establishing Priorities," by Jared M. Spool: www.uie.com/articles/kj_technique.

This kind of technique can help you jump-start the prioritization process or reset a process that has stalled due to disagreement. Once you've achieved momentum and a common understanding, completing the prioritization document (such as the one we saw in Figure 9.3) will become much easier.

In parallel with your prioritization activities you should be preparing for the full design effort that will soon follow. Having a plan for your work will help you estimate the effort that will be involved in creating detailed designs, integrate your work with that of others on your project team, and coordinate efforts to align with project milestones. The next section covers some of the considerations that will help you plan.

Plan Your Activities and Documentation

Once you have a prioritized list of requirements and, ideally, some early conceptual work complete (such as the storyboards illustrated earlier in the chapter), your project manager will probably start asking you for details on what you're going to do as you design.

There are several types of design activities, and each will have a different impact on how you design, the amount of time it will take, and the type of document you'll end up with. This is a "document" in a general sense; it could vary from a whiteboard sketch, to a wireframe, to a prototype.

We'll be covering some interaction design activities in the next three chapters. As you plan the activities to use, keep these questions in mind:

▶ **How iterative will the overall process be?** Ideally you can begin by exploring several different concepts quickly (for example through sketches), then agreeing on one to develop in further detail. This approach could also involve taking one or more design concepts to users (see Chapter 13 for more on design testing).

▶ **How will collaboration happen during design?** If you're working closely with a team at the same location, you can include more collaborative whiteboarding sessions. If the team is dispersed, consider Web conferencing sessions with tools that allow a high degree of collaboration despite the distance.

▶ **How will your design documents be shared with the larger team?** Are you e-mailing them out to a small team or posting them to an online collaboration site? What does that mean in terms of size limitations and your process of tracking versions?

▶ **How much detail will your designs need to carry, later in the development process?** If your documents are part of a formal quality assurance (QA) process, you should make sure you involve someone from the QA team early on so they understand what kinds of detail they'll be receiving from you.

▶ **How long do your documents need to "live"?** With complex projects, the minute you stop updating a document such as a set of wireframes, it starts to "die"—the details become more inaccurate as time goes on. (This isn't always a bad thing, as long as you're involved in the discussion of those changes.) Documents that are focused on providing general guidelines, such as a brand guideline document or a library of interaction design patterns, tend to live longer.

▶ **Who are the primary users of each type of documentation?** This answer may be different at different points in the project. The primary users of your conceptual design documents are usually business stakeholders and the design team, who use them for communicating and socializing ideas. Detailed design documents are primarily for the developers who need to implement the designs; those docs provide specific direction.

▶ **What other types of documentation will yours need to align with?** You'll need to provide some kind of tie between the prioritized list of features you created above and the designs you create. You may need to keep an eye on several other kinds of documents, as well, to ensure everyone is on the same page. These docs may include brand guidelines, content development plans, functional specifications, or use cases (see Chapter 2 for an overview of different roles and the types of documentation they may be producing).

▶ **How can you estimate the effort needed for each type of document?** This one is tricky since there are a lot of variables on a project that can affect the time. But, by setting a baseline for a rough estimate, you'll have a place to start, and you can validate the numbers as you get more information. For example, you could set a baseline estimate that each detailed wireframe will take you about 6 hours to create. If you estimate a particular feature will require about five pages (for example, based on the results of the sto-ryboarding sessions described earlier in this chapter), you'll have an initial estimate of 30 hours for that feature. If it ends up taking you eight pages per wireframe, try to figure out why. If it's something that you think that will continue, you'll need to revise your estimate and possibly reprioritize.

▶ **What additional factors will affect the timing of the document?** Total time includes review time with the team and with stakeholders, as well as the time for the number of revisions you think you'll need to make. For detailed sites, it could also include time needed to reconcile your design documents with other documents, like detailed functional requirements (such as use cases). Write those assumptions down for yourself so you can check against them later.

▶ **Will you be working with multiple designers and, if so, how are you going to split up the work?** If you're working on parallel but distinct areas of the site, you can be working fairly independently on the documents you create. If you're breaking up work in a way that's very interdependent, you'll need to plan for time to reconcile your designs, and you may also need a way to track and merge different versions on documents. Save yourself a big headache later by working out a process at the beginning, and set some design guidelines early on so you're on the same page about such key elements as navigation.

Now that we've talked about some of the things you should consider when choosing your design activities, let's explore those activities. In the next three chapters we'll discuss a variety of documents, including site maps, task flows, sketches, wireframes, and prototypes.

10 Site Maps and Task Flows
Structuring Your Project from Here to There and Back Again

Site maps help to identify the structure of Web sites and applications. They can show hierarchies and connections that allow your audience to gain an understanding of where users may locate content. Task flows take site maps a step further by identifying the various courses of action that a user may traverse within a section of the site. Task flows also draw the connections to error states, content, or page views based on decision points throughout the process. When used together, site maps and task flows can provide your audience with a clear picture of content structures and how users may navigate through them.

Russ Unger

What Is a Site Map?

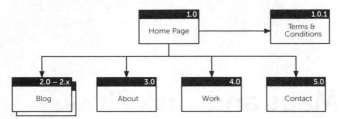

Figure 10.1 *A site map for a basic Web site with blog functionality*

Starting with the most basic of definitions, a *site map* is simply a visual way to display representative pages of a Web site (Figure 10.1). A simple site map generally fits on a single sheet of paper and resembles an employer's organizational chart. Site maps are not just for Web sites, however; you can use them for any type of application that would benefit from identifying pages, views, states, and instances of whatever is being displayed.

In most cases, you will use a site map to show teammates and clients how content will be organized for a Web site. It will provide an overview of the Web site navigation and, in some cases, will display all the connections each page can have.

What Is a Task Flow?

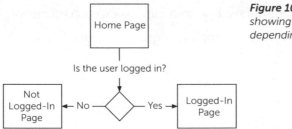

Figure 10.2 *A basic task flow showing the path for a user depending on login status*

Task flows identify paths or processes that users (and sometimes a system) will take as they progress through your Web site or application (Figure 10.2). Although site maps and task flows may look similar at first, the two types of diagrams serve different purposes: A site map tells you the visual hierarchy of a site's or application's layout, while a task flow gives you details of users' options and the paths they will be able to take.

Tools of the Trade

If you are just getting your start in the user experience design field and need a tool to start creating work product, you have many options:

▶ Microsoft Visio (http://office.microsoft.com/visio)

▶ Axure RP Pro (www.axure.com)

▶ OmniGraffle (www.omnigroup.com/applications/OmniGraffle)

▶ Adobe InDesign (www.adobe.com/products/indesign)

▶ Adobe Illustrator (www.adobe.com/products/illustrator)

▶ Microsoft PowerPoint (http://office.microsoft.com/powerpoint)

▶ OpenOffice Draw (www.openoffice.org)

▶ HTML

▶ Blueprint CSS (www.blueprintcss.org)

So how do you choose? You can ask other designers; everyone has a favorite and they're usually happy to name it. Just don't be surprised if they, like your authors, answer "good ol' pencil and paper." You can also test out free trials online or opt for a no-cost solution, such as OpenOffice Draw, which is part of the OpenOffice.org suite of tools and outputs the same formats as popular office suites.

Beyond pencil and paper, what do we use? Many of the examples in this book were generated with Microsoft Visio 2003, using stencils created by Nick Finck, director of user experience at Blue Flavor (www.blueflavor.com) and publisher of Digital Web Magazine (www.digital-web.com). You can download Nick's outstanding stencils from www.nickfinck.com/stencils.html. Such ready-made stencils, shapes, and samples are invaluable to new and experienced practitioners alike. In addition to Nick's, check out the offerings of the Information Architecture Institute, which houses many of these tools on its Learning IA page: http://iainstitute.org/en/learn/tools.php.

Note *Microsoft currently offers a 2007 version of Visio; however, many companies still have not upgraded to the product and for the sake of not dealing with version differences, we currently recommend Microsoft Visio 2003.*

Whatever tools you decide to use, there are countless examples online from other professionals who are happy to share them and help you along in your career. These are largely free and can provide you with the framework you need to create—at the barest minimum—very professional-looking documentation. Unfortunately, many people are not taking advantage of these resources. Don't be like those people!

Basic Elements of Site Maps and Task Flows

The most basic of elements within your drawing program will be more than enough to get you started creating site maps and task flows. To ensure that your creations can be easily interpreted by a wide audience, however, it's best to use a standard set of shapes.

The Visual Vocabulary for Information Architecture is one such standard, and the one used in this book. Created by Jesse James Garrett, one of the founders of Adaptive Path (www.adaptivepath.com), it is available online at www.jjg.net/ia/visvocab. The site provides many elements to help you articulate your site maps and task flows, all of which are available with detailed descriptions and as downloadable stencils for many of the popular drawing and sketching programs (more on these in a bit).

To help you get started and become familiar with the basics, the next sections take a look at the Visual Vocabulary's core set of elements and what they represent.

Figure 10.3 Page element from Jesse James Garrett's Visual Vocabulary

Figure 10.4 Pagestack element from Jesse James Garrett's Visual Vocabulary

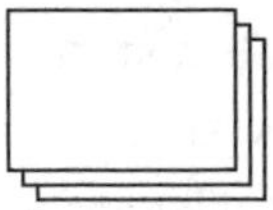

Page

According to Jesse James Garrett, a *page* is "the basic unit of user experience on the Web." "Instances" or "views" of content may be more realistic today, but a page is still very meaningful. There are a number of ways to draw these pages, but the simplest, most commonly used format is a plain rectangle (Figure 10.3). As you progress through creating site maps and task flows, you will want to find the style that best suits you for labeling and numbering your pages.

Pagestack

A *pagestack* represents multiple pages of similar content (Figure 10.4). An easy way to comprehend pagestacks is to think of dynamic content, such as a common blog page created using a publishing system. These pages are designed once and are in a design template, but you have the ability to click through many different pages of content—without actually leaving the original template design.

Decision Point

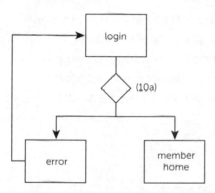

Figure 10.5 *Decision point element from Jesse James Garrett's Visual Vocabulary*

A *decision point* is used to show the path that a user can take depending on the answer to a question (Figure 10.5). The decision point 10a might be "Are the user's login credentials correct?" The answer to that question would determine which page (or content view) would be displayed. A failed login results in an error message, while a successful one takes the user to the site members' home page. Take the time to appropriately label decision points; you'll be glad you did, particularly when sharing your work product with teammates or clients.

Connectors and Arrows

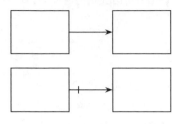

Figure 10.6 *Connector and arrow elements from Jesse James Garrett's Visual Vocabulary*

Connectors and arrows are used to show movement or progress between pages, pagestacks, decision points, and so on. Connectors generally appear where there is a call to action from one page to another. For example, a link to the About Us page from the Home page could be the connector between the two pages. Arrows (top of Figure 10.6) indicate "downstream" movement toward task completion.

Connectors with the crossbar (bottom of Figure 10.6) can be used to identify when movement back to the page you originated from ("upstream" movement) is no longer available. For example, once a user is logged into a Web site, what was the home page content may now be personalized for the user, and the generic page, or the login page, will no longer be available to the user from the path they just followed.

Conditions

Figure 10.7 *Condition element from Jesse James Garrett's Visual Vocabulary*

A dashed line is a fairly common way to display a condition. It can appear in site maps, task flows, and other work product you may create or invent.

You can use a dashed line as a connector (as in Figure 10.7) or as a box around an area to highlight that a connection to a page—or an entire section of pages—is conditional based on some other action or event.

Common Mistakes

You wouldn't go into a presentation with a lump of peanut butter on your chin or a coffee-stained shirt. Not only would such a blunder undermine all your hard work, it could also prevent you from landing a good project. A sloppy site map or a task flow that looks unprofessional can do just as much damage.

To help you recognize those little lapses with big consequences, the next sections take a close look at some bad designs. Learn to spot these common mistakes—then avoid them.

Sloppy Connections

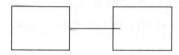

Figure 10.8 *A missed connection between two pages*

Sloppy connections are just that: Sloppy. They're badly drawn. They look very amateurish, and they give you—the author—the appearance of not paying a lot of attention to detail in your work, to say the least. Most tools have some method of assisting you with connecting your lines to your boxes. Please take advantage of it.

Do *not* get lazy, regardless of the time constraints and pressure that you might be under. In most applications, using a combination of Shift and other keys allows you to drag elements from a starting point in 45 degree angle increments. Take advantage of this built-in functionality and ensure that your connections are, well, connected. If you are showing pencil sketches, you should have an eraser on hand just in case.

Make it a rule: Always make sure any lines that touch any other object are connected with accuracy.

Misaligned and Unevenly Spaced Objects

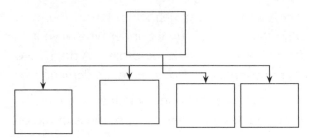

Figure 10.9 *Pages that are not aligned and are unevenly spaced*

Depending on the tool you are using, it can be difficult to ensure that your objects are accurately aligned or evenly spaced apart on your site map or task flow. There are some fairly simple ways to ensure that you get this basic rule down.

For starters, turn on the grid in whatever application you're using. That way, regardless of whether the tool offers options that ensure evenly spaced, appropriately aligned objects, you can always *count* the number of grids between your objects. Fortunately, when you are using pencil and paper, you can use graph paper and apply the same basic principle.

It is that easy to make your documents look professional. Unfortunately, it is also that easy to make your documents look like you really don't care about the quality of your work.

Poorly Placed Text

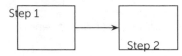

Figure 10.10 *Inconsistently placed text*

Careless text placement (as in Figure 10.10) seems simple to avoid, yet it is another common mistake. Find a way to make your text fit nicely in the shape you have created, and make sure any labels that are placed outside of their elements have appropriate connections (Figure 10.11).

Figure 10.11 *Well-placed text*

It may seem basic, but proper placement of your text—along with appropriate font size and usage—will make your documents easier to read and use.

Lack of Page Numbering

It's time to establish another rule: Number every page of every site map that you create. Don't create a vague, numberless map like Figure 10.12.

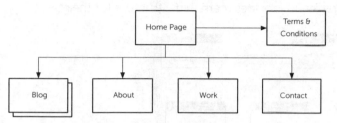

Figure 10.12 *Site map without a numbering structure*

Any page that you identify on your site map needs to be given a number, and your numbering system must allow for downstream changes to occur as new iterations and versions of your project are created.

You can use a variety of approaches for numbering pages; the most common is to identify your home page as either 1.0 or 0.0.0.0 (Figure 10.13). Over time, you will be able to determine which of these works best for you, but until you get comfortable and understand the advantages and disadvantages of both approaches, start by identifying your home page as 1.0. This method allows you to account for any decisions and pages that may occur prior to your home page—such as a Flash preloader, a login or register screen, or a number of other page types—as 0.X.

A numbering system on your site maps allows other documentation to sync up with it. The numbering system can proliferate to other documents, such as

▶ **Content matrix.** Content creators can map their copy and other content to specific pages (and to a specific element in a wireframe; more on that later).

▶ **Task flows.** Task flows can use the same numbering system to show how a user will proceed through the pages of a specific task.

▶ **Wireframes** (see Chapter 11). The pages of your wireframes should share the same numbering system as the pages on your site map to provide a clear connection between the two documents.

▶ **Visual design.** Visual designers can sync design pages and elements to specific pages on your site map. This allows them to segment their inventory when it is time to hand off their designs to developers.

▶ **Quality assurance documents.** Quality assurance teams may author testing scripts that are dedicated to a specific page or pages on the site map.

Your attention to detail and structure at this point helps keep everyone else who touches the project on track and provides them with structure for their tasks.

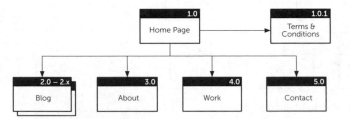

Figure 10.13 *Site map that correctly connects pages, with elements that are aligned, evenly spaced, and appropriately numbered*

In short, numbering the pages on your site map will make everyone else's life easier—and that means your life will be easier, too.

The Simple Site Map

In addition to containing page numbers, Figure 10.13 is a good model for creating the map of a basic Web site that has limited dynamic functionality and a mostly static nature. The pages identified for this Web site were

▶ Home

▶ Blog

▶ About

▶ Samples of work

▶ Contact

As you can see, this simple site map incorporates the core elements from the visual vocabulary and maintains a professional style and appearance. Most importantly, it provides a very clear picture of the navigation, pages, and conditions available to users of the Web site.

Advanced Site Maps

A simple site map can generally fit on a single sheet of paper and most likely it looks something like an employer's organization chart. More advanced site maps, however, can expand to multiple pages.

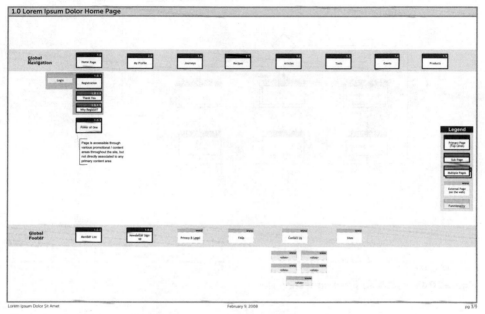

Figure 10.14 *Advanced site map home page view*

When creating site maps that are more advanced or for larger scale Web sites and applications, one approach is to use your first page to identify any of the steps required to reach the site's home page. (That's correct, we're suggesting you use a task flow as part of your advanced site map.) In addition, you should identify all your top-level pages, global navigation elements, and footer elements. This allows you to show a very high-level overview of the site up front and provides your team and clients with a clear picture of the project.

The first page is also an appropriate place to include a legend or key to help in reading your site map (see Figure 10.14). Your team and your clients will need one. Don't skip this step!

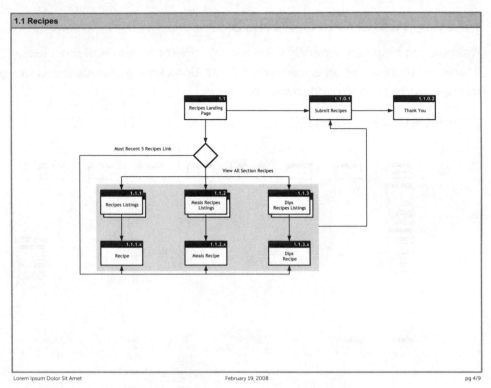

Figure 10.15 *Advanced site map section view*

Pages that you create after your first page should essentially map back to it. For every top-level page, you should have at least one page following that identifies all the pages, pagestacks, and external content that will be required for the Web site or application (Figure 10.15). If necessary, do not be afraid to connect subpages together. Site maps can grow to become more expansive than any single sheet of paper of standard size will allow. This is nothing to worry about, as long as your site map is well organized and the connections are clearly documented for your audience.

These examples are more than enough to get you started in the world of creating site maps. As you begin to make your way through a variety of projects and you find that your skills—and often your team or client needs—are growing, you will find that there are vastly different approaches and methods you can take toward delivering site maps.

Breaking the Site Map Mold

You have now seen solid examples of site maps that should fit most of your needs in getting your primary tasks accomplished. Don't let those models prevent you from exploring ways that work better for you—and please share them with us! Different approaches can highlight information beyond basic site architecture. For example, consider the site map in Figure 10.16, which was kindly provided by Andrew Hinton, senior information architect at Vanguard.

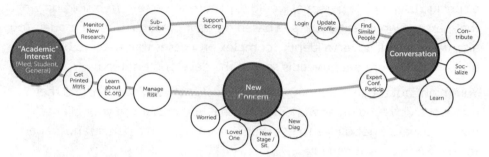

Figure 10.16 *Advanced site map. Courtesy of Andrew Hinton.*

This site map not only shows the various pages of the Web site, it also serves to provide insight into user paths and priorities. Andrew (www.inkblurt.com) says he created the site map after seeing an example from Wolf Noeding that sparked his creative flame. Andrew uses this site map to show various user scenarios and mental models related to the Web site. The larger circles on the map perform an additional function: They highlight top-level areas of the site that receive the most traffic.

Like all good user experience practitioners, Andrew borrowed—but also gave credit. There are limitless ways that you can expand your site maps as you begin to get more comfortable using the tools and identifying your work product—and client—needs. Let inspiration strike you where you find it! Don't be afraid to try something new, but take your time to make sure the time you spend is useful and valuable.

Task Flows

Using many of the same basic elements as site maps, task flows are diagrams that identify a path or a process that users (and sometimes a system) will take as they progress through your Web site or application.

You can use task flows in a number of different ways. When used in conjunction with a site map they can show how a user arrives at a page with a specific set of information displayed. Sometimes they are used to show how a specific user type (a persona) would expect to traverse a Web site and what that persona would expect to see based on their personal mental model. You also can use task flows to identify complex processes that need to be clearly understood before the project is sent to the development team.

You might not use task flows on every project that you work on, and they may not always end up as work product that you present to your clients, but it is always a good idea to use them—even if just in a pencil-and-paper format for your own benefit.

A little clarity can go a long way.

In order to create a task flow, you need to have an understanding of the user's objective. In some cases you will receive a requirements document, and in other cases you may receive (or author) a use case. Although a use case consists of just a few sentences summarizing tasks and goals, it will allow you to synthesize the user's view into the experience.

The use case for the scenario in Figure 10.17 might look like this:

▶ System displays project list.

▶ User selects a project.

▶ System displays basic project information, in Write mode.

▶ User changes status of project to Closed.

▶ System checks for pending tasks.

  ▶ If there are pending tasks, system displays error notice.

  ▶ If there are no pending tasks...

▶ System checks for pending payments.

   ▶ If there are pending payments, system displays error notice.

   ▶ If there are no pending payments...

▶ System displays summary page.

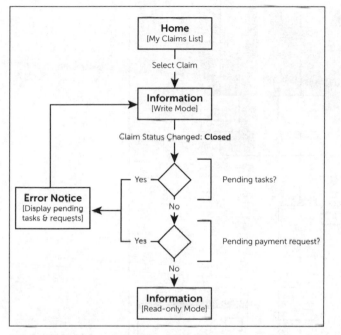

Figure 10.17 *This task flow identifies how a system displays information to a user based on the responses to multiple conditions.*

The task flow in the figure depicts the sequence of information displayed to a user based on whether a variety of conditions from the use case are met. If either question in the center ("Pending tasks?" or "Pending payment request?") is answered with a yes, the system displays an error notice, potentially delivering additional information to help the user complete the required tasks prior to making forward progress. If both conditions are answered no, the system provides the user with a display that identifies success.

The task flow in Figure 10.18 shows the paths that a user could take from a calendar application through a travel shopping site. The task flow is very high level in that it identifies three very different paths that require testing by users to ensure that the detailed flow for each path meets user needs.

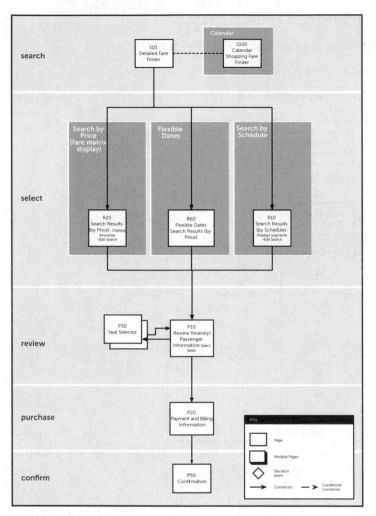

Figure 10.18 *Task flow used to demonstrate the path of a user through the phases of a purchase process*

Users of this application are able to enter a set of dates for their travel and then make purchases based on their own priorities. After users set their dates to search for travel, they can prioritize their results according to what is most important to them: price, flexibility of travel dates, or travel times (schedule).

The task flow identifies the high-level paths that a user could take in order to provide direction to the persons facilitating the testing. Detailed task flows could be created for each of the paths in the groupings and then provided to the development team to create the pages necessary for testing.

Taking Task Flows to the Next Level

As with all the topics in this book, don't feel as if what you are seeing here is the beginning and end of the universe of task flows. Explore new uses and expand your use of the basics outlined here as much as possible—as long as there is a good purpose for it.

As your skills with creating task flows continue to grow, you may find yourself creating a work product that is a bit more colorful, has more options, includes modified or improved language rules, and so on.

Process Flow

Figure 10.19 shows a task flow Will Evans (www.semanticfoundry.com) took to the next level and turned into a process flow diagram.

His process flow is very high level and flexible and is used here to show that in the many steps of a project process, the first phase of the project only appears to be a single step, however, in this particular case, it is important to understand that phase does not consist of a single event. Instead, the first phase of the project, in this case, is actually composed of many different activities:

▶ User research

▶ Market research

▶ Ethnography and contextual Inquiry

▶ Usability testing

▶ Competitive analysis

▶ Market analysis

▶ Culture analysis

▶ Log file analysis

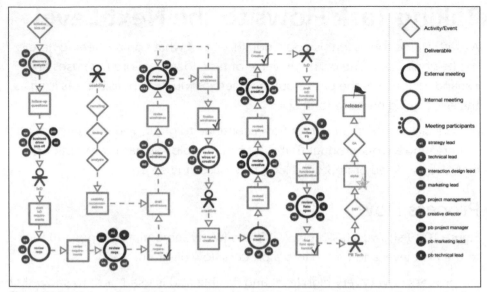

Figure 10.19 *This process flow diagram takes task flows to the next level to articulate complex scenarios. Courtesy of Will Evans.*

For each of those activities, reports are generated that feed into other various documents prior to the project kickoff, where the necessary stakeholders would gather to determine the scope, priority, and dates. All of this is shown in the process flow diagram.

As you can see from this example, the sky is the limit when it comes to creating task flows. Look at the example above and consider ways to take your deliverables to the next level. It may take a bit of practice, but with a little finesse you can create task flows that will blow away your clients!

Swimlanes

James Melzer (www.jamesmelzer.com), principal information architect at SRA International Inc. (www.sra.com), has created a number of diagrams that extend far beyond the basic task flows. The diagram in Figure 10.20 shows a task flow that was extended to show "swimlanes" of actions, notifications, and so on in a process that had a lot of events happening at the same time—with this project a traditional approach to task flows could have been a nightmare!

Instead, James explored extending the basic task flow to encompass all the various steps and actions taking place in a format that was much easier to understand.

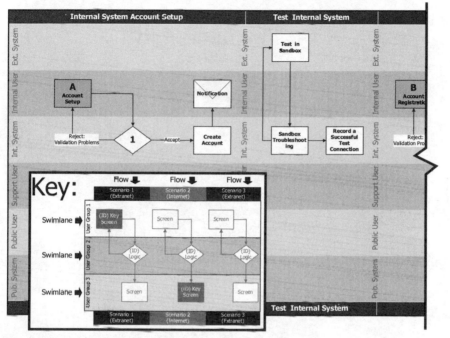

Figure 10.20 *This swimlanes diagram is an example of expanding task flows to illustrate complex scenarios with multiple actions in many places. Courtesy of James Melzer.*

James described the project and swimlanes as follows:

> The system lets people manage information about buildings they own. This extension would allow building services partners to provide data system-to-system on behalf of their customers, reducing the data entry needed from the owners. The project had three parts: partners configuring the presentation and operation of their data services, customers signing up and using the partner data services, and ongoing partner data management and troubleshooting on the back end.
>
> We were planning out a major extension to an existing system. We knew early on that nearly all the service scenarios involved multiple users and multiple systems. There were a number of notifications, and a lot of the processes were asynchronous. This diagram helped us identify, design, and explain the service scenarios needed for the project. In the full version of this work product, we actually had detailed wireframes arranged underneath the flows in this diagram. The whole thing covered a wall. Once we were fairly confident in the design concept, we chopped it up into a more traditional multipage specification.

The important thing to remember here is to not limit yourself in your uses of task flows or site maps. Stretch the boundaries of the basics that you've been shown in this chapter. In the event you really need something to test your mettle, spend some time creating a task flow for how to tie your shoes.

Good luck!

11 Wireframes and Annotations

Design and Direction—Before the Visual Design Begins

Wireframes and annotations are ways to identify the proposed content and structure, as well as functional behaviors, of a view of a Web page or an application. When combined with site maps and task flows, these documents are also extremely useful for identifying prototyping scenarios and proof of concepts. Wireframes are typically presented in grayscale, bereft of graphical elements or finalized content; instead they use placeholder content to highlight representative locations that can be used as guidance in the visual design.

Russ Unger

What Is a Wireframe?

Basically a low-fidelity prototype of a Web page or application screen, a *wireframe* is used to identify the elements that will be displayed on the page or screen, such as

▶ Navigation

▶ Content sections

▶ Imagery and/or media needs

▶ Form elements

▶ Calls to action (CTAs)

Wireframes are typically created in black and white or shades of gray, use placeholders for images, and do not get into specifics of fonts (although many apply font sizing to convey separations of copy types). They come in all shapes and sizes—from the very basic to so advanced that they nearly replicate full-screen design.

Wireframes are evolving; no longer are they merely provided to designers and developers as outlines for their tasks. Wireframes are now used to represent the site or application to clients, designers, developers, and any other team members who have a stake in it at its very core level. It is common to show them to clients to get validation on the "design thinking" before the visual design and development phases are started. Often the people who are creating the wireframes are working hand in hand with those who create the business requirements (in some cases, they are the same people).

It should also be noted that some of the best wireframes and annotations are the result of direct interaction and collaboration among the various work partners—from business analysts to developers and other designers. Some companies are shifting toward using their wireframes and annotations in place of business requirements documents (BRDs). Although the world is far from claiming that BRDs are extinct, the beginnings of this shift are enough to show just how important it is to be very thorough and thoughtful as you create your wireframes and annotations.

In many cases, users will be shown wireframes to elicit feedback that can validate the page elements or to request modifications. Wireframes that are placed in front of users typically have a different name: prototypes. (For more information on prototyping, see Chapter 12.)

To help you identify the approach that works best for you, this chapter discusses the basics of creating wireframes and shows examples from designers in the field. Like the rest of this book, these examples are just the beginning—don't be afraid to explore and innovate on your own.

What Are Annotations?

Annotations are, quite simply, explanations and notes about an element or an interaction on a wireframe. They typically contain such information as

▶ Content Identification or labeling

▶ Content source(s)

▶ Display rules

▶ Interaction rules

▶ Interaction destinations

▶ Process rules

▶ Error content/messaging

It's best to author annotations with very direct—if not terse—tone and clear explanations. Do not leave anything to chance in an annotation; there is a *very* big difference between *should* and *shall.*

> **Bad:** "Triggering this call to action (CTA) *should* result in the display of the home page."

> **Good:** "Triggering this call to action (CTA) *shall* result in the display of the home page."

OK, to be fair, the first example isn't exactly horrible, but the word *should* could leave room for confusion for a developer downstream in the process, who may not have the luxury of his favorite UX designer standing by to answer questions. Ensure that your annotation style is succinct and leaves zero ambiguity for anyone who may need to read—and rely upon—your instructions.

Who Uses Wireframes?

With their clear, concise annotations, wireframes are very nice, but who is really the audience for these outputs? Unfortunately, there is no simple answer to that. From project to project your audience may vary from a single person to any combination of several groups. Table 11.1 outlines the potential audiences for your wireframes.

TABLE 11.1 Wireframe Audiences	
AUDIENCE	**PURPOSE**
Project Management	Project managers may use wireframes as discussion points within the team to highlight strategy, technology needs, and a very high-level user experience.
Business Analysts	Business analysts may use wireframes to ensure that their requirements are being met and to validate that they have not missed requirements that need to be included.
Visual Designers	Visual designers may use wireframes as a blueprint for their output. Wireframes provide them with an accounting of page elements and behaviors that need to be included.
Content Creators	Copywriters, content strategists, editors, and other people responsible for copy may use wireframes to map to a content matrix and identify content needs throughout a project.
Search Engine Optimization (SEO) Specialists	SEO specialists can use wireframes to help identify appropriate naming schemes, copy needs, and enhancements to the overall SEO strategy. (For more information on SEO, see Chapter 8.)
Developers	Developers often use wireframes in conjunction with (and sometimes instead of) business requirements to understand the expected functions and behaviors of the design. In some cases, the wireframes may be used as the basis for a proof of concept.
Quality Assurance	A QA team can use wireframes as the basis for authoring its testing scripts. Once wireframes have been approved by the client, the variation should be minimal, and this allows the QA team to begin working on their tasks earlier.
Users	Users may see wireframes in very early stages, sometimes in the form of "paper prototypes," as a mechanism to test the design direction. (See Chapter 12.)
Clients	Clients are increasingly more involved in the review of wireframes to validate whether the business requirements, goals, and objectives are met and to provide approval to move forward into the visual design phase.

Creating Wireframes

To create a wireframe, you typically need a set of requirements. These can come in the form of a formal business requirements document from a client, a creative brief or project brief, meeting notes, a well-articulated site map or task flow, or even notes on a napkin that provide direction. One way or another, you need an understanding of what it is that you are trying to create for a user, what the connections are, and a general understanding of the technological limitations and expectations.

Note *For more information on defining business requirements, see Chapters 4 and 5. For suggestions on effective meeting notes, see the online bonus chapter, "A Brief Guide to Meetings," at www.projectuxd.com.*

After you compile the necessary information, take the time to carefully read through all the requirements, ask questions, and consider the answers to obtain any additional clarity, you're ready to begin creating your wireframes!

Tools of the Trade

Chapter 10's "Tools of the Trade" section listed the many design tools that you can use to create site maps and task flows. The good news is that you can use basically the same applications for wireframes and annotations. The bad news is that if this is your first experience in creating wireframes, you may feel just a little bit lost about where to begin.

But wait—there is still more good news. Nearly every seasoned user experience professional gets started with pencil and paper, so you should not feel as if you need to immediately choose a technology solution (although it is entirely possible that you'll need to translate from sketches to something digital rather quickly).

Leah Buley, experience designer at Adaptive Path, highlights the importance of using pencil and paper (much like the authors) in her "How to Be a UX Team of One" presentation. Leah says,

> When you first start sketching ideas for a wireframe, here's what often happens: You have one or two good ideas, and then you hit a wall. These ideas will probably come from something that you've seen and liked, or from something you've designed in the past. That's not an ending point; it's a good starting point.

The mind tends to race to what's familiar, but what's familiar may not always be the best solution to the problem. When you force yourself to seek more varied ideas, often by idea 4 or 5, you've come up with something new and interesting. I don't know why it happens that way. It just does.

Templates can be useful for guiding yourself through this process. At Adaptive Path, we use a six-up template, which simply provides a space to do six little thumbnail sketches. The number of sketches isn't actually all that important. What is important is forcing yourself to move beyond the first few obvious ideas. Six is a magic number (for me) because the six-up template, with its six little boxes, encourages me to keep going until all the little thumbnails are filled in.

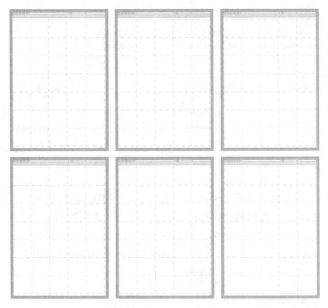

Figure 11.1 *Adaptive Path's six-up template*

These are sound words to live by—especially if you are just getting familiar with the work you are doing in the world of UX design. As times passes, you will begin to identify an approach that works best for you, but there's not much better advice than Leah's. For additional insight into her approach, the entire "How to Be a UX Team of One" presentation is available online at www.slideshare.net/ugleah/how-to-be-a-ux-team-of-one.

Don't be afraid to get started with pencil and paper—just be sure to bring a lot of erasers. Mistakes are a part of the process, and you should expect that even after you have committed to a pencil sketch you will make modifications as you move to digital.

Few professions operate within the realm of iterations as frequently and consistently as UX designers. Very rarely, if ever, is design work accepted on the first pass, and sometimes you can only hope to be "wrong in the right direction." Because of this, start small: Take a single page or small portion of a section of a project, review it first with your internal team, and then with your client team to ensure that your understanding is on track. Getting your designs in line with the client's way of thinking about their business objectives up front saves you a lot of rework moving forward. The same approach can apply to design testing with users—seek validation early!

Start Simply: Design a Basic Wireframe

In this section, you will see how to create a wireframe at a very basic level. Often you may start with nothing more than a simple site map and some additional requirements, but with these you can build a wireframe for a Web site's home page.

Remember the basic site map from Chapter 10, which showed how a very simple Web site might be structured? Figure 11.2 presents a refresher—as you can see there is a degree of navigational hierarchy shown. Every X.0 page identified is most likely a top-level, or primary, page. You can use this as a jumping off point for defining a portion of the business requirements and a wireframe.

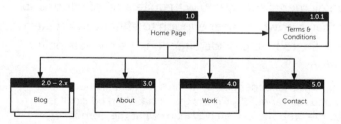

Figure 11.2 *A site map for a basic Web site with blog functionality*

Getting Started

It is not uncommon that you may be the author of your own business requirements document, and that can be a blessing and a curse. When you are the author of the requirements, essentially you have only yourself—or your client—with whom to discuss the meaning of anything vague or relatively undefined. Often it may feel as if you are making it up as you go—but don't let that deter you.

In many instances, your wireframes will help you identify gaps in the information you are working with. This can help you create the best solution—eventually. Remember, user experience practitioners work toward putting forth the best possible solution for the users, and your first versions of any project are always going to be used to solicit feedback and influence the next iteration of design. Your design does not have to be perfect, but you do want to make sure it looks clean and professional, and that in the worst case it's wrong in the right direction.

The requirements for this home page design are limited and very brief. Fortunately, the site map in Figure 11.2 provides enough information to formulate the navigation that could be used for the Web site:

▶ The home page (numbered 1.0) is the topmost level of navigation. Terms & Conditions (1.0.1) is most likely a common footer element, or at least it should not be considered part of the primary navigation.

▶ The other primary navigation elements are About (3.0), Work (4.0), Contact (5.0), and Blog (2.0–2.x)—which is depicted as a pagestack, so you can ascertain that it will be viewed as multiple dynamic pages and may have a "previous" and "next" form of navigation.

These primary navigation elements supply you with quite a bit of information to get started with—but that is nowhere near enough to effectively create a home page for a Web site. So, to help provide direction, the client supplied some additional information:

> The company is a boutique user experience design firm that has gained exposure due to its blogging and the range of projects that it has worked on. It is important that visitors to the Web site can quickly learn what the company/Web site is about through limited text and strong, evocative imagery that works in conjunction with user experience design. Additionally, it is important that the navigation is clear (would prefer reusable header and footer, if possible) and

that there is a call to action to most recent blog postings so that visitors can quickly read a summary of our latest take on current issues in the user experience world. If possible, it would be nice to be able to highlight recent work on the home page, but this is secondary, as much of our work is often in development or under strict nondisclosure.

The Wireframes and Annotations

There are a number of ways to interpret these requirements, and the first wireframe presentation to the client could be very similar to Figure 11.3.

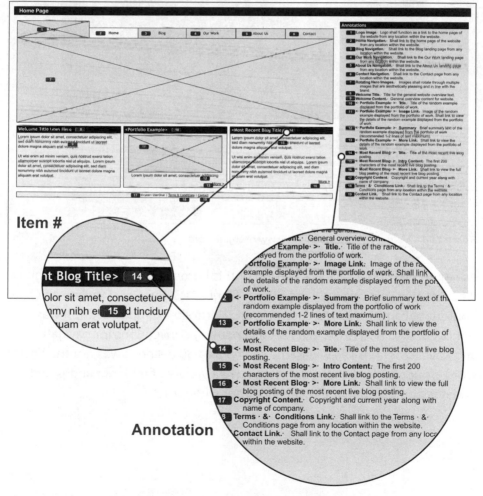

Figure 11.3 *Wireframes with annotations submitted for home page design*

The wireframe with annotations details every element on the page, as well as expected calls to action and the action results (such as loading a specific page). This particular example works very well because of the limited number of elements and the limited amount of detail required.

Figure 11.4 *Live home page design for www.userglue.com*

As Figure 11.4 shows, the live version of this home page today is only slightly different than the original wireframe in Figure 11.3. Because timeline and content became issues, for instance, the Portfolio Examples section was removed. Also notice the difference in naming conventions for navigation and calls to action: The wireframe served as a guideline, it was not the final word. Your end result, too, will often have a variety of minor changes and updates compared to the content of your wireframe.

An Exercise: Design a Home Page Wireframe

You've seen an example, now it's time to dive right in and create a wireframe on your own. Your assignment is to redesign the home page for Global Cruises, a fictitious international cruise line. Global Cruises wants its home page to become more effective as a sales tool and information resource for returning visitors—which frequently appear to be those who have booked a cruise and are interested in learning more about other opportunities and add-ons, updates to travel conditions, and so forth.

The exercise is to use the requirements below to create one home page wireframe with annotations on the document or in a separate document (your choice). Nothing more.

Requirements

The main *must-have* requirement is that the global header and footer (Figure 11.5) remain the same—absolutely unchanged.

GLOBAL HEADER

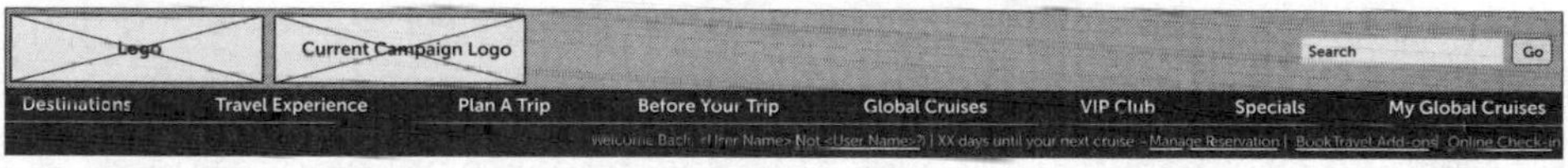

GLOBAL FOOTER

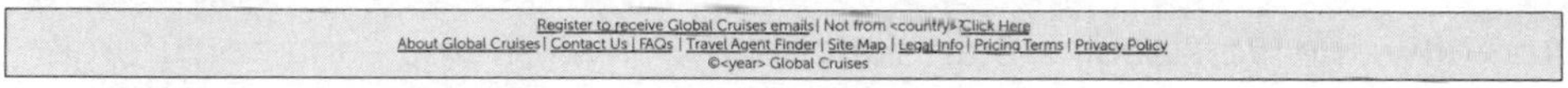

Figure 11.5 *Existing Global Cruises global header and footer*

The header/navigation must be

> Destinations | Travel Experience | Plan a Trip | Before Your Trip | Global Cruises VIP Club | Specials | My Global Cruises
>
> Welcome Back <User Name> (Not <User Name>?)
>
> XX days until your trip | Manage Reservation | Book Travel Add-Ons | Online Check-in

The footer must be

> Register to receive Global Cruises emails

> About Global Cruises | Contact Us | FAQs | Travel Agent Finder | Site Map | Legal Info | Pricing Terms | Privacy Policy

> Copyright Information

In addition, the site must have

▶ Ability to feature multiple promotions

▶ Ability to display headlines/news

▶ CTA for customer service

▶ CTA for Travel Agent Finder

▶ CTA to browse popular trip itineraries

The "nice to haves" are

▶ Ability to display newest, most popular, and/or sale itineraries

▶ Ability to display itinerary geolocations and trip points

▶ Ability to, if logged in, view itinerary (MY ITINERARY/IES)

▶ Ability to view upsell items, such as additional stops (for example, if going to Hawaii, book an island tour), onboard dining experiences, and so on

▶ Anything else that you may think of to add in that might be of value to Global Cruises

And now, the work begins. Start sketching your wireframe—and don't forget to annotate accordingly!

When you have completed your wireframe, look at the next page to see examples from other top professionals who received the same set of requirements.

The Results: Design a Home Page Wireframe

Will Evans, a user experience architect at Semantic Foundry (www .semanticfoundry.com) was kind enough to create wireframes based upon the Global Cruise exercise requirements.

Compare your own work to his designs in Figures 11.6 and 11.7 to see how his approach compares to yours. An explanation of how he pieced together his wireframe and annotations follows.

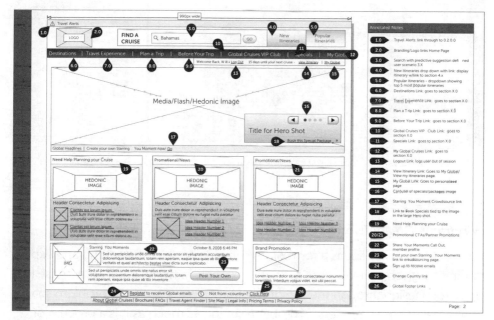

Figure 11.6 *Global Cruises home page wireframe by Will Evans*

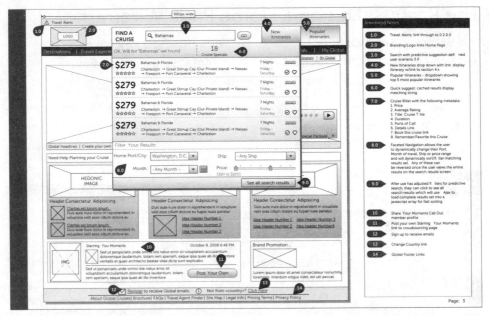

Figure 11.7 *Will Evans's Global Cruises home page wireframe with search activated*

Wireframe Creation in Will's Words

For me, wireframes act as a form of "thinking device" for the setting and exploration of a given problem space—in this example, a home page for a cruise line operator. Design through the use of wireframes is a search in a problem space of alternatives; it's a process of problem setting as much as it is a process of problem solving, which means that I always start with the context.

In this case the primary audience wants to easily find the best cruise, at the right time, for the right price. To simplify, I pick my primary audience and the one activity that allows them to solve one goal quickly, effortlessly, elegantly.

By sketching a number of wireframes, I can explore alternatives, and both impossible and conceivable ideas are presented, tested, and in many cases, tossed away. I already knew that I wanted to design the best cruise line search interface possible, and I wanted that activity to be brought front and center in the design. It was here that I sketched the concept of providing immediate suggested cruises even before the user had committed to seeing a complete search results screen. I wanted the user to be pulled into a conversation and engaged with the process of finding a great cruise.

FIND A CRUISE

Q Bahamas   GO

OK, Will for "Bahamas" we found   **18**
                                   Cruise Specials

$279 Bahamas & Florida   7 Nights   details
☆☆☆☆☆   Charleston → Great Stirrup Cay (Our Private Island) → Nassau   Friday -
         → Freeport → Port Canaveral → Charleston   Saturday

$279 Bahamas & Florida   7 Nights   details
☆☆☆☆☆   Charleston → Great Stirrup Cay (Our Private Island) → Nassau   Friday -
         → Freeport → Port Canaveral → Charleston   Saturday

$279 Bahamas & Florida   7 Nights   details
☆☆☆☆☆   Charleston → Great Stirrup Cay (Our Private Island) → Nassau   Friday -
         → Freeport → Port Canaveral → Charleston   Saturday

$279 Bahamas & Florida   7 Nights   details
☆☆☆☆☆   Charleston → Great Stirrup Cay (Our Private Island) → Nassau   Friday -
         → Freeport → Port Canaveral → Charleston   Saturday

Filter Your Results

Home Port/City: Washington, D.C. ▼   Ship: - Any Ship ▼

Month: - Any Month - ▼ 🗓   Price: ●━━━━●━━━
                                            $190 to $1650

                                    See all search results

Figure 11.8 Will Evans's front page cruise search results feature

In the case of the cruise line operator, I sketched out the header, footer, static content, and the need to block out areas in the design for content modules such as CTAs and promotions. I share the output from this stage with the key stakeholders, but I also bring in the visual designer and development lead, as well as the quality assurance, so they can contribute to the process, provide more ideas, and begin documenting pitfalls and constraints.

Finally, as the designer, I had to make the decision to implement the design in a specification. I created two or three candidates for final consideration and, through the use of annotations, empowered the wireframe to plead its case to stakeholders and targeted testers. The wireframes you see in Figures 11.6 and 11.7 are now at this stage, where the design changes are small and the details are being polished.

Compare and Contrast

It is important to note that the example in Figure 11.3 and the work by Will Evans are fairly similar—yet different—styles of creating wireframes. It is easy to look at both now and proudly announce, "Those are wireframes!" They both have elements of their own style and approach, but the core is very similar. The examples in this chapter are great places to start finding the style of wireframing that works best for you.

Visual Design: When Wireframes Grow Up and Find Their Own Way in the World

Figure 11.9 *Global Cruises home page visual design by Mark Brooks*

Photos courtesy of Maciej Piwowarczyk

From the requirements and Will Evans's wireframe, Mark Brooks (www .markpbrooks.com) created a home page design for the fictional Global Cruise Lines. As you review the visual design in Figure 11.9, note how he accounted for the layout and content of the page. Once the design moves through the process and into development, the interaction models will begin to come to life.

Design Exercise Follow-up: Which Design Is Right?

There is no right—or wrong—design, as long as the requirements are met. At times you may feel compelled to create multiple wireframes for a single page to explore various approaches, work through the details, and to present to potential users, teammates, and possibly your clients.

This is completely acceptable.

Remember that this is an exercise in iterations. The work that you present to a client is almost always guaranteed to not be considered "correct" or "final" on the first try. More often than not, you will find yourself working through at least one round of iterations and updates. Unfortunately, that can sometimes extend to multiple rounds—but that is the nature of projects, and it should ultimately lead to less exploration for your downstream work partners.

As you compare your wireframe and annotations to the two examples provided, examine the difference in approach and style of presentation. Compare these to the home page example earlier in the chapter and to the work that you did. Find the similarities and differences and create the approach that works best for you, unless there's an established template in place for you already.

In many cases, the hardest part about creating a wireframe is getting your pencil to your paper for the first time. Follow Leah Buley's advice and start sketching out multiple ideas—doodle and draw, explore different approaches, and test your designs with coworkers, peers, and family members until you feel confident that you can defend your design (without being defensive), and you will find yourself moving in the right direction.

A Final Note on Presenting Wireframes

Once you start creating wireframes and become more comfortable with the work product—and understand how valuable they are to your workflow—it's easy to forget that not everyone understands the amount of thought and time that goes into creating them. Often, clients and work partners may have been exposed to wireframes of a completely different quality level, complexity, or with a different style of annotations.

In fact, you may find that many of your work partners and clients have never seen a wireframe before (even if they say that they have). It's also not uncommon for clients and work partners to get confused about the differences between site maps and wireframes, and the purpose of each.

In other words, your first wireframe could potentially be your client's first wireframe as well! This makes it extremely important to accurately set the stage for what you are going to present. Before presenting the wireframes you need to clearly explain what they are, what they will look like in comparison to a final visual design, and what their purpose is.

Here's some additional advice for presenting wireframes:

▶ If possible, engage your client's team during discovery; try to get them involved in actively drawing on a whiteboard. Explain that they are contributing to the wireframing process and that the end result will look similar, but it will be produced in an electronic format. It is very important to explain that this is an activity that will lead to wireframes that may look completely different as you explore design options.

▶ Find strong metaphors to convey the differences between your wireframes and the final design of the project. A popular metaphor is "Wireframes are to applications/Web sites what blueprints/floorplans are to a house." Wireframes allow changes to be implemented more easily and efficiently, and at a stage when changes are generally less expensive (prior to engaging the build teams and pouring the foundation).

▶ Tell your meeting attendees that the wireframes are *not* a final representation of the graphical treatment of the site. The wireframes are being presented to account for content, general layout, and interaction of the elements of the pages. Once wireframes have been approved, the building can begin. (Oh, and subtle changes may still occur!)

▶ Engage your visual designers—if there is time and budget—to provide design mock-ups to show the differences between your wireframes and a final design. If possible, show the client examples from other projects that demonstrate how wireframes and final designs are similar and different at the same time.

▶ Explain how other members of your project team will use the wireframes—it never hurts for a client to understand the importance of their review and approval of this milestone, as well as how wireframes inform the rest of the project.

Once your clients and work partners start to understand and appreciate the value of wireframes and where they live in the design process, it becomes easier to move your projects along.

Why?

Because wireframes help create visual clarity and direction throughout the rest of the project. In many cases, work partners and clients may even evangelize the usefulness of wireframes on your behalf. This allows you to spend more time focusing on user experience design and less time selling it!

12 Prototyping

Breathing (Some Sort of) Life into Your Designs

Prototyping is an effective way of testing and validating proposed functionality and designs before you invest in development. You can use a number of tools and approaches to create prototypes, from the quick and dirty (but we prefer quick and clean) to the interactive and robust. The method you use will largely be determined by two factors: the time and the materials you have available to dedicate to prototype development.

Russ Unger and Jono Kane

What Is Prototyping?

In the context of user experience design, prototyping is the act of (and in many cases, the art of) creating and testing all or part of the functionality of an application or Web site with users. Prototypes can be made with analog tools (such as whiteboards or pencil and paper) or digitally with PowerPoint, Acrobat, Visio, OmniGraffle, HTML, or other technology-based tools.

Prototyping can be an iterative process, as prototypes are generally created to identify issues with—or validate—the user experience. Once you gather feedback, you can make modifications to the prototype for additional testing. In other cases, a successful (enough) prototype can keep a project moving forward into other phases of the development lifecycle.

Remember that prototyping is a *process* and not an artifact. You may end up creating screens and (sometimes mock) functionality that you *call* a prototype, but these are a part of prototyping, and not the end result. The outcome of the prototyping process is actionable feedback from concepts that can be used to enhance and improve the design.

This chapter, however, focuses on creation of the prototype only, leaving the details of testing to Chapter 13.

How Much Prototype Do I Need?

Any user experience design process should include some degree of prototyping—whether it is formal or informal, interactive or static. Prototyping does not have to be performed for an entire Web site or application. In fact, prototyping can be very effective when it uses only a representative sampling of a system—in other words, you don't have to create a simulation of the entire system but only key parts. In most cases, you will want to test a handful of concepts, and your prototype should include those concepts and little more.

You can do prototyping using any number of methods that are readily available to you: whiteboarding, pencil-and-paper sketching, storyboarding, cardboard cutouts, and so on. In addition, a number of digital tools are available that allow you to create interactive prototypes and engage your test users in a more realistic environment.

The method of prototyping you choose will largely depend on the time and materials available to you. Following are some of the more popular methods available to meet many of your prototyping needs.

Paper Prototyping

Few activities can take you back your early years quite like the hands-on, arts-and-crafts approach of paper prototyping. The only tools needed are pencils and pens, paper, scissors, and anything you can swipe from the art department or buy at a local office supply store.

Paper prototyping is flexible. As long as you have an eraser or more materials, you can create as many scenarios as you need. You can also revise rapidly from test to test—that is, if a potential user calls out a glaring error in something you have created, it is not a complex process to update the design before showing to the next potential user.

It's also cheap. Beyond the amount of time you invest in paper prototyping, you can generally create any scenario for much less than the cost of a couple of highbrow lattes. Paper, Post-it notes, index cards, pencils, and the like should already be at your disposal, and if they aren't, you won't break the bank by stocking up.

The process is simple: Sketch the portion of the functionality you want to test. Present the functionality to the user(s). Document the feedback (it's paper, so flip your prototype over and start writing). Then move on to the next user, or make updates and start over.

Simple. Fun. Effective.

Used early in the process, paper prototyping can help uncover design-related issues before you've become heavily invested. Changes at this stage can be made quickly and efficiently, reducing your risk. This allows you to make efficient changes prior to investing too much in the design.

Using three sheets of different colored paper, each tab in Figure 12.1 was sketched as it would display on the Web site and stacked on top of each other. The Global Now tab is placed on top to display its content as if the user had just visited the home page for the first time. Each tab shows the navigation available to the users and allows them to select a different viewing option.

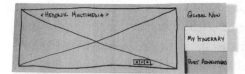

Figure 12.1 *Paper prototype of a vertical, tab-based navigation*

Figure 12.2 *Paper prototype of a vertical tab-based navigation with the My Itinerary tab activated*

When a user selects a different tab, that particular tab is moved to the front of the stack to show the newly active tab's view of the content area, such as the My Itinerary tab displayed in Figure 12.2.

Paper prototyping is about as low-budget as you can get and can be as simple as the exercise above. When you start exploring full systems, the hours you invest can become substantial (though your material costs increase only slightly). If you need to change the primary navigation on a hundred pages of paper prototypes, this method becomes costly. While paper prototyping is essentially low cost, it does not scale well for reuse when pieces need to be updated. At that point you should consider whether moving to digital tools would be more beneficial.

Digital Prototyping

If your prototyping needs are greater than paper can handle, you may find that a technology-based solution works better for you and your audience. These tools can enable you to showcase exactly how interactive portions of the site or application will appear to users.

Digital prototyping pulls from many other aspects of the design process. You'll be able to refer to your personas when presenting or testing your digital prototype, to your wireframes for blocking and visual treatment of the prototype, and to visual design assets (if they are available at this point in the process) for a realistic fit and finish to your prototype.

Wireframe vs. Realistic Prototypes

Just as with paper prototyping methods, your mileage may vary with digital prototypes. Depending on the tools, resources, and skills you have at your disposal, as well as the requirements you are dealing with, you may find that having your prototype look like wireframes is good enough for your project. In fact, it may be preferable. Wireframes can show the audience that the project is still a work in progress and not the final, production-ready site.

On the other hand, sometimes during design testing with users, you will find that the most important aspect of the prototype is how realistically it represents the final system.

The outcome of your digital prototype rests on three factors:

▶ **What does your timeline look like?**

Do you have the time to pull together a team and build an amazing, almost production-ready prototype that will show the users who sit in front of it a crystal-clear vision of the production-ready site? Do you have a few hours to export your wireframes as HTML or build a very simple Flash project to simply show the page flow and basic interactive elements within the project?

Both types of digital prototypes can be very useful. However, just as with any real project with a deadline looming, it's important to set expectations based on the time and materials available to you.

▶ **Who are you building this prototype for, and why?**

It is vital to the success of your prototype to know what you're doing with it before you get too deep into the project. Are you building a prototype for design testing with users? If so, what is important to focus on for the testing? Does it matter if the prototype is a black-and-white wireframe, or does it need to resemble a live Web site? Are you testing for discoverability of buttons and links?

Are you building the prototype for a business pitch that needs buy-in from a team of executives, managers, investors, or others who may be signing your check at the end of the day? If so, what are you trying to communicate to them? What needs to be functional and what simply needs to *look* functional? These questions may help determine the requirements for your digital prototype.

► **What types of resources, tools, and skills do you have available?**

If you are not an HTML or Flash expert, and don't have the budget to engage someone who is, you can still build a very functional prototype using a simple presentation tool like PowerPoint or Keynote, or a wire-framing tool like Visio or OmniGraffle. Even a simple PDF may do.

HTML vs. WYSIWYG Editors

HTML is the digital equivalent of a paper prototype. It is (sometimes) free and (somewhat) easy. If you aren't an HTML wizard or a front-end code expert, you can still be an HTML prototype wizard with just some basic knowledge of HTML.

There are essentially two ways to build an HTML prototype: either by hand-coding the HTML or by using a WYSIWYG editor, such as Adobe Dream-weaver, Realmac's RapidWeaver, or Microsoft Visual Studio. These tools have a code view as well as a layout view that allows you to visualize your code efforts without opening a browser.

Creating a Prototype with a WYSIWYG Editor

The great thing about using the layout view in a WYSIWYG HTML editor is that you can build a page layout with about the same amount of effort as it would take to lay out a page in Microsoft PowerPoint, Apple's Keynote, or any other simple graphical layout application (more on these later). And it's just as easy to add interactivity such as links, mouse events, and so on.

One of the most impressive aspects of Dreamweaver CS4 (Figure 12.3) is that it features what Adobe calls the Live View, which is based on the open source WebKit rendering engine. What does this mean? Quite simply, it means that what you see in Live View is exactly what you'll get in Apple's Safari and Google's Chrome browsers—assuming you've been meticulous with the details in your prototype. Dreamweaver CS4 is a very powerful prototyping tool, especially when used in conjunction with Adobe Fireworks CS4.

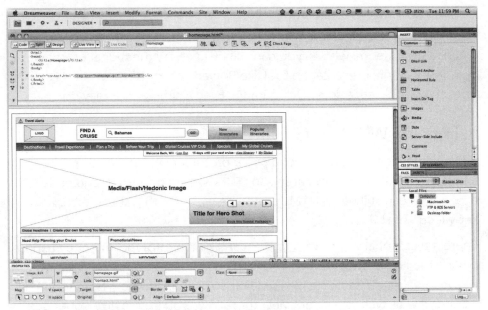

Figure 12.3 *A simple example prototype created in Dreamweaver CS4*

Creating a Basic HTML Prototype

Possibly the least expensive way to build a simple, quick-and-dirty HTML prototype is to do it "by hand"—to type in the code manually in a text-editing tool.

One of the most common reasons for transitioning a design from wireframe to prototype is the requirement to show or test the proposed flow and navigation of the site. By taking blocks of elements or even full pages from your wireframe (or design mock-up) and setting them up as clickable images in your HTML prototype, you can very quickly and easily build a functioning prototype.

A very simple prototype that allows you to click full-page images in a browser and then load different pages is fairly straightforward. In the following exercise, you will need to have a home page and a search results wireframe at your disposal, or you can download sample images from www.projectuxd.com.

> **Note** *Typos are the most common mistakes made in HTML coding, so pay close attention to the accuracy of your typing.*

1. Export your home page wireframe from your preferred tool (such as Visio or OmniGraffle) or your design comp from your visual design tool. You should save the entire page as a GIF image named homepage.gif; create a new folder named Prototype and store homepage.gif there.

Note *The JPEG format works great for raster and photolike images; GIF works better for wireframes and line drawings.*

2. In your WYSIWYG HTML editor or a simple text editor, such as Notepad (Windows) or TextEdit (Mac), create a new document and save it as homepage.html in the same Prototype folder. If you are using TextEdit, make sure you select HTML as the file format.

3. In your new document, insert the following HTML code:

```
<html>
<head>
    <title>Homepage</title>
</head>
<body>
</body>
</html>
```

4. Save the document, and then open the file in your Web browser. You should see a blank page, but notice the title bar in the browser. It should say "Homepage."

5. In your text editor, modify the homepage.html code. Between the <body> and </body> tags, enter the following HTML:

```
<a href="searchresults.html"><img src="homepage.gif" border="0"></a>
```

This code will turn your entire homepage.gif image into a clickable button that will load the searchresults.html page (which you will need to create to see if the functionality works successfully).

6. Save your document and reload the page in your browser. You should see the new home page that you just created in your browser, in all its glory (Figure 12.4). When you click on the image in the browser, the browser will try to load the searchresults.html page (which does not exist yet).

7. Repeat step 1 for your search results wireframe content. Save this page as a GIF image, name it searchresults.gif, and save it in the Prototype folder. Save a new copy of the current homepage.html document as searchresults.html. Select "Save as" for the current "homepage.html" page, and save it instead as "searchreseults.html." Then update your HTML to display it and link back to the home page (homepage.html).

You will need to replace this line of code:

```
<a href="searchresults.html"><img src="homepage.gif" border="0"></a>
```

With this:

```
<a href="homepage.html"><img src="searchresults.gif" border="0"></a>
```

8. Once this page has been created, you will have a very basic HTML prototype that shows how two pages can link back and forth to each other.

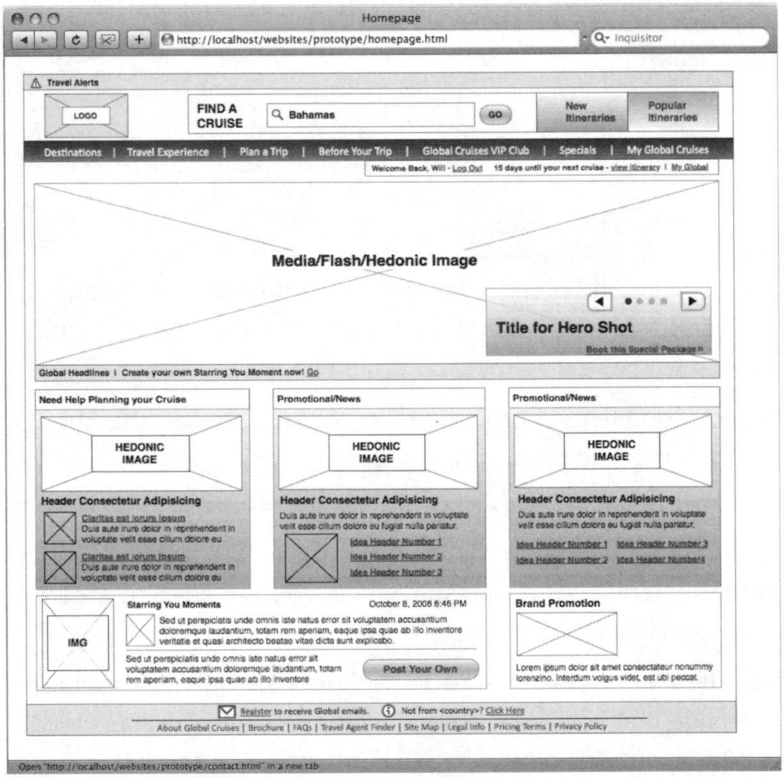

Figure 12.4 HTML prototype of the home page, as viewed in a Web browser

Breaking Down the Code

Now that you've created a basic prototype using a very limited amount of HTML, let's briefly walk through the code, or HTML tags, you used, so you can have a better understanding of you just did.

The *HTML*, *head*, and *title tags*

```
<html>
<head>
    <title>About</title>
</head>
```

are basic tags that are required in any HTML document. The important item to note here is the title tag, which allows you to specify the name of the page.

An *image tag*

```
<img src="homepage.gif">
```

is also a simple tag; it's all you need to view an image in a browser.

Anchor tags, like this one,

```
<a href="searchresults.html"></a>
```

are used to set up links in your HTML document. For simplicity's sake the example's anchor tag uses a *relative path*—"relative" because the tutorial project is in the same folder. An absolute path looks like this:

```
<a href="http://www.userglue.com/contact.php"></a>
```

Although this HTML isn't stylized or standards-compliant (don't show this to a developer—he may be prompted to give you a harsh lesson in code development practices!), it is more than enough to get your prototype working in a browser. Remember, this prototype doesn't have to be perfect: The goal is simply to communicate your ideas to your audience.

This simple markup example created linked HTML files that allow for page-to-page click-through, but what if you want to get more granular with the clickable areas within the layout? The answer: image maps. With image maps, you can designate areas of an image to link to and display different pages when clicked. The easiest way to create image maps is to use a WYSIWYG tool such as Dreamweaver to assign linkable parts of an image without any real knowledge of how to create the HTML code. For more information on how to create image maps, see the "How do I create an image map for

my Web page" tutorial by Dave Taylor at: www.askdavetaylor.com/
how_do_i_create_an_image_map_for_my_web_page.html.

HTML prototypes are only one approach to digital prototyping. Many different frameworks and dynamic coding languages can be used to create very
robust prototypes to meet almost any need. If HTML prototyping is an area
you want to explore and expand upon, you may want to seek out tutorials
and other resources for more of a deep dive in that area. To get started, you
might want to research JavaScript, PHP (or other dynamic coding languages),
jQuery (http://jquery.com) or the Yahoo! Interface Library (http://developer
.yahoo.com/yu).

> **Note** *For a deeper exploration into HTML, see* HTML Dog: The Best-Practice Guide to
> XHTML and CSS, *by Patrick Griffiths (New Riders, 2006).*

Additional Tools for Prototyping

You've now explored hands-on options that can help you create prototypes
in both analog and digital spaces. In addition to these methods, there are a
number of other software tools that you can use to create prototypes that
range from the basic "getting the job done" to ones that are more robust and
filled with interaction and intelligence. The following list is far from inclusive,
but it will provide you with a variety of options for creating the right prototype for your situation.

PowerPoint and Keynote

A PowerPoint or Keynote prototype falls into the quick-and-dirty category,
and sometimes that's all you need. You can build your PowerPoint or Keynote prototype as if you were building a basic slide show, with simple
interactions. Both tools allow you to create interactions to simulate the
click-through of a flow that you want to validate with your users. If you are
a PowerPoint or Keynote "power user," you can embed animation and other
elements to make your prototype a bit more interactive.

Adobe Acrobat PDFs

Exporting your wireframes or visual design comps as a multipage PDF may
be all you need to show what the product could look like and how it might
navigate in a linear page-to-page format. Remember that many applications

export to PDF, and if you're on a Mac, you can choose Print to PDF for pretty much any document or file in any application that allows for a print function. A lot of applications, including Visio and OmniGraffle allow you to specify hot spots and actions, such as link location, for interactivity.

Visio and OmniGraffle

Both Microsoft Visio and The Omni Group's OmniGraffle are well-known tools for creating wireframes. Both allow you to create click-through prototypes via their ability to export to HTML and PDF formats. In OmniGraffle, you can easily assign actions and specify a jump-to point within a PDF or to a URL, if you're exporting as HTML. Visio has prototyping kits available for download on the Web that allow for easy export to HTML or PDF with clickable areas, for page-to-page navigation.

Visio and OmniGraffle can also export popular vector and raster formats, such as EPS, GIF, and JPEG, which allow you to easily import your images into Flash, use them as images for HTML prototypes, and so on.

Axure RP

The "RP" in Axure RP stands for *rapid prototyping*, which is what makes the tool popular with many user experience designers. The tool offers drawing capabilities similar to those in Visio and OmniGraffle, but it adds a relatively easy-to-learn set of tools that allow you to create a variety of navigation styles, forms, pop-ups, and other typical page-based interactivity. In addition, its flexible integration of specifications, comments, assignments, and progress markers enable you to produce document-based specifications directly from the prototype. Axure is a Windows-only tool, however, which may be a challenge if you are working with a Mac and aren't using any applications that allow you to launch Windows.

Fireworks CS4

Adobe's Fireworks CS4 has recently become more popular as a tool for creating a variety of design components from wireframes to visual designs. It has a standard set of Windows and Mac form elements and controls that allow for easily defined interactions that can highlight functionality without requiring an external developer. The Common Library stores elements that can be added and shared across multiple documents, so you can reuse components. Fireworks also has a Pages feature that enables you to create sets of elements that are common to all pages within a specific document—similar to the way developers use "includes" or how some documentation systems allow you to create backgrounds for reuse in document pages. This feature is useful for identifying repeatable page-level content areas such as the header, footer, and navigation while still maintaining unique content areas on each page.

Balsamiq Mockups

Balsamiq Studios' Mockups is a wireframing and prototyping tool that provides an experience similar to sketching wireframes with pencil and paper—only you use a computer. A variety of predesigned common user interface controls are available (over 60 at the time of writing) that you can drag and drop to a screen and customize for your project.

Your mockups are styled as if they were hand-drawn, which gives a bit more of an organic feel to the digitally created screens, yet the digital platform allows you to quickly modify the designs for rapid iterations.

Flash and Flash Catalyst

Prototyping with Adobe Flash is a great way to communicate interactive concepts beyond just a basic click-through prototype. Flash allows you to easily build click-through prototypes, but it also allows you to add other elements of interactivity, including mouse-over or hover events, click events, video, and animation. If you have the ability to explore Flash in more detail, it also has a core set of user interface components that can be programmed to respond to user interactions and display a desired result.

For a primer on prototyping in Flash, seek out Alexa Andrzejeski's article "Quick and Easy Flash Prototypes" on Boxes and Arrows: www.boxesand arrows.com/view/quick-and-easy-flash.

As this book was going to press, Adobe announced a new prototyping tool called Flash Catalyst. Flash Catalyst is a development environment that works with the other Adobe CS4 suite applications to act as a conduit between the design and the development process. This allows you to export your designs to browser-ready format with little effort. For more information, visit www. adobe.com.

Working with a Developer

If you have the resources available to you, you may want to engage a developer to create a prototype for you based on your wireframes or designs. Note that the developer will need to have a firm understanding of what you are trying to accomplish, so this approach may require that you also create development specifications and requirements for the process to be efficient and effective.

If your prototype is being used for iterative testing, make sure that you communicate which parts of the prototype you are focusing on for testing and will therefore require changes to be implemented quickly. It is advisable to spend time with the developer during the development process and identify key areas of the code that should be flagged (with comments in the code) as susceptible to change. Be sure to remain engaged with your developer during the prototype development to keep the lines of communication open and ensure accuracy of the output.

Note For greater detail on a variety of prototyping approaches, see the forthcoming book, A Practitioner's Guide to Prototyping, by Todd Zaki Warfel (Rosenfeld Media, to be published in 2009: www.rosenfeldmedia.com/books/prototyping).

Prototype Examples

The simple, easy-to-execute examples of prototyping in this chapter are far from a complete set of approaches that you should use for every situation. To highlight some real-world uses of prototyping, Keith Tatum and Jon Hadden generously shared from their experiences.

Keith Tatum, senior user experience strategist at Slingthought (www .slingthought.com), created the paper prototype in Figure 12.5 to explain the left-hand navigation links and identify the navigation hierarchies and categorizations to his collaboration partners at Align Interactive (www .aligninteractive.com). In addition, the paper prototyping process allowed him to bypass the wireframe phase and move into visual design and layout (Figure 12.6).

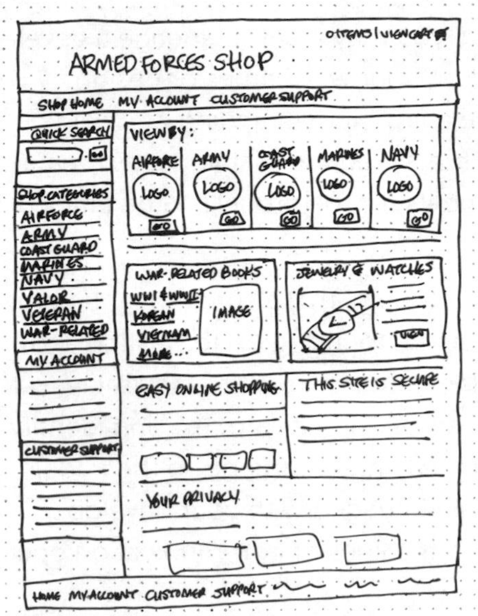

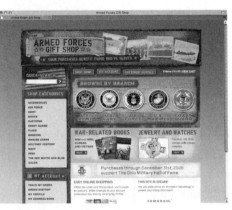

Figure 12.5 *Paper prototype used to explain navigation concepts to development team*

Figure 12.6 *Live Web site design based on paper prototype*

Keith took advantage of his team's common understanding of the design and development tasks to quickly create a design within two workdays. This allowed the team to proceed with development quickly upon approval of the visual design concept.

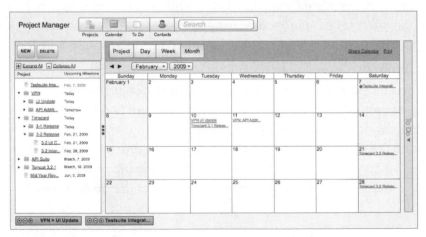

Figure 12.7 *Functional prototype of a calendar tool, mocked up using high-fidelity XHTML, CSS, and JavaScript; courtesy of Jon Hadden*

Jon Hadden (www.jonhadden.com), a senior visual designer at Yahoo, created a prototype of the calendaring functionality for a tool he is building called Project Manager. Project Manager is a collaborative, Web-based application for managing projects. It began as OmniGraffle wireframes and was then built as a high-fidelity XHTML prototype to help determine if the functionality was both usable and affordable.

Affordability is an important point: In some cases, portions of an application or project can be put to the prototype test to see if the functionality is cost effective. If the cost of creating functionality becomes a concern and prototype development exceeds time-and-materials expectations, you may need to evaluate the viability of your project.

What Happens After Prototyping?

Once you have completed your prototyping process, you will need to synthesize your results and turn them into something actionable. If you were paper prototyping, you might need to begin creating digital wireframes based on the feedback you received. If you are already in a digital wireframe mode, you may need to update your wireframes and proceed through your project process. Or, you may need to take your feedback and update your prototype for another round of reviews.

Todd Zaki Warfel, president of Messagefirst (www.messagefirst.com), shared the following:

> Prototypes are a way to achieve one or more of the following goals:
> ▶ Work your way through a design
> ▶ Create a common communication platform
> ▶ Sell your design ideas internally (e.g., to your boss, other designers, etc.)
> ▶ Test technical feasibility
> ▶ Test design concepts with end users/customers
>
> Prototyping serves as a feedback mechanism. Through prototyping, you can determine whether to continue with a particular design direction or explore a different one, prior to moving on to the next phases of your project.

Remember: Regardless of where you are in the process, prototyping is just a piece of the process, and as with any other piece, you need to be aware of when you have reached the point of maximum effectiveness and are ready to move on to the next stage of the user experience process.

13 Design Testing with Users

Break Away from What You Think You Know—And Find Out How They Think

In Chapter 6 we covered several UX design techniques that can help you understand your user groups—their needs, attitudes, and preferences as they relate to the overall subject matter represented by your site.

This chapter discusses techniques that will help you gather user information about particular designs or elements of designs. We'll focus on exploratory techniques often used early in the design phase and on usability testing, which can be used at many points in your project. First, let's talk about exploring design concepts with your users.

Carolyn Chandler

Concept Exploration

Concept is generally the word used to describe an abstract idea, such as happiness, collaboration, or efficiency. In the field of UX design, *concept* is also used to refer to design elements that are meant to represent one or more abstract ideas to the project team or a potential user. In this sense of the word, a conceptual design element can be visual (for example, a photo of a machine to represent the concept of efficiency) or it can be text-based (for example, a short collection of sentences written to express a company's focus on efficiency, using words such as *timely* and *responsive*). *Concept* can also mean the exploration of wireframes, visual design mock-ups, or rough prototypes that are meant to express the general messaging on the site (see Chapter 12 for more on prototyping).

Concept exploration typically happens early in the design process, after you've defined your user groups but before you've gotten into the detail of each page or screen. The research can provide inspiration for designers and reduce some of the risk of bringing a new product to market, because you'll be able to hear (and then plan for) the kinds of reactions you may get from potential users.

The primary purpose of concept exploration is to understand the kinds of responses and ideas that are elicited from your user groups when faced with a set of design elements.

Concept exploration may consist of one-on-one discussions or may take place in a group but include some individual activities aimed at gathering and discussing a variety of viewpoints. The latter can be set up like a focus group, with a portion of the time dedicated to concept-testing activities, followed by a group discussion (see Chapter 6 for more on focus groups).

Let's look at an example of concept exploration that was performed for a nonprofit microfinance organization.

Potential Pitfalls of Concept Exploration

Henry Ford once said, "If I asked my customers what they wanted, they would have asked for a faster horse." Although you may get some great ideas out of exploring concepts with potential users, you don't want to rely on them to stand in for designers. After all, the most memorable designs are often very different from what has gone before, and research participants may not be comfortable with a large degree of change.

Participant responses will be rooted in their current understanding. What you're collecting are reactions, not predictions of what they will or will not want in the future. Also keep in mind that many other factors outside of the design itself will influence future behavior (such as positive word of mouth).

Avoid asking participants to make direct choices (like "Which concept is better, A or B?"); instead listen to how they use their own words to describe the concepts presented. The results should be thought of as input into the design process, not a mandate to designers.

For an excellent overview of the potential pitfalls of testing design concepts and for recommendations on how to use the technique well, take a look at this article on the AIGA Web site: "Design Meets Research," by Debbie Millman and Mike Bainbridge: http://www.aiga.org/content.cfm/design-meets-research

Microfinance is the funding of very small loans for entrepreneurs in impoverished countries. These loans can allow the borrowers to build businesses and as a result improve the lives of their families and communities. The loan funds come from individuals who come together to lend or donate small amounts to make up a larger loan (for example, $25 each to fund a loan of $800 needed by a store owner in Kenya). The entrepreneurs pay back the loan as the business grows.

The funding model is very powerful, but the organization sometimes found it challenging to explain the concept in simple terms.

In addition to having the challenge of describing microfinance, the organization was also unsure about how to handle messaging and design with regard to religion. This particular microfinance organization was inspired by the faith of the founders and employees. Many in the organization wanted to make this inspiration apparent in the design of the site, but they were unsure about how to hit the right balance: If the presentation of religious messages was too strong, it could alienate potential givers who were not members of that faith. Too subtle, and the organization would not be truly representing its values.

The UX designers on the project decided to explore the possible ways that imagery and text could be used to both explain the microfinance model and represent the religious inspiration of the organization without alienating potential donors. To do this, they chose photos and words that could be used to explain concepts related to the model (such as *self-reliant* and *investment*), and others that represented various degrees of religious messaging (for example, *faith* and *spirituality*).

Focus groups were then planned with participants who fell into the site's target user groups. Two user groups were included: those who indicated that they donate as an expression of their religious beliefs, and those who did not.

For each group, the facilitator explained the donation model (saying nothing about religion). Then each participant was given a sheet of poster board, a set of photos, and a set of words to use, plus additional blank cards for filling in their own words if they chose. They were asked to create a collage that displayed the images and words they would use to explain the model to their friends and family. When they were finished, the participants came together again to present their collages, explaining why they chose certain images and text and why they chose not to include others. Figure 13.1 shows an example of a collage created in this exercise.

Figure 13.1 *An example of a collage created by a participant during concept testing*

The project team gained valuable insight from these collages and the discussion that followed. Insights included

▶ Participants shied away from imagery that represented success in "Western" terms (for example, business suits and briefcases). They wanted to improve the lives of entrepreneurs without changing their culture.

▶ All user groups agreed that the focus of the site should be on the goal of the organization (providing entrepreneurs with the funding to grow and prosper) rather than the motivation behind it (religious inspiration). Participants believed it was important that the organization remain true to who they were but that those messages could be provided in an area set aside for describing the organization itself (such as an About Us area).

The attitudes and interests that surfaced helped the team decide on a direction for site messaging—and provided a good example of the value of concept testing!

Tips on Exploring Visual Design Mock-Ups

At some point in the project, you may have mock-ups that represent the potential design of pages of the site. If you decide to explore designs with participants, it's best to have two or more variations available for them to compare and contrast. With just one, you're more likely to get the "nice" bias: people don't want to sound overly critical of the mock-up because they don't want to hurt the designer's feelings. However, with two or more mock-ups, they will generally feel more comfortable being critical because they're more focused on comparing designs than directly critiquing them.

You can give the participants each design separately (either on a monitor or as a paper printout) and ask a set of questions. For example, you might ask participants to look at each design for a minute and then choose at least three terms from a list that best describe the design. They could circle their choices on a sheet with 20 words such as *boring, trendy, conservative, loud, safe,* and so on in random order.

Responses to open-ended questions could also be gathered. For example, you could give participants five blank lines to write down their general impressions on the design.

Some of the information you might gather includes

▶ Common brand associations made by your participants:
"Pseudo Corporation is the Rolls Royce of widget makers: It looks great but you probably can't afford it."

- Design and lifestyle fit:
  "I don't think I'd let my son go to this site. He's only 8, and these images look too adult for him."

- Effectiveness of a particular mock-up in explaining a new concept:
  "Oh, I get it—this site is like a wedding registry, but you're registering for charity donations instead of dishware."

- Ways that participants define some of the key terms you're using:
  "When I see the word *solution* on this site, it makes me think I'm going to find all the products and the services I need to track my shipments."

- Questions or concerns about how a particular set of tools would be used or the impact of introducing them (the following section illustrates several examples of participant concerns).

Designers can use these responses to judge if the reactions they are getting are along the lines of what they intended or if they may need to try another approach.

Keep in mind that participants (and project stakeholders, for that matter) often cherry-pick different elements from different designs: "I like this part of concept A, and I like this part of concept B." This is a natural reaction, but it shouldn't be taken too literally. You don't want an unnatural melding of two different design directions. If the visual designer does feel that the popular elements blend well together, then go for it. But leave room for her to tell you it's less "chocolate-and–peanut butter" than "chocolate-and-pickle."

Overall, there are no hard-and-fast rules for the activities included in concept tests or the types of elements you can test. Rather, the key is to make sure that you set the right expectations with the project team about the kind of information that will be coming out of the tests and how that information will be used to inform design decisions without stifling creativity.

Usability Testing

Usability testing is one of the most frequently used UX design testing methods. It's also the most well known among those who aren't UX designers themselves, so your business stakeholders and project team may already be familiar with it. The concept itself is elegantly simple: create a prioritized set of tasks for your site, ask some users to perform them, and note where they have issues and successes.

Usability Testing vs. User Acceptance Testing

Some people in your organization may have the misconception that usability testing only happens near the end of development or beginning of deployment, when there's a functioning version of the site or application—perhaps something in beta mode. This impression may also be related to the common practice of conducting user acceptance testing (UAT) at this later point. The similarity of the names can cause the two to be confused.

For applications that go through a formal QA process, UAT is one of the later stages of testing, and is rarely conducted by actual users. The main purpose of UAT is often to serve as a final check on whether the application has met the functional requirements set out by stakeholders; it can also catch any errors or bugs participants report.

Although UAT can bring out usability issues, it should not be relied on as the only method for catching them on a project. Because it occurs so late in the process, changes based on feedback from UAT are much more costly. It's far better to catch major issues earlier in the process, before much time is spent in development. Usability testing is designed to provide more true-to-life performance information earlier in the process.

The following sections discuss common steps involved in usability testing, such as

▶ Choosing an approach

▶ Planning the research

▶ Recruiting and logistics

▶ Writing discussion guides

▶ Facilitating

▶ Analyzing and presenting results

▶ Creating recommendations

Before you get started, consider your project objectives. They'll help you maintain focus throughout but will be especially helpful in the early stages as you choose an approach and plan the test.

Choosing an Approach

Research approaches are often described as being either quantitative or qualitative. *Quantitative* research is focused on numerical data and are meant to provide *high-confidence*, *repeatable results* among your target user group. It relies on your inclusion of a large enough set of users within that group (called the *sample size*) that you can take findings from that smaller set and make inferences about the way the user group as a whole will respond, within a certain range of error. Overall, it's a more scientific approach to research, with a formality to the test design and analysis. The focus is on *assessing* the current design—in particular, against other iterations of the site, against competitors, or against a set of benchmarks.

Performing quantitative research means involving a higher number of participants to account for variations you'll find from individual to individual, like speed of typing, familiarity with similar sites, and so on. Surveys are an example of a method of information gathering that can be expanded to a larger audience, resulting in quantitative data— if you ask the right questions, that is (see Chapter 6 for more on surveys).

Qualitative research, on the other hand, is not as focused on confidence levels and repeatability, but rather on gaining *context* and *insight* regarding user behavior. It relies on the designer's interpretation of findings, intuition, and common sense. (Contextual inquiry, discussed in Chapter 6, is an example of qualitative research.) A qualitative approach allows an openness to the testing that's conducive to exploring ideas and gaining insights; the discussion with the user is as important as her performance, if not more so. The focus is on *improving* the current design—gaining insight and reactions to what is presented in order to generate ideas.

So is usability testing a quantitative method or a qualitative method? That's one of the longest running discussions in the field of UX design.

Either approach is possible and can bring back useful results. Proponents of a more quantitative approach say:

▶ It allows for setting of measurable benchmarks that can be tested against in later iterations, showing progress toward a goal (for example, reducing the time it takes to check out by 20 percent or catching 80 percent of the usability issues in a site). This also makes it a good approach when you want to perform a formal comparison of two sites or evaluate a particular site.

▶ It provides results that can be validated statistically, which can be important when recommendations need to be defended to stakeholders who trust data-driven decisions.

▶ It reduces the likelihood of an individual UX designer's bias affecting the results.

▶ It provides a higher degree of confidence that the results obtained will be reflected by results among the entire user base.

▶ It offers a clear, numerical method of validating a finding (for example, how many users encountered the same issue).

Proponents of qualitative usability testing say:

▶ Qualitative research builds up experience and empathy in the designer, promoting creative solutions focused on the user.

▶ It relies heavily on the UX designer's intuition to make reasonable recommendations, which is a large part of why she's on the team.

▶ For usability testing in particular, a qualitative approach is often less costly than a quantitative one, both because fewer users are required and because qualitative research does not require a knowledge of formal scientific design and analysis (such as statistics).

▶ It's very easy to analyze the results of quantitative studies incorrectly, lying (however unintentionally) with data, so a quantitative approach can actually introduce more risk than a qualitative test if it's not run correctly.

▶ Although findings are not validated numerically, they can be validated by a designer, who will make the call about the issue's likely impact using his informed rationale and build the case with user stories.

Qualitative usability testing is the more accessible approach for those who haven't had training in formal scientific methods and provides a rich source of data for informing design. For these reasons, we'll be focusing on the design of qualitative testing for the rest of this chapter.

How Many Users Are "Enough"?

Asking "How many users are enough?" in a group of UX designers is like bringing up religion at a political rally—it's a subject of hot debate.

It's also a question that can't be avoided, because you'll need a framework to start from in order to plan your research. It's tied to the approach you use: quantitative or qualitative.

To give the short answer, here are the guidelines that seem to have gotten the most consensus in the UX field, provided by Jakob Nielsen:

For a *quantitative test*, plan for a higher number of participants: *20 participants per round* of research (see http://www.useit.com/alertbox/quantitative_testing.html).

For a *qualitative test*, *five to eight users per group for each round* of research is usually sufficient. Ideally, more than one round of research is conducted to uncover issues that may have been "hiding" under other issues or unintentionally introduced in the new design (see http://www.useit.com/alertbox/20000319.html).

Planning the Research

When designing a usability test, there are a few questions you should answer early on to provide focus and scope. This could be provided as a document written for and discussed with the project team and key stakeholders, often called a *user research plan*. The plan should outline your approach as chosen above.

Why Are You Testing?

Write a clear statement outlining the objectives of the test, based on one or more of the goals of the overall project. See Chapter 2 for examples of design goals and how they vary based on project type.

Who Are You Testing?

Once you've created your user model (see Chapters 6 and 7) you can use it as the basis for your decisions on which users to test. If you haven't already, meet with the project team and relevant stakeholders to prioritize the user groups. This information will feed into your screener (discussed under "Recruiting and Logistics").

This point is also where you should choose the user groups to be represented and the number of users to include in each group.

What Are You Testing?

The question of what you are testing includes two interrelated questions: What method will you use to represent the site or application? and What tasks do you plan to include?

If you have an existing application for redesign, you may choose to run the whole test on the current version first to find major usability issues to address.

If you're working with a new design, you can use sketches or paper prototypes (for example, a packet of printed wireframes) to represent new interface elements like pages. These low-fidelity representations of the UI allow you to quickly generate and discuss ideas among the project team, and iterate on them quickly with participants (see Chapters 10 and 11 for more on sketches and wireframing).

When you're working with a new design that includes highly interactive elements, it may be better to create a prototype that simulates the navigation flow of the design realistically but can still be created quickly, before full-scale development begins (see Chapter 12 for more on prototyping).

The pages you include will be closely tied to the tasks that you pick. If you plan on using prototypes to test with users, you'll need to plan for the main pages of the task as well as intermediate pages and alternate paths. You may not need to detail each one, but you'll need to plan for a response if a user goes in that direction. Sometimes this can be as simple as a page that states a certain path is not available and requests the user to return to the previous page to try again.

The specifics of your tasks will go into the discussion guide (discussed below), but because the scope can vary greatly depending on the type of tasks you include, it's helpful to have the list outlined during planning.

Deep Diving

For more on iterative designing and testing with sketches, as well as truly inspirational insights into creativity in the design process, read *Sketching User Experiences: Getting the Design Right and the Right Design*, by Bill Buxton (Morgan Kaufmann, 2007).

For more about techniques in paper prototyping, check out *Paper Prototyping: The Fast and Easy Way to Design and Refine User Interfaces*, by Carolyn Snyder (Morgan Kaufmann, 2003).

If the list is too long and you're not sure how to prioritize, here are some possible priorities to consider:

▶ Areas where the design breaks some established conventions. Are you calling it a "goody bag" instead of a "shopping cart"? It's probably a good idea to see if that's clear to your users.

▶ Areas where design decisions are politically charged. You may have a strong feeling that a particular design direction is the right one, but you know there are a lot of disagreements among stakeholders or other members of the project team. Seeing is believing.

▶ Areas where usability issues can have critical consequences, such as lost sales or, in the worst case, lost lives (health care applications involving medication dosage are a good example of this).

Next, you'll determine the information he wants to gather while a user is trying to perform each task.

What Information Are You Gathering?

We're focusing on qualitative usability tests, which tend to have a smaller set of measurements. For the most part you want to understand the issues users may encounter, the different levels of frustration they may experience, and the severity of a particular problem. For example, maybe there's an intermittent problem (not experienced by all users) that results in the irretrievable loss of a posted story. That should definitely be a high-concern problem in your report!

To get some perspective across the users you are testing, or across rounds of testing, there are some measurements to consider gathering as part of your test. Again, if you're conducting a qualitative test with a smaller number of users, don't take these numbers too far (calculating an average number doesn't make a lot of sense if you're only testing five users), but the following measures can help you understand the severity of some of the issues users are encountering.

Success—The degree to which a user was able to complete a task. If you're looking across users, you could also refer to "success rate"—the number of users who are able to complete the task successfully. It sounds simple, but this means you need to define the meaning of *success*!

For less formal tests you may say a task is successful if the user achieves the end state (for example, an editor successfully approves a story). You can track success more formally by noting the different levels of intervention needed by the facilitator:

Level 1 Prompt: The test facilitator responds to a participant's question but doesn't provide any additional detail. For example, a participant asks, "I think it would be this button, should I click on it?" and the facilitator responds, "Go ahead and try it." A Level 1 prompt alone doesn't mean a failed task, but it is good to note because the participant is probably experiencing some uncertainty at that point. (Although if this is the first task, it could also just be that he is unfamiliar with usability tests).

If a user needs no prompting to complete the task, or needs only one or two Level 1 prompts, you may consider that step a success—unless you feel the amount of time it took the user was well beyond the level of patience likely for your users.

Level 2 Prompt: The test facilitator sees a participant is struggling and gives a hint in response to a question. This level doesn't include giving the answer directly, but the response may affect the user's approach. For example, the facilitator might say, "Is there anything else on this page that you think may relate to this task?" Here you could set a limit on how many Level 2 prompts may be given before the task is marked as failed (for example, at the second prompt) or as "succeeded with difficulty."

Level 3 Prompt: The participant has given up in frustration or has struggled to the point where he would likely have given up if faced with the task in real life. In this case, the facilitator gives a direct answer to part of the task—for example, saying, "To approve this story, you would click on the Submit button." If a participant requires a Level 3 prompt, the task is typically marked as failed.

User satisfaction—Sure, he completed the task successfully, but how did he feel about it? It can be helpful to include a few follow-up questions after each task (with the timer off) so you can understand how happy or frustrated your users are afterwards. If you get someone who doesn't like to talk, this may be the main window you'll have into their soul.

Table 13.1 shows examples of some of the post-task questions you could include.

TABLE 13.1: User Satisfaction Questions

	STRONGLY DISAGREE	DISAGREE	NEITHER AGREE NOR DISAGREE	AGREE	STRONGLY AGREE
The task took longer to finish than I expected	1	2	3	4	5
The task was easy to complete	1	2	3	4	5
I felt frustrated when try-ing to complete this task	1	2	3	4	5

User Satisfaction Questions

User statements—This isn't a metric, but what users volunteer is a key set of details to collect. Adding user quotes to a report is a powerful way to bring the human element to the results so that stakeholders aren't just interpreting data but are understanding perceptions that lead to insights. During the test you may just mark statements as either questions or comments; we'll be splitting those out in the report (see the later section "Generating Insights").

Recruiting and Logistics

Now that you have the outline of the research and you know how many participants you need from each group, it's time to get some tests scheduled!

Generating a List

When you created your research plan, you outlined the types of users you were looking to include. You can use that outline as a focus to generate a list of potential participants. Ideally, you're looking for names, e-mail addresses, and phone numbers. Here are some of the sources you can draw from to gather that list:

▶ Registered users of a related company site

▶ Customer contact information

▶ Responses to postings about the research sent to sites or groups relevant to your topic of research. This can be broad, such as postings to Craigslist, or targeted, such as discussion groups centered around your company's industry.

▶ E-mails to acquaintances with a connection to the subject of the test. You want to ask them to forward the invitation to others who may be interested, since using subjects whom you know personally could bias the results. This kind of word of mouth is a great way to find pockets of potential participants, but keep in mind that these candidates still need to be screened. (If you or others on the team know people well, it can be tempting to let them slip through.)

▶ Requests in the form of short surveys that prequalify participants, either in ad space on relevant sites or on the company site

▶ Postings or prequalification questionnaires in public places where potential participants may be found. For sites with a strong association to a physical place, you could do the majority of your screening and scheduling on site as well.

▶ Third-party recruiting firms, who may also run your screener for you and help with scheduling. This can be an expensive option, but if you're looking for a specific participant type that's hard to recruit or you need to recruit a lot of people, you can save a lot of time by outsourcing this part of the process. Some firms specialize in certain fields as well (such as medical) and can give you pointers on how to encourage a high participation rate.

Be prepared to get creative here. Use your empathetic skills to think like your target users—where can you find them and what may motivate them to join? This last question leads us to the next topic.

Choosing the Compensation

What will motivate members of your user group to participate in the research? It may or may not be money, but participants want something of value for their time.

If you're working on a site for internal users, you'll need to demonstrate that value to the managers who need to approve the use of company time for participation in research. In this case, you might focus on how a better system directly relates to benefits for his or her group.

If you're working with potential external users, here are some variables to keep in mind when determining how you'll compensate:

How general or specific is the audience? For a widely used e-commerce site your audience is likely to be general and you can often offer a lower rate of compensation in the form of a check or gift card. For an application used by lawyers, your compensation will need to be high value, and it is often better to use something other than money as compensation (for example, access to a premium service). In those cases a check may actually seem like an insult—someone who bills $250 an hour isn't likely to participate for money. If you're working with customers of big-ticket items, treat them as a specific audience and compensate them well.

How much interest is the topic likely to generate? Some participants will join because they want to see what's coming in the area you're testing. If it's a high-interest area, you may not need to provide much extra compensation at all—the reward is having access to something no one else can see yet. But be realistic here: *You* may be that enthusiastic about the topic, but will your users be?

Will people participate mainly because they want to contribute something to the cause? Some groups will be motivated by altruistic purposes, and may be turned off by the offer of money to participate. If you're testing something that betters the community (online or off) you may get more participation— and happier participants—if the experience is about coming together rather than getting paid. In this case you can show your appreciation with public acknowledgment and by letting them know, once the site is complete, the contribution they were able to make by participating.

How inconvenient will participation be? If participants need to travel to your site, be prepared to provide greater compensation. If they're participating in remote testing from the comfort of their own home or office, less is required. Time also comes into this equation, of course, and people will expect to be compensated more highly for 2 hours than for 30 minutes.

Possible Forms of Compensation

Your situation will vary, but here are some things you could offer:

► $50 for a half-hour remote test with a general user group

► $80–$120 for an hour-long, in-person test with a general user group

► $180–$250 for an hour-long test with a specific user group that you determine will respond well to monetary compensation

► Free service for three months, free products made by the company (ideally ones that are not yet available to everyone), membership to an exclusive group for six months, and the like for a specific user group that is unlikely to be impressed with a check, for instance, lawyers, doctors, and sales executives

Here again is where it helps to be creative and to focus on your personas. What will motivate your user group?

Screening

A *screener* is a type of questionnaire you can use with potential participants before you schedule them. It ensures they fit within your definition of a representative user. Questions are meant to

► Ensure the respondent is either a current user of the features you're testing or a likely future user

► Determine his fit into one or more of your user group(s)

► Help you get a good mix of participants within that user group

- Exclude particular respondents who may have experience that could skew your results

- Gather key details you need to know about before a participant arrives (optional)

Your screener should include an introductory script that your recruiter can read over the phone, along with directions on when to qualify the participant (if they fit) or terminate the call (if they don't).

The end users of your screener will be the people recruiting your participants— or the potential participant if you're using an online form to screen. Either can work, but generally it's best to gather a list of those interested using a form or e-mails and then screen them by phone. Why? Because, unfortunately, it's usually easier for people to misrepresent themselves on paper than when answering someone directly, and it's not unusual for someone to try to join a study even if they don't qualify for it. Especially if compensation is involved!

Your screener should also weed out those who have knowledge that may affect your results. For example, a common question to ask is if the respondent works in the field of market research, because they are probably too familiar with research in general and as a result aren't as likely to give you genuine reactions. You may also want to screen out those who work for competitors if there are concerns about sharing design information.

Following are some examples of questions you might see on a screener for a business-to-business Web ordering application. In this case, we're targeting a user group that is comfortable with using and purchasing via the Web and is likely to do so on their own as well. Note that some questions are meant to screen participants in or out, while others (like question 4) are more geared toward placing qualified participants into the correct user group.

1. What age range do you fall into? [mix of ages above 18]

   a. Under 18   TERMINATE

   b. 18–24

   c. 25–34

   d. 35–44

   e. 45–54

   f. 55 or above

2. How often do you use the Internet at home?

    a. Never   TERMINATE

    b. Less than once a month   TERMINATE

    c. A few times a month

    d. At least once a week

    e. Several times a week

    f. Once a day or more

3. When was the last time you made a personal purchase of a product online?

    a. Within the past month

    b. 1–3 months ago

    c. 3–6 months ago

    d. 6–12 months ago   TERMINATE

    e. Over 12 months ago   TERMINATE

    f. I've never made a personal purchase online   TERMINATE

4. When was the last time you visited pseudocorporation.com? [Group A are infrequent or nonusers; Group B are frequent users]

    a. I've never visited the site   CHECK for GROUP A

    b. Within the past month   CHECK for GROUP B

    c. 1–3 months ago   CHECK for GROUP B

    d. 3–6 months ago   CHECK for GROUP B

    e. 6–12 months ago   CHECK for A or B

    f. Over 12 months ago   CHECK for GROUP A

You've Been Terminated

Terminate is a harsh-sounding word. It means the call should be ended because the respondent doesn't fit the test. You don't want the respondent to feel bad about this, but you also don't to waste her time asking follow-up questions when you know she doesn't fit. There are many ways to handle this. One favorite is to simply say that the group she qualifies for has already been filled, and ask if you can contact her in the future if there's another test she would be interested in.

Planning for Space and Equipment

By this point you know whether you're testing remotely or in person and the amount of time you need for each participant. Here are some of the other decisions you should finalize:

Where you're testing: In a rented space with an observation room, in a conference room at the company site, or on location where potential users will be? Plan for a quiet place that can fit two or three people comfortably along with the computer setup you'll be testing on.

What staff you'll need besides the facilitator: You can save time and increase accuracy by having a note-taker log information during the test, for example. Other possibilities include a greeter (to meet incoming participants, hand out questionnaires while people are waiting, and escort participants into and out of the test room) and someone to provide IT support should something come up during the test.

How you'll be recording the test: You can use a variety of methods, but software such as TechSmith's Morae and Camtasia Studio make screen recording easy, and Morae has additional Webcam video and audio integration features.

Writing Discussion Guides

Finally, you'll need to assemble the materials you need for the test itself. You have your general tasks listed in the research plan; now you need to finalize the actual text and instructions for the task. You'll have at least two packets here—one for the test facilitator and one for the participant (with enough copies for each test to include one of each).

Begin with an introductory script that the facilitator can read to the participant. Lots of good examples are available at http://usability.gov/templates.

> ### Surfing
>
> Usability.gov is a site developed through the U.S. Department of Health and Human Services as part of an initiative to encourage the development of sites accessible to a broad audience. It has an excellent set of reference materials to help with user-centered design, including an example of a video consent form (in Microsoft Word format), which you should have participants sign before you record them: http://www.usability.gov/templates/docs/release.doc

Your instructions should include all the specific information that the participant needs to successfully complete the task or tasks you're testing.

If your tasks require a lot of data entry and personalization, set some information up ahead of time and give your participants predetermined data to use. For example, if a login is involved, you will probably have all participants use the same set of login credentials. Make sure the instructions for the task include all of this information clearly so that it's easy to fill in.

Here's an example of how a task for a content editor becomes more specific in the discussion guide. The original task in the plan is

"Find an article that's ready for editing."

In the discussion guide this becomes the following:

INTRODUCTION

Your manager has asked you to take on a new role: editing and approving articles posted by writers contributing to the company Web site. Once you approve an article it will be posted to the site in the News area.

You and three other editors will be approving the items to make sure they fit with the company's message. You've been given the following login information for the editing tool:

Username: **grobertson**

Password: **come2gether**

Please read each task out loud, and then complete it using the editing tool.

Task 1

Log into the tool and open an article that's ready for editing.

As you can see above, we've altered the task somewhat to end with a clear final state—an open article. This kind of tweaking will be common as you move to this level of detail and think about how you'll be measuring success. You can also follow each task with the user satisfaction questions discussed in the planning section. In general it's best to give each task its own page so the user isn't tempted to look ahead.

In summary, your test materials should include the following:

▶ Consent form for videotaping (see the Surfing sidebar on the previous page for more information)

▶ Discussion guide for the facilitator, with introductory script

▶ Discussion guide for participant, with detailed tasks and user satisfaction questions

▶ A format for note taking, if you have someone dedicated to it. This can vary from a logging tool built into testing software to a spreadsheet for typing in responses to a printed template for checking off key information (such as types of prompts required). Spending a little extra time before the test In setting this up will ensure you get consistent results and save you a lot of time in reviewing recordings.

▶ Optionally, a questionnaire. Sometimes participants come early and have a little wait time—this is an excellent opportunity to gather a little extra information. If you've designed a survey previously, why not reuse it here?

▶ The method of compensation, to be given to the participant at the end of the test (money in an envelope, a widely accepted gift card such as a Visa gift card, etc). If you've chosen compensation such as free services, where nothing is handed out after the test, reassure the participant that they'll be receiving follow-up no later than the next day.

If you're using paper prototyping during the test, you'll also have those materials to work with. Make sure you have the sets prepared for easy handling before your first test begins.

Facilitating

The job of the facilitator is to introduce the participant to the process, answer their initial questions, and then glean what insights you can while still trying to allow the participant to act as naturally as possible.

Be sure to ask users to think out loud during the test, as if they were talking to themselves (and gently remind them to do so if they start to work silently). The "think aloud" technique is the way you gain the most insight into users' behavior. You'll learn a lot about their problem solving and thought processes if you hear about them during the task itself, versus asking participants to recreate them later when their recollection may not be as accurate.

Also, be careful not to give the participant the "right" answer too quickly! One of the hardest parts of conducting a usability test is watching your carefully selected participant struggle mightily with a task and just letting them struggle.

After all, you're probably in this field because you're an empathetic individual. You want to help people. So it can feel a little sadistic to watch someone get increasingly frustrated, have them turn to you for help, and then respond, "What would you do if you were trying this on your own?"

Whenever a participant asks you a question as he works, hold back a few beats before answering. Participants are most likely to ask questions right at the beginning of the test, especially if they feel awkward about working with you sitting next to them. Once they realize you're there for observation more than for conversation, they'll often start to focus on the task more than your presence.

Here are some examples of participant questions and suggested responses:

Participant: "It looks like it may be this tab, should I go here?"

Facilitator: "Go ahead and try it."

Participant: "Am I supposed to go here?"

Facilitator: "Is that what you think you'd do at this point?"

Participant: "Is this the way to submit comments?"

Facilitator: *Silence*. Has a friendly and relaxed look on her face as she smiles at the participant, then looks at his screen expectantly.

So when *do* you intervene?

If the user has already given more effort than you think he realistically would when working on his own, and you feel you've learned why he ended up down the wrong path, it's time to move on—especially if you have more tasks to get through and you don't want him to carry his frustration through to the rest of the test.

In Chapter 6 we mentioned the importance of avoiding leading questions in user interviews. The same applies here as well. If you feel you're too close to the design and that criticism might make you respond defensively, consider coaching someone else to facilitate while you take notes.

Analyzing and Presenting Results

You've finished all the tests and now have a mountain of data to wade through. But there are some key findings that you already think are relevant, and your project team is dying to know how it went.

You may want to schedule a casual verbal overview of your top-of-mind takeaways for the team. It can help you verbalize some of the trends you noticed and help set the stage for your later report. Be sure to communicate that these are initial impressions and you'll need time to analyze your data in more detail. You don't necessarily want to jump into recommendations here before you have a full picture of where any problems may lie.

Once you have time to sit down with the data, review it with a couple of things in mind:

The amount of time you have for analysis. It's easy to get lost in the details and try to include everything. As always, keep an eye on your test and objectives as you tease out the important findings. If you have ten hours of test recording and five days to write the full report, you probably don't want to take the time to watch the video of every test. Rely on your note taker and go back to the videos mainly to make sure the key quotes you remember are recorded correctly.

How your results will be used. This is an important detail that can often be underestimated. You may create a beautiful 20-page report, but only one of those pages is likely to get a lot of mileage: the executive summary.

If your business stakeholders are going to want to see the details, the report itself can be the main way to communicate results. If you think you'll need two levels of detail—one for stakeholders and another for the project team—consider creating a presentation version of the report as well, which hits on key findings in a more visible, digestible, and prioritized way. Those who are interested in more detail can then refer to the full report.

Prioritizing Issues

At the end of the test you'll potentially have a long list of usability issues to understand and prioritize. Here are some characteristics that will help you determine how severe an error is:

Consequences. The negative results of encountering the issue. For example, if a participant loses data because of a usability issue, that warrants a High rating. Let's say she spends ten minutes filling out a complex form and accidentally chooses a link taking her to another page. If she hits a browser's Back button, is her data gone?

Recoverability. The degree to which the participant can recover after encountering the issue—for example, is he able to easily get back via an alternate path?

Frequency of occurrence. Because you're not working with a large number of people this doesn't stand alone as a mark of severity. But if five people make the same mistake and it leads them down a less optimal path, that's a good sign you should consider making it a higher priority.

Rational cause. If the issue wasn't encountered frequently but it was made by someone who fit within your user group, she made it for a rational reason, and there was a clear cause for the error, that issue should be considered as you make your recommendations.

Generating Insights

Aside from the issues you've gathered, you'll have a wealth of statements made by users that can bring out valuable insights for the project team. As described in Chapter 6, an affinity diagramming exercise is an excellent way to gather these statements and collaboratively identify patterns.

Here are some of the ways you could categorize user statements (see the "Contextual Inquiry" section in Chapter 6 for more detail):

▶ Goals

▶ Mental models

▶ Ideas and feature requests

▶ Frustrations

▶ Workarounds

▶ Value statements

▶ Delights (don't leave these out—you don't want to lose the good stuff!)

▶ Expectations (especially when they are missed)

Both in insights and In recommendations be sure to include the positive findings as well. Usability test reports are often seen as being too negative, mainly because the researcher prioritizes discussion of the things that need to be fixed over the things that are going well. Taking time to discuss the good things will make the overall report experience better for everyone. It also helps the design team get engaged with the results—and excited to make the design even better.

Creating Recommendations

Even before you start analysis you probably already have some good ideas in your head for fixing the issues encountered in the test. Sketch them out along the way as you identify issues and insights, so you don't lose them. Just be careful a single idea doesn't take over too early and sway your view of other potential approaches that may resolve more issues.

A good recommendation should

▶ Resolve more than one issue, if possible. You may want to group issues together under one larger recommendation, depending on how detailed and specific you get with your issue descriptions.

▶ Be actionable and simple—avoiding prematurely detailed designs.

▶ Use verbiage that is straightforward but doesn't condescend. Receiving criticism is a difficult thing, especially for those who were directly involved in the design tested. Don't underplay issues, but keep in mind that your words need to come across as constructive and respectful.

Remember that recommendations need to be targeted to their end users just as much as the system does. As you finalize your report, circle back and ask yourself if the original objectives were met and how to best provide your results to the variety of people who will be using them: stakeholders, designers, and developers.

Speaking of developers, it's time to bring them into the forefront again. In the next chapter, we'll be covering the things to keep in mind as you transition from design into development, and beyond.

14 Transition: From Design to Development and Beyond

Where Do We Go from Here?

The Define and Design phases of your project are over. Now what? A good user experience design process never ends. After you've been through so much defining and designing, how do you remain engaged to ensure that the final project deliverable is the user experience you've designed—and where do you go from there?

Russ Unger

This Is the End...

...of the book.

This is the very last chapter.

It is not, however, the end of the user experience design process, although it may seem like it on the surface. Once you've been through all of the previous phases of a project, you might think your work is done and you don't have anything more to contribute. In many cases, UX design efforts end up as tasks on someone's project plan somewhere, and after your work product is handed over to the rest of the team, you invariably get shuffled to another project. Time to close that door and start on something new, right? Very wrong!

You still can do a lot to ensure that the best possible user experience design is produced.

Visual Design, Development, and Quality Assurance

In some cases, working with a design or development team that receives your project-based work product is seamless. Sometimes, downstream work partners rely on you to answer questions, provide input, and help them with some of the design concepts they are working on. (This may even sound a lot like prototyping to you!) In these work environments user experience design is already being embraced, and the team probably has had the foresight to give you the time to perform these consultative tasks.

In many organizations, however, the roles of user experience designers, information architects, interaction designers, and so on are still very new. How to manage these roles can be unclear, and the decision about how engaged you should be may fall upon someone who does not fully understand user experience design. It may be up to you to find ways to continually remain engaged.

Here are some suggestions:

1. Buy them a copy of this book, please.

2. Don't be shy.

3. Read through the rest of this chapter and look for opportunities in which you can be engaged and useful.

4. Ask to be engaged and be ready to defend your request.

There are other cases where you may find that the visual design or development team is the king of the company and their projects, and you may find it challenging to remain engaged. You may find yourself trying to break down walls just to be able to review the work and ensure compliancy. This is not always the case, but it does happen.

Christopher Fahey, founding partner at Behavlor (www.behaviordesign.com), is no stranger to overcoming this challenge. He offers this advice:

> Some organizations are tightly compartmentalized. In order to keep engaged in the development of the project after the initial design phases are complete, you will need to be proactive and demand the opportunity to give feedback and correction to the visual design and development teams. They often simply won't even think to ask you to be there.

> Ideally, you will do this during the planning and budgeting stages of the project. If not, you may have to literally volunteer your services to ensure that the design doesn't degrade during subsequent development.

> One trick is to simply ask to be added, even informally, to the Quality Assurance team (assuming you have one—if not, definitely ask this of the visual designers and developers!) and to be given access and passwords to any development locations and bug tracking tools. Then you are able to add your critiques and deviations to the same bug-fixing queue the developers are looking at every day.

Of course, many projects won't have the luxury of a quality assurance team. In a perfect world, every project would have such a team; however, in reality QA is not always available. Sometimes, developers are performing QA themselves, as they develop. In addition to making you cringe, knowing this should make you try even harder to work with developers.

The Art of Negotiation

The art of negotiation may become a critical aspect of your role as a user experience designer. Downstream work partners, such as visual designers and developers, may take liberties with their changes to your work without realizing how it affects key parts of the user experience. In the event that someone tells you something "can't" be done, you must be prepared to come up with a Plan B. Good negotiation skills will help you defend your design decision (which should be based on the research that you've done) and convince others that the user experience *can* be done. Alternatively, those skills will help you work with your partners to create a satisfactory Plan B approach that meets as many of everyone's needs as possible.

For additional insights on negotiating, check out *Getting to Yes: Negotiating Agreement Without Giving In,* by Roger Fisher, William L. Ury, and Bruce Patton (Penguin, 1991) and *Selling to the VP of No,* by Dave Gray (XPLANE Corp., 2003).

It is especially true in many small companies: QA is a luxury. QA is "performed by everyone, but especially the developer," says Troy Lucht, principal and director of development of Ascend Realty Solutions (www .ascendrealtysolutions.com).

> Everyone tries to—and wants to—pitch in, but without resources dedicated to authoring test scripts, it can be impossible to inform people as to what they should test when development is often performed until the last possible minute. In many cases, our in-house designer is the person who knows the application as well as I do, so he is able to provide more informed feedback. Adding a user experience designer to the mix would really round things out for our small team.

Although your user experience design work product may not include creating test scripts, in some cases you can test against the wireframes and annotations you created to ensure that all elements are accounted for and all the defined calls to action are functioning correctly. This situation is not perfect, but it is an approach that can be useful when QA does not exist.

The key takeaway here is that user experience design does not end just because you have turned over your work product and performed a knowledge transfer. Your role may temporarily assume more of a consulting nature, but you are far from done.

Design Testing with Users (Again)

Didn't we already do user testing?

Hopefully, you can answer yes to this question, but it does not always happen. Unfortunately, neither does this particular step of testing, which is designated for testing the final, designed and developed, site with real users prior to launching.

This allows you to take one final look at the Web site and find the last-minute bugs and errors that you might have overlooked during QA testing. Once you identify your target set of users, you can test the Web site against any scenarios that appear to be high risk or that may have issues in previous iterations of the site. This round of testing can provide you with the information necessary to determine whether or not your site is ready to launch. If there are significant issues uncovered during this round of testing, it may be important to make updates and test again.

10, 9, 8, 7, 6, 5, 4, 3, 2, 1 ... Launch!

"If you build it, they will come. ..."

That theory gets mentioned a lot—and disproved nearly as often. You can build the most beautiful, satisfying, usable application possible, launch it into the world, and find out two months later that almost no one is adopting it.

What gives?

User adoption is the degree to which the user base you're targeting ends up using the site or application. Some adoption issues can be avoided if you follow good practices in search engine optimization (Chapter 8) to make sure your users can find the new site.

User adoption also means good user experience design doesn't stop once the project is over—or that it's limited to the project you're working on.

You can help the marketing, customer support, public relations, and training teams ensure a smooth deployment and user base that's excited about the site or project by helping them with three factors that often affect user adoption:

▶ Personal advantage

- Support
- Network opinion

Let's take a closer look at each of these in turn.

Personal Advantage

One of the most important questions to answer for the users will be "What's in it for me?"

As great as your site may be, if you can't quickly explain the unique benefit it brings to a particular type of user (or one of the personas you have identified), you may struggle to engage users.

Some advantages are direct: "By using this camera feature, you can post photos to your online account with one click of a button."

Some are indirect: "By using this timesheet tool, the company can more easily track the time you're spending on each project."

You've spent valuable time gaining insights into your users; now use that insight to help the marketing department tailor its messages.

Support

When your users need help with the site, how do they get it? Beyond the contextual assistance that your excellent user experience design efforts will strive to provide, the answer to this question also includes training and customer support.

Do you feel your users may respond better to classroom training instead of online training? Will some of your users bypass training and expect to have all they need within the site itself? Is live chat an important option to your users for customer support, or will they be satisfied with telephone and e-mail support?

Support efforts are tricky, and understanding the users allows you to be effective in helping your customer support and training departments.

Network Opinion

Word of mouth is the most important influencer around. What kind of reputation does your client's company and its current Web site have within the target user groups?

Even if the answer here is positive, that doesn't mean that no effort is required—maintenance is always important when it comes to reputation. Don't use a positive response as an excuse to skip to the next section: The effort involved in maintenance does not have to be substantial, but the effort required to rebound from a reputation nosedive can be staggering. A little TLC can go a long way, so keep reading.

If the answer is negative, then serious effort must be made to improve perceptions. You may need to reach out to the user community and identify who the influencers are, how they prefer to communicate, and how they influence their audience—and then engage them. There are many ways to engage your users via social networking and influence the opinions held about your client, company, and Web site. Help your client identify opportunities to engage these communities and attempt to steer them in a positive direction.

If all three of these factors are in place and you still notice a low degree of usage, consider how and what your competitors are doing to meet users' needs. How can you differentiate the product or site?

Postlaunch Activities

These are interesting times that we're living in: So many companies are launching with themselves—or their products—in a "beta" state. A *beta launch* typically means that real, unfiltered users are the audience for live testing of the Web site to help identify bugs, errors, crashes, or any other problems. At one time betas were typically offered up only to developers, but it has now become a common practice to open betas up to the user community as a whole.

During a beta phase, it is imperative that communication methods are set up to record and report any issues that users may have. Any type of system malfunction that occurs must be recorded and made available to the project team. There must also be a mechanism in place to let users report issues they encounter to the appropriate members of the project team. If this kind of communication doesn't happen—if the user experience designers, visual designers, and developers don't know what's going on during the often rigorous and fast-paced beta phase—the Web site may be updated and redeployed to users without much of the strategy implemented.

Postlaunch Analytics

After you've launched your site, one of the first things you should do is begin to accumulate data on site usage. The best source for this is your site's log file. Unfortunately, user experience designers probably aren't at the top of the list to receive or review this information, so seek out whoever is in charge of hosting the site and apply those negotiating skills of yours.

Web site analytics can give you some insight into the visitors to your site. Among other aspects, you can get an understanding of

▶ Who new site visitors are

▶ Who repeat site visitors are

▶ Number of page views

▶ Page view duration

▶ Page depth

▶ Where visitors exit the site (which pages)

▶ Session duration

▶ Advertising impressions

▶ Search terms used, results, and re-searches

This information can help you understand where users are having problems by highlighting trouble spots on the site. Although analytics may come across as dry and numbers heavy, the data and insights will help you put together appropriate questions when you do your postlaunch testing.

Note *For more information on Web site analytics, Avinash Kaushik's* Web Analytics: An Hour a Day *(Sybex, 2007) is a good place to start.*

Postlaunch Design Testing with Users (Again, Again)

After you accumulate data from your Web site analytics and gather information from customer support or other departments interacting with users, you can begin to compile a list of questions to use in another round of design testing with users. In other words, use the data you have collected to create a new set of questions to ask users of the site, and use the skills you learned in Chapter 13.

One of the benefits of this round of testing is that you have an opportunity to test the same batch of users that you worked with previously to determine if their opinions have changed after launch and more usage of the Web site. This can be quite helpful: If you retest the same batch of users (or a portion thereof) you can re-ask some of the original questions (opinions about functionality, ability to achieve specific tasks, and so forth) and analyze the variance in responses over time.

This potential for variance can help you uncover new areas for improvement in the site, as well as gain some insights into the users' learning curve, based on previous rounds. As an added benefit, analyzing the differences in responses may also help you identify new questions that were not considered previously.

All Done, Right?

Nope.

Just Like Starting Over...

Through your collection of analytical data and design testing with research data, you can begin to compile a list of enhancements and improvements that would be beneficial for the Web site. Once you have fully compiled these, you can put together a new proposal (Chapter 3) based upon your recommendations. This proposal could lead you to a brand new project, which could send you all the way back to defining a new set of project objectives (Chapter 4) and business requirements (Chapter 5). You can then move forward into additional research (Chapter 6), creating personas (Chapter 7) for newly identified targets, enhancing your SEO (Chapter 8), updating or creating new site maps and task flows (Chapter 10), updating or creating new wireframes and annotations (Chapter 11), launching into additional rounds of prototyping (Chapter 12), and more design testing with users (Chapter 13)...

You get the idea.

Projects should not die. They should be the springboard into new projects that are geared toward continually improving the user experience design.

Index

A

absolute path, using in HTML prototype 213

acknowledgement and sign-off, including in proposals 53–54

ACSI (American Customer Satisfaction Index) 103

activities, planning 162–164

Adaptive Path
> use of pencil and paper at 189–190
> Web site 168

additional costs and fees, including in proposals 50

Adobe Acrobat PDFs prototyping tool, features of 214–215

Adobe Illustrator Web site 167

Adobe InDesign Web site 167

advocates, priorities of 150–151, 154

affinity diagramming
> applying to feature conflicts 160–161
> steps for 99–100
> using in usability testing 244

agile approaches
> overview of 63–64
> resource for 65

AIGA Web site 51

Ajax, problems with 132

Align Interactive Web site 217

alt attributes, using 139

American Customer Satisfaction Index (ACSI) 103

analytics tools
> availability of 24
> benefits of 254

annotations
> overview of 187
> tools for 189–190
> and wireframes 186–187, 193–194, 201

Aquent talent agency Web site 51

arrows and connectors, defined 170

Ascend Reality Solutions Web site 250

Ash, Tim 16

Ashton, Jonathan 143

Ask.com, searches performed by 128

assumptions, including in proposals 47–48

attributes
> comparing 90
> prioritizing and defining 89–91

Axure RP prototyping tool
> features of 215
> Web site 167

B

Babyhold Web site 118

BabyNames Web site 118

balance, achieving in UX design 6–7

Balsamiq Mockups prototyping tool, features of 216

Baty, Steve 12, 95

Behavior Web site 249

beta launch, defined 253–254

billing rate, determining 51

black hat
> defined 130–131
> versus white hat 141–142

blog functionality, site map for 166, 191

Blue Flavor Web site 167

Blueprint CSS Web site 167

body language, interpreting in focus groups 106

bot, explained 129

brand presence sites
> described 11
> examples of 13
> features of 12–13
> goals for 13–14

brand strategist/steward, role of 26–27

Brooks, Mark 200–201

building ownership, system for 183

Buley, Leah 189–190, 201

business advocate
> concerns of 154
> versus development and user advocates 155

business analysis
> role of 27–28
> use of wireframes in 188

business requirements 73
> *See also* requirements gathering
> clarifying 68–69
> coalescing 82–84
> conducting heuristic analysis for 70–73
> creating plans for meetings 78–79